AIRCRAFT CASUALTIES IN KENT
Part I: 1939 to 1940

Compiled by:G.G. Baxter
K.A. Owen
P. Baldock
Kent Aviation Historical Research Society

Dedicated to those who failed to
return to base, R.A.F.,
Allied Commonwealth and Luftwaffe.

Meresborough Books
1990

ACKNOWLEDGEMENTS

Air Historical Branch, Ministry of Defence
Australian High Commission
Mrs E.S. Baxter — checking
J. Bentley-Beard Esq.
Bexley Public Library
C. Blomfield Esq. of Rye
Bromley Public Library
Canadian High Commission
Commonwealth War Graves Commission
Department of Registrar of Graves; Ashford, Canterbury, Folkestone, Maidstone, Margate
    and Tunbridge Wells
Fleet Air Arm Museum, Yeovilton
Kent County Archives
'Kent Messenger' (Mr Mellor)
Cav. Nicola Malizia, Forli, Italy.
Imperial War Museum
Naval Historical Branch, Ministry of Defence
New Zealand High Commission
Mrs P. Owen, for Research and Checking
Michael Payne Esq.
Public Records Office, Kew
Royal Air Force Museum Archives
R.N.L.I., Headquarters and Dungeness and Margate Stations
Kenneth Wynn Esq.
Messrs Oldfield, McPhun and Taylor

The above have all contributed information and/or photographs, for which we are duly grateful.

Published by Meresborough Books
17 Station Road, Rainham, Kent. ME8 7RS.

ISBN 0948193 506

Printed by Mackays of Chatham plc.

Front cover: Me110C of 6/ZG26 which crashed near Lenham. Incident No. 434
(SE Press)

Back cover: An Me110 of ZG26 being re-armed, probably at St Omer-Arques.

CONTENTS

EXPLANATION OF LAYOUT

The information is presented in semi tabular form to provide a concise and clear layout.

Date Given only at the beginning of each day's entry, in bold type.

Incident number On the left hand side. Some numbers are missing because after the general format was established the information was found incorrect and the entry deleted.

Identification of the aircraft This is by the service number in the case of the R.A.F. or the Werke Nummer for the Luftwaffe, followed by the identifying letters where known.

Parent Unit Is given in the bold type figures on the right.
In British aircraft it is the squadron number unless otherwise stated.
Luftwafe unit designation is at once more informative and complicated but a full explanation appears in the appendix. Sufficient to say here that bomber units have KG in the title, fighters JG, twin engined fighters ZG, dive bombers StG and training units LG.

Location of the Incident Given in bold type under the incident number on the left. The nearest town or village that might be found in a map gazeteer is followed by more exact information if known.
Finally the airfield base is included and the category of the damage i.e. Cat 2 repairable, Cat 3 written off.

ABBREVIATIONS

A.A.	anti aircraft artillery	Nav.	navigator
A.A.C.U.	A.A. co-operation units	O.T.U.	Operational Training Unit
a/c	aircraft	POW	Prisoner of War
Adv.	advanced base	P.D.U.	Photographic Development
a/f	airfield		Unit
A/G	air gunner	P.I.	Practice Interception
ALG	advanced landing ground	Pol.	Polish
A.S.R.	air/sea rescue	P.R.O.	Public Records Office
Bel	Belgian	P.R.U.	Photo. Reconnaisance Unit
C.F.I.	chief flying instructor	RAAF	Royal Australian Air Force
C.G.	Coastguard	RCAF	Royal Canadian Air Force
Cz	Czechoslovakia	R.N.Z.A.F.	Royal New Zealand Air Force
Do	Dornier	R.N.	Royal Navy
e/a	enemy aircraft	R/T	Radio Telephone
FFAF	Free French Air Force	r/w	runway
flak	enemy A.A.	Seenotflkdo Lw A.S.R.	
H.E.	high explosive	Stab	unit H.Q.'s
He	Heinkel	u/i	unidentified
H.S.L.	High speed launch	u/s	unserviceable
Inc.	incendiaries	W/Opr	radio operator
I.W.M.	Imperial War Museum	W/T	wireless telegraphy
Ju	Junkers		
L.A.A.	light A.A.	(?) indicates a degree of doubt about the	
L.B.	lifeboat	item of information.	
Lw	Luftwaffe		
M.C.U.	Marine craft unit	**Dunkirk** To avoid confusion between the	
Me	Messerschmitt	village in Kent and the port in France the lat-	
		ter is given the French spelling 'Dunkerque'.	

INTRODUCTION

The purpose of this work is to provide as full an account as possible, of aircraft casualties and their crews that crashed or force landed in Kent. This between 1939 and 1940.

It is not a narrative of flying during those times, but as accurate a compilation of the facts as is possible, after the passage of nearly fifty years.

Each year more of the memories of the period are lost, and it is hoped that this will stimulate a further flow of information from readers to fill any gaps.

These records start with the pre-war defence exercise in the summer of 1939, which preceded mobilisation of the reserves, and contains some 1500 incidents, roughly half of the total for the whole War.

Each incident has its number; the date; type of aircraft; aircraft number and identification letters, if known; location of the crash site; details of the crew and their condition; cause and category of the crash.

The compilers, all members of the Kent Aviation Historical Research Society approached the work from different view-points.

Phillip Baldock, who is the secretary of the Robertsbridge Aviation Society and Museum is concerned with the location and preservation of aircraft material.

Ken Owen, secretary of the K.A.H.R.S. lived through the early years of the war in Canterbury, and saw much of the Battle of Britain from the ground and subsequently served in the Royal Engineers. Post war he spent much of his spare time in researching the records of the Kent Civil Defence.

Geoff Baxter served in R.A.F. Operations/Intelligence from the outbreak of war, and as an Intelligence Officer from 1943-1959 in the R.A.F. and R.Aux.A.F., has an especial interest in the Order of Battle of the Western Adversaries.

Many publications have been used as references and these are listed in the bibliography.

The Public Records Office at Kew, whose staff have been always most helpful, provided access to Forms 540 & 541 (Operations Record Books) of the flying units.

Much information has come from our own society members, many of whom have studied one or other of the wartime county airfields in great detail.

A considerable loss of sources has occurred as a result of organisations failing to keep their wartime records. For example those of the Kent Police would have been invaluable as would those of the National Fire Service. However some, such as the Royal National Lifeboat Institute still hold records, and the Headquarters and some of the local stations kindly allowed us access.

Much of the Luftwaffe records were lost or destroyed during late 1944 and 1945, but the Imperial War Museum holds photocopies of the Daily Returns of the Quartermaster General of the Luftwaffe. Unfortunately at best these have only limited facts and some are missing.

We expect and hope for a feedback from readers of additional information and corrections, because our researches have shown that very many doubts remain as to the accuracy of some of the information recorded. This with any further details that come to hand will be incorporated in an Addendum to Part II: 1941-45.

EINLEITUNG

Der Zweck dieses Buches ist alle mögliche Auskunft zu geben über die Flugzeuge und Mannschaften, die während des zweiten Weltkrieges in Kent notlanden mßten oder abgestürzt sind.

Es ist keine Schilderung über das Fliegen zu der Zeit, sondern eine Zusammenstellung der Tatsachen, so exakt wie möglich nach fast 50 Jahren. Jedes Jahr geht mehr von der Information verloren, weil viele Organisationen keine Aufzeichnungen gemacht haben. Es wäre z. B. sehr wertvoll gewesen, Aufzeichnungen von der Polizei in Kent wie auch der Feuerwehr und Küstenwache zu haben.

Als Informationsquelle dienten viele Veröffentlichungen und sie werden in der Bibliographie aufgefürht. Diese Angaben sind dann mit den Aufzeichnungen der Einheiten verglichen worden, die im 'Public Records' Büro, Kew und dem 'Imperial War Museum', London aufbewahrt werden.

Es wird gehofft, daß, als Ergebnis dieser Veröffentlichung, von seiten der Leser weitere Informationen zutage kommen, die in einem zweiten Buch veröffentlicht werden können.

Viel Information, die die Luftwaffe betrifft, ist verloren gegangen oder zu Ende des Krieges zerstört worden und es war besonders schwer über die Verluste der Mannschaften und die Standorte der Einheiten Bestätigungen zu finden.

Die Verfasser dieses Buches, alle Mitglieder der 'Kent Aviation Historical Research Society', haben ihre Arbeit in diesem Buch von verschiedenen Gesichtspunkten her angegriffen.

Phil Baldock, Sekretär vom 'Robertsbridge Aviation Society and Museum' befaßt sich mit dem Ausfindigmachen und der Erhaltung von Luftwaffenmaterial.

Ken Owen, Sekretär von der K.A.H.R.S. wohnte während der ersten Kriegsjahre in Canterbury, wo er viel von der 'Battle of Britain' gesehen hat. Später hat er die Aufzeichnungen vom 'Civil Defense' und die damit verbundenen Themen aufgeschrieben.

Geoff Baxter hat in 'Operational Intelligence' schon vor Kriegsausbruch gedient und also Stabsoffizier von 1943-1959 in der R.A.F. (Luftwaffe) und R.Aux.A.F. und ist besonders an der Schlachtordnung der westlichen Gegner interessiert.

Andere Mitglieder der K.A.H.R.S. sowie Verfasser von Kriegsbüchern haben viel mit ihrem Spezialwissen beigetragen.

Die ersten Aufzeichnungen im Text stammen noch aus der Vorkriegszeit vor der Mobilisierung.

CALENDAR OF EVENTS AFFECTING THE AIR WAR IN BRITAIN

1939

September   Invasion of Poland by the Wehrmacht, and destruction of the Polish Air Force by the Luftwaffe, followed by the exodus of P.A.F. personnel to the Middle East and then France.

Commencement of the U-boat War in the Atlantic.

R.A.F. attacks on naval targets in daylight with prohibitive losses.

The transfer of the Advanced Air Striking Force of Battle and Blenheim squadrons to French bases together with Gladiator and Hurricane fighter squadrons (continuing into October).

Flying restricted during December and January by the very hard winter weather.

November   Russian attack on Finland and the tentative formation of an R.A.F. force to support the Finns.

1940

April   German invasion of Denmark and Norway leading to the abortive occupation of Narvik by British forces including fighter support.

British forces in Iceland.

May   German invasion of Belgium and Holland.

Battle for France (by now 16 Hurricane Sqdns on French bases).

The Battle squadrons almost wiped out. Other units lost men and equipment.

Evacuation through Dunkerque, with 11 Group responsible for air cover.

June   Italy invades Southern France.

July   The battle of the convoys in the Channel.

August   Battle of Britain starts.

Attacks on fighter and radar stations.

First Stirlings into service.

First raid on Berlin.

September   Attacks on major British cities, in daylight.

Beginning of Anglo/U.S.A. arms deals.

October   Night attacks on British major cities with little success in defence.

November   Destruction of most of Coventry.

December   Formation of Army Co-operation Command.

THE BALANCE OF AIRPOWER
and how it was affected by the Battle for France, Dunkerque, and the Battle of Britain

Neither the Army nor Air Councils had correctly envisaged the need for air support for the ground forces in France, despite the lessons of the Spanish Civil War.

The Fairey Battle intended to be the power of the Advanced Air Striking Force was totally inadequate, under-powered and so lacking speed, altitude and bomb capacity. Despite the gallantry of the aircrews in the face of appalling losses, despite the efforts of the Hurricane squadrons the Battle units were to all intents wiped out, for very little in the way of results.

The Advanced Air Striking force lost 248 aircraft in a matter of days and by the 18th May had fallen its Rear H.Q. back to Boulogne, and in the process practically lost control of the scattered squadrons. The 20th saw a considerable part of the R.A.F. Component withdrawn to the U.K.

In the week before the Commencement of Operation Dynamo the only air cover flown over France was from the S.E. of England in support of the Army forces concentrated in a long narrow pocket stretching 70 miles from Dunkerque.

The outward and inward flights totalled about 100 miles so that a large proportion of the single engined fighters' endurance was consumed, leaving little time over the target. This was further exacerbated by the lack of range of the CH radar chain which could not cover the pocket. These deficiencies gave rise to the bitter complaints of the soldiers that the R.A.F. was failing in its support.

Records show that on the 26th and 27th May there were 45 patrols at squadron strength and on the 28th 11 patrols at double or treble that strength.

The Official Historian of the R.A.F. wrote at the time: "Even so a daily average of about 300 sorties at a period of crisis may seem less than might have been expected from a force of 600-700 fighter aircraft".

He further concludes that it would have been operationally feasible to have increased the effort considerably. However it was largely due to the foresight of Air Chief Marshal Sir Hugh Dowding, AOC in C Fighter Command that the increase was not allowed and so the Command's strength was maintained allowing it to win the coming Battle of Britain. With hindsight it is easy to conclude that an increase in effort would not have improved the chances of the evacuation, but would have seriously if not fatally depleted the fighters, this especially as current Spitfires and Hurricanes were not armed for ground support work.

When all the Intelligence reports were in it was clear that the Command had lost 106 s.e.f. during the cover operations in addition to the A.A.S.F.'s Hurricane losses. Coastal Command and 2 Group, Bomber Command also had considerable casualties.

Against this the Luftwaffe losses were variously assessed as follows:

Churchill   424 lost
Air Ministry   262 lost
Luftwaffe   156 lost. This was from the Q.M. General's returns and not just for Dunkerque.

Royal Navy claimed 35 and the Army and the French Navy a few. Therefore the R.A.F. successes could not have amounted to more than 100.

What cannot be estimated is the effect on the efficiency of the German force of a short very intensive, highly mobile period of continuous operations.

A German estimate was that by the end of the Battle for France many of the front line Luftwaffe units were down to 50% strength with exhausted flying and ground staffs.

Line of communication units had their transport facilities so elongated and over-worked that reinforcement was practically at a standstill. Field Marshal Kesselring, Commanding General of Luftflotte 2, said: "These operations exhausted our men and materials reducing air strength to 30-50%".

BATTLE of BRITAIN

The dates given for this vary according to source. Air Chief Marshal Sir Hugh Dowding said that for him it started in the autumn of 1939.

Churchill broadcast on the 8th June 1940: "The Battle for France is over, I expect that the Battle for Britain is about to begin".

The Luftwaffe High Command considered that it started later 'Der Adlertag' being the 13th August 1940, but many historians agree that it began on or soon after the 5th August and continued until late October.

THE AIRCRAFT CASUALTIES

1. **2.7.39** Gladiator II, K7958 **615**
Ide Hill. Crash landed, causes not known. Based Kenley. Cat 3

2. **9.7.39** Hurricane I, L1661 **32**
Herne Bay. 5 miles S. Pilot baled out. Based Biggin Hill. Cat 3

3. **21.7.39** DH60G Moth, G-ABJZ
Kent Flying Club, **Tilmanstone.** In collision. K.K. Brown (C.F.I.) and W.A. Pragnell (pupil) killed.

Hind O.U. AirSq.
As above D.C. Lewis killed.

4. **9.8.39** Hurricane I, L1557 **111**
Biggin Hill. 2 miles SW. Crashed on take off. Based Northolt. Cat 3

5. **11.8.39** Hurricane I, L1662 **32**
Tatsfield. Hit a hill in cloud. Based Biggin Hill. Cat 3

6. **9.9.39** Anson I, N5066 **500**
Whitstable. Ditched off the town. Crew P/O Harris and Lane.

7. **10.9.39** Hurricane I, L1939 **3**
Sittingbourne. Hit trees in poor visibility. Sgt A.F. Butterick condition not known. Based Croydon. Cat 2

8. **7.10.39** Anson I, N5233, MK-O **500**
Benenden. On returning from ops. over the Channel this Coastal Command a/c had engine trouble and the crew were ordered to bale out. F/O Mabey, P/O Patterson and Cpl Drew were killed but LAC Messent landed safely. Based Detling. Cat 3

9. **2.11.39** Hurricane I, L1649 **3**
Manston. Crash landed. Sgt Sillence killed. Det. Hawkinge. Cat 3

10. **8.11.39** Anson I, MK-D **500**
Littlestone G.C. Had been on a convoy patrol and whilst returning to base had to force land for unknown reasons. Later they were able to take off and return to base. Crew F/O Balston, P/O Pain, Sgt Jones, A/C's O'Kelly and Simmonds all unhurt. Based Detling. Cat 1

11. **15.11.39** Magister **3**
Lydd. P/O C.G. Jeffries had collected this a/c from No.10 M.U. but had to force land in poor weather conditions, damaging the airscrew and undercarriage. Based Biggin Hill. Cat 2

12. **21.11.39** Do17Z **3(F)122**
off Dover. Shot down by 79Sq Hurricanes (F/O J. Davies and Sgt Brown). The wreckage was picked up by HMS Boreas.

13. **10.12.39** Anson I, N5231 **500**
nr Detling. Crashed on take off. P/O Arkill, Sgt Braybrook, LAC le Gassick and Walton all safe. (This incident may have been on the 9th or 10th.) Cat 3(?)

14. **2.1.40** Magister **79**
Margate, Garlinge. On air familiarisation flight when it failed to recover from a roll and flew into the ground. P/O T.S. Lewis and A/C2 S. Smith were killed. Based Manston. Cat 3

15. **15/16.1.40** Anson I, N5226, MK-E **500**
Swingfield. Returning from ops. in very bad weather force landed in heavy snow. P/O Pain, Sgt Rayner, A/C's Combe & Ridley safe. Based Detling. Cat ?

16. **16.1.40** Battle, N2258 **253**
Manston (Base), Westmarsh. Crashed in snow. Crew condition not known. Cat 3

17. **13.2.40** He111 **Stab/Kgr100**
Margate. 8 miles E. This was one of the first operations flown by this Unit after a long layoff during the bad winter of 1939/40.

The Commanding Officer of the Gruppe, a special signals unit, Oberst Lt Joachim Stollbrock was a very experienced ex Luft Hansa pilot and a most popular C.O. with all ranks. On this day he was captain of the aircraft, the other members being Lt Weckner, pilot Lt Gudenatz, Nav. of the Stab Staffel with Uffz K. Beisser W/Opr., and Uffz Bohlmann bombaimer from the 1st Staffel.

The object of the mission was to check the X-Verfahren beam, a secret nav. device, over the Thames Estuary.

By the time the aircraft was in position it was late on a cold dark winter's evening with night falling rapidly. Under these conditions the crew no doubt felt safe, being unaware that they were being plotted by the East Coast CH radar, and that a section of Spitfires had been scrambled from Rochford to intercept. The Heinkel was sighted at 2000ft by F/L Leathart and the section closed to about 200yds and opened fire together, silencing the rear gunner. The e/a then dived through the clouds and mist to crash eventually in the Estuary. F/L Leathart and P/O J.D. McKenzie claimed a shared probable.

The loss of this crew with the much admired Gruppen Kdr. was a severe blow to the morale of this small elite unit, but it was fortunate for Germany that the secret apparatus was lost at sea and not on land. Based Vannes-Meucon.

11

18. **16.2.40** Hurricane I, L1699 **79** **Reculver.** Was reported by the C.G. as fallen into the sea, and a search was carried out by the Margate L.B. and H.M. Minesweeper H67. P/O Tarlington was posted missing. Based Manston. Cat 3

19 **22.2.40** Blenheim IF, L8400 **23** **Tonbridge.** Sgt Macrae with A/C's Cullen and Penleve became lost in this night fighter and had to abandon. The aircraft crashed hitting a house and causing civilian casualties. Based Wittering. Cat 3

20. **23.2.40** Battle, L5005 **235** **Penshurst ALG.** Force landed in very bad weather conditions whilst on a delivery flight to R.A.F. Brize Norton. Based Manston. Cat 2

21. Blenheim, K7122 **235** **Manston** (Base). Crashed on landing due to undercarriage failing to lock down. F/L R.P. Cross and P/O W. Smith unhurt. Cat 2

Blenheim, L6792 **235** Also crashed on landing. Pilot Sgt J.C. Blessey unhurt. Cat 2

22. **3.3.40** Hudson, N7334 **P.D.U.** **S. of Gravesend.** This was a type new to the R.A.F. at the time, and its loss was due to poor aircaft recognition as it was shot down by Hurricanes. F/L Slocum and 2 crew members were killed, but J. Reid (rank not known) baled out burnt. Based Heston.
Cat 3

23. **11.3.40** Hurricane I, L2123 **3** **Folkestone G.C.** Sgt Lomax who was killed seemed to lose control and spin in from 1500ft, whilst on an exercise with 16Sq Lysanders, crashing and burning. Based Hawkinge. Cat 3

24. Blenheim, L6682 **600** **Dover,** W. Cliffe Road. This aircraft was on an A.A. co-operation exercise with Lt Sperling of the Welsh Guards as a passenger. It hit a tree on approach to Manston its base, crashing and burning. The crew F/O Tollemache and LAC Smith escaped but returned to the wreck in an unsuccessful attempt to rescue the Army Officer. Cat 3

25. Battle **?** **Margate,** Fleets Fm. One of the crew was killed. No other details found.

26. **24.3.40** Hurricane I, N2531 **32** **Folkestone.** Crashed in the sea. Cause unknown and also pilot state. Based Gravesend. F/O Bowler(?) Cat 3

27. **25.3.40** Spitfire I, N3291 **92** **Edenbridge.** Crashed whilst attempting a forced landing on the racecourse. F/L Byrne was baulked at the last moment by the sudden appearance of horses and riders, and had to divert to a small nearby field. He was bruised and slightly concussed. Based Croydon. Cat 3

28. **28.3.40** A.W.27, Ensign **G-ADTA** **Lympne.** The R.A.F. had impressed this Imperial Airways plane as a military transport. It was flak damaged whilst returning from Merville and had to force land on one wheel and only two engines. It was finally destroyed during an air-raid on the airfield 12.8.40.

29. **13.4.40** Hurricane I, L1719- **79** **Biggin Hill** (Base). Belly landed. No details of pilot and his condition on record. Cat 3

31. **10.5.40** Hurricane I, N2333 **3** **St Margaret's Bay.** 3Sq were posted to Merville. They had just landed and refuelled when the airfield was attacked by a staffel of He111's. As the attackers flew away into the evening dusk the Hurricanes took off in pursuit. With no ground control one of them became lost and headed north west across the Channel. Running out of fuel the pilot baled out near the radar unit at Swingate. The next day he returned to Merville in a new aircraft. Cat 3

31A. **13.5.40** Defiant I, L6955 **264** **Manston.** The pilot of this aircraft retracted the undercarriage instead of the flaps, when it was taxiing. This was due to faulty cockpit drill. He was returned to O.T.U. Crew unhurt. Based Duxford. Cat 3

32. **22.5.40** Lysander II, P1672 **2** **Bekesbourne** (Base). Had been on a raid against enemy motor transport near Boulogne. As it landed a bomb that had hung up fell off and exploded. P/O G. Grant-Govern was wounded and LAC Jones killed.
Cat 3

33. Ju88 **3/KG30** **Dover.** 10 miles S. Seen by 74Sq whilst on a northerly heading at 12000ft towards the town and attacked. Claimed as shot down by S/L A. Malan and P/O P. Stevenson. Three crew killed.

34 Spitfire I, K9920 **65** **N. Foreland.** A flight lead by F/L G.A. Saunders was on a Dunkirk patrol when this aircraft flown by P/O K. Hart had engine trouble and had to force land with undercarriage up on the clifftop and caught fire. Based Hornchurch. Cat 3

35. Blenheim IV, R3596 **53** **Hawkinge.** Sustained flak damage between Arras and Cambrai during a bombing attack. It crashed whilst attempting a force landing. P/O Tiptree unhurt, Sgt Williamson and LAC Jeffreys slightly injured. Based Andover.
Cat 3

36. Blenheims **107 & 110** **Manston.** A flight made up of aircraft from the two squadrons led by W/C B. Embry attacked a German Army H.Q. at Ribeaucourt. They were forced to land at Manston due to adverse met. conditions. Based Wattisham.

37.   Blenheim, P4925 **107**
Channel. Whilst on the above operation received flak damage to engine and hydraulics, which forced them to ditch. P/O Miller and crew were picked up by the R.N. after sometime in the water. Based Wattisham.   Cat 3

38. **23.5.40**   Spitfire I, N3167 **92**
Hawkinge. Force landed after a defensive patrol over Dunkirk. F/L C.P. Green was wounded in the leg. Based Hornchurch.
                                             Cat 2

39. **25.5.40**   Hurricane I, P3319 **151**
off Dover. Had a mid-air collision with P3323. F/L Ives missing. Based Martlesham.
                                             Cat 3

40.   Hurricane I, P3323 **151**
As above. P/O Bushell missing.

41. **26.5.40**   Spitfire I, K9827 **616**
Dungeness. Shot down by Me109's. Pilot picked up dead by the L.B. Based Northolt.
                                             Cat 3

42.   Spitfire I, L1031 **19**
Deal on the beach. Engine failed after shooting a Ju87B. P/O M.D. Lyne had a bullet in his knee. Based Hornchurch.   Cat 2

43.   Hurricane I, P2589 **145**
nr Dover. Received hits in the wings and coolant tank from return fire of a He111, and had to force land. P/O P.L. Parrott unhurt. Based Tangmere.   Cat 2

44.   Hector, K8111 **613**
Herne Bay G.C. Was on its way to Calais to carry out a supply drop to soldiers cut off in the town. The pilot tested his guns and part of one came adrift and pierced the main fuel tank. The aircraft force landed, later returning to Hawkinge on the reserve. P/O Brown and gunner safe. Based Odiham Adv. Hawkinge.   Cat 2

45. **27.5.40**   Me110 **2(F)122**
S.E. Coast. Shot down by the R.A.F. whilst on a recce. flight. Lw Q.M's records do not give the names of crew or a/c number.

46.   Hector, K8116 **613**
nr Dover, Shakespear Cliff. With Lysanders had been on a supply dropping mission to beleagured British rearguard in Calais. When a/c crashed P/O Jenkyns was safe but LAC Brown (903229) killed. Based Odiham.
                                             Cat 3

47.   Spitfire I **610**
Gravesend (Base). After combat with Ju88's and Me110's over Dunkerque was combat damaged and out of fuel. Only just reached the end of the runway, shed a landing wheel and ended on its nose. F/O Kerr-Wilson safe.
                                             Cat 2

48.   Blenheim IV, R3703 **53**
St Margarets Bay. Damaged by enemy fighters when one of 48 Blenheims attacking Dunkerque area. Crew abandoned. P/O

Aldridge and A/C Trafford injured, Sgt Macrae not. Based Andover.   Cat 3

49. **28.5.40**   Blenheim, -E **235**
nr Goodwins. Shot up by Me109's and had to ditch, but crew were picked up. (There are conflicting reports about this.) Based Detling.   Cat 3

50.   Spitfire I **616**
Manston. Crash landed after ops. over Dunkerque. S/L Robinson unhurt. Based Rochford.   Cat 2

51. **29.5.40**   Blenheim IVF, P6909 **235**
Detling (Base). Crashed on take off due to engine failure. F/L R. Cross and Sgt A.V. Slocombe killed. A/C North died later in hospital.   Cat 3

52.   Defiant I, L6956 **264**
Manston. Crash landed with only one wheel and a leaking fuel tank, after a defensive action over Dunkerque. Sgt Thorn and LAC F. Barker safe. Based Duxford.   Cat 2

53.   Hurricane I, L1666 **242**
Biggin Hill (Base). Took hits from a Me109 over Dunkerque and had to land on one main wheel, crumpling the wing. P/O J. Latta unhurt. (Also reported at Manston.)
                                             Cat 2

54.   Hurricane I, P2769 **242**
Manston. Landed with high coolant temperature after above action. F/O G. Plinston hurt. Based Biggin Hill.   Cat 2

55.   Hurricane I, L1756 **242**
Hawkinge. Crashed on take off hitting a parked Blenheim. P/O J. Howitt unhurt.
                                             Cat 3(?)

56.   Blenheim, L9470 **53**
Involved in the above incident,

57.   Anson I, K8771(?) **48**
off Deal. Damaged by enemy action and forced to ditch. F/L Astley, P/O Dunn, LAC McIlvenny and Hill safe. Based Detling.
                                             Cat 3
(There is doubt about the a/c No. given in Form 541 as K8771 was not written off until 23.6.41.)

58.   Blenheim IF, L9260 **235**
off Dover. Shot up by Me109's whilst on patrol Dunkerque to Dover. P/O Cronan, Sgt Lancaster and LAC Peebles rescued from their dinghy. Based Detling.   Cat 3

                       Blenheim IV, L9397 **235**
As above. P/O Booth, Sgt Elliott and LAC Scott killed.

59.   Spitfire I, N3289 **610**
Channel. Was providing air cover Dunkerque when it crashed in the sea. F/O Kerr-Wilson missing. Based Gravesend.   Cat 3

60.   Defiant I, L6957 **264**
Manston. Shot up by a Me109E and had to force land. P/O Kay's condition not known. LAC Jones baled out, missing. Based Duxford.
                                             Cat 3

13

61.   Hurricane I, P2854 **242**
Manston. Force landed with engine trouble. P/O Stansfield safe. Based Biggin Hill. Cat 2

62   Anson I, K8773 **48**
off Deal. Had been on a Dunkerque patrol when it was shot down by a Me109E and had to ditch, but not before the gunner A/C Harding had shot down one and damaged two more. He was later awarded the D.F.M. Crew P/O's Allington, Wharry and AC Dilnutt. Based Detling.   Cat 3

63.   Defiant, L6986 **264**
Manston. Forgot to lower undercarriage on landing. Crew unhurt. Based Duxford. Cat 2

                 Defiant, L7006 **264**
Manston. Swung on landing and undercarriage collapsed, due to crew fatigue. P/O's Barwell and Williams unhurt.   Cat 2

64. **30.5.40**   Hurricane I, N2455 **245**
Dymchurch (Base). Force landed after a patrol over Dunkerque. P/O R. West unhurt.
                                 Cat 3

65.   Hurricane I, N2596 **245**
Lydd. As above. Sgt P. Banks unhurt.   Cat 2

66.   Hurricane I, N2597 **245**
Lydd (Base). As above. P/O Marsland unhurt.
                                 Cat 2

67.   Spitfire I, N3203 **609**
Manston(?). On return from Dunkerque had to force land. F/O F. Howell unhurt. Based Northolt.   Cat ?

31.5.40
On this day Fighter Command lost 21 a/c + one written off, but only 8 pilots and 1 gunner. *Claims* against the Lw were 40-50.

68.   Spitfire I, L1087 **609**
Dover. 3 miles off. Whilst flying as an escort for 264Sq Defiants at 2700ft, 3 miles north of Dunkerque sighted a number of He111's 2000ft lower. The bombers were engaged but the Me110 escort intervened. F/O J.C. Gilbert disappeared and L1087 flown by Sgt Bennett was shot up. Turning for home, escorted by F/L Russell he reached a point only 3 miles short of the English coast when he had to ditch. Russell flew on to Dover and guided HMS Playboy back to pick up Bennett. Based Northolt.   Cat 3

69.   Hurricane I, L2117 **605**
Folkestone. 6 miles N. P/O Dini was killed when he crashed into a field. Cause not known. Based Hawkinge.   Cat 3

70.   Defiant I, L6972 **264**
Dover. 5 miles off. Having shot down a He111 and attacked two others, it was itself hit by return fire damaging the radiator. The cockpit filled with smoke forcing the last attack to be broken off. Eventually the Defiant had to ditch between 2 destroyers. P/O Barwell and Williams were picked up safely. Based Duxford.   Cat 3

71.   Hurricane I, N2423 **229**
Biggin Hill (Base). Was attacked by 4 Me109's and Sgt D.F. Edgehill was badly wounded remaining in hospital for a long time, only returning to flying duties in 1941.
                                 Cat 2

71A.   Anson I, N5232 **500**
Detling. Overshot on landing and finished in a hedge. Sgt D.C. Spencer and crew unhurt.
                               Cat 2(?)

72.   Defiant I, L7019 **264**
Manston. Crash landed after a Dunkerque patrol. P/O R.W. Stokes unhurt. LAC Fairbrother baled out safely.   Cat 2

73.   Anson I, R3389 **500**
Detling (Base). Had engine trouble and made a wheels up landing. As the bomb load was still on the aircraft it burst into flames. The crew escaped except the Nav. F/O Chambers. Cpl Pearson, a WAAF medical orderly managed to pull out the badly burnt man. Later she was awarded the B.E.M.   Cat 3

74.   Spitfire I, (?)R6629 **610**
off Ramsgate. The squadron had been in combat with Me110's over Dunkerque. P/O G. Keighley badly shot up. He managed to keep the a/c flying for most of the Channel crossing, finally baling out from 3000ft. After some time in the sea he was picked up and landed at Ramsgate. Based Gravesend.   Cat 3

75.   Spitfire I, N3274 **610**
Channel. After the above action. F/O G.L. Chambers was missing.   Cat 3

76.   Hurricane I, L1973 **111**
Manston. Had been part of top cover over Dunkerque and became involved in the general melee. Sgt Robinson had a bullet in his ankle and crash landed. Based N. Weald.
                                 Cat 2(?)

77. **1.6.40**   Spitfire I **616**
Rochester a/f. Had attacked two Me109's circling a naval vessel, but ran short of fuel on return and had to crash land. P/O K. Holden unhurt. Based Rochford.   Cat 2(?)

78.   Me109E   **I/JG26**
Straits of Dover. Shot down by the gunner of an Anson. Lt Gruel killed.

79.
2 × Blenheims, -A & -O, 1 of them R3630 **254**
Goodwin Sands. These aircraft were on a patrol when they were attacked by 11 × Me109's, whilst they were trying to drive off a Ju87B. One was shot down at once and the other failed to return to base. F/O Spiers was the sole survivor. Based Sumburgh. det. Manston. (There is no record of this in the unit's F541. May have been due to the detachment.)

80.   Blenheim **254**
Goodwins. This is a separate incident to the

above, but also due to enemy action.   Cat 3

82.   Lysander II, N1253   **26**
Hawkinge. Crashed on landing, cause not known. P/O Patterson safe, LAC Carter killed. Based Lympne.   Cat 3

83.   Hurricane I, N2497   **145**
Manston. Was hit in the radiator during a Dunkerque patrol, but just managed to reach the airfield. P/O L.D. Scott unhurt. Based Tangmere.   Cat 2

84.   2.6.40   Spitfire I, K9924   **72**
Gravesend (Base). Damaged whilst on patrol over Dunkerque. As a result it had to belly land at base. F/O O. Pigg slightly injured in the leg.   Cat 3

85.   2.6.40   Hurricane I   **111**
Margate-Ramsgate. Badly damaged after an evacuation patrol and P/O R.R. Wilson had to bale out over the sea but landed near the airfield. Based Croydon.   Cat 3

86.   Blenheim, L9476   **53**
Goodwin Sands. Shot up by L.A.A. and whilst taking evasive action hit the sand with the starboard propellor, and had to force land on the Sands. Crew F/L Brown, Sgt Brooks and A/C Knowles were picked up by HMS Shipmate.   Cat(?)

87.   4.6.40   Blenheim IV, R3697   **59**
Eastchurch (Adv. Base). 1 mile N. Crashed on take off. P/O Ashton and crew killed. Based Odiham.   Cat 3

88.   Hurricane I, N2460   **32**
Hawkinge. Pilot reported that he had been shot up by three He113's whilst intercepting a raid at 5000ft. P/O Smythe had to force land. Based Biggin Hill.   Cat 2(?)

89.   Hurricane I, N2463   **32**
Manston. As above P/O Grice unhurt.   Cat 2

90.   Hurricane I, N2724   **32**
Hawkinge. As above P/O Gillman.   Cat 2(?)

At this time faked photographs had convinced A.M. Intelligence that the Luftwaffe had He113's in squadron service. In fact only a few of the prototypes had been produced before the High Command abandoned the design. Later Heinkels sold 17 to Spain, 24 to Rumania and 16 to Japan.

91.   6.6.40   Hurricane I
Dungeness. 6 miles SSW. The lifeboat was led to the position of a ditched aircraft by two others and the pilot picked up. (From the Dungeness L.B. log. It has not been possible to identify the pilot or unit.)

92.   Hurricane I   **79**
Hawkinge a/f. Crashed badly on landing but S/L Joslin unhurt. (Perhaps a non-op. flight for not recorded in F.541.)   Cat 3

93.   12.6.40   Spitfire I, P9451(?)   **610**
off Margate. Lost in combat with Me109's

when it was shot down into the sea. F/L J. Ellis safe. Based Gravesend.   Cat 3

94.   Spitfire I,   **610**
As above. Sgt Arnfield picked up unhurt.
                              Cat 3

95.   19.6.40   He111   **6/KG4**
Margate, Palm Bay. Found on the beach by the lifeboat which had been launched to investigate a series of flares NNE of Foreness. This aircraft was inspected and recovered for R.A.E. Farnborough. Lt J. Bachaus, Uffz T. Kuhn and F. Boeck all POW's. Later the body of Fw A. Reitzig was recovered.

96.   19.6.40   He111   **4/KG4**
nr Felixstowe. Crashed into the sea. Hptm Prochnow and his crew killed. They were initially buried in Sheppey Cemetery, later transferred to the Soldaten Friedhof at Cannock Chase. Based Amsterdam-Schipol. Hptm Prochnow's body was washed ashore on the Isle of Sheppey.

97.   22.6.40   Hurricane I, P2764   **615**
Kent. P/O Lloyd crashed. No further details in unit records. Based Kenley.   Cat ?

99.   23.6.40   Hurricane I, P2698   **79**
Biggin Hill (Base). Overshot in fog and crashed attempting a landing.   Cat 3

100.   27.6.40   Hurricane I, P3591   **79**
Dungeness. 6 miles SSW. Ditched after being shot up by a Me109. Sgt McQueen was picked up unconscious by the Lifeboat and given artificial respiration. After transfer to a R.N. launch he was dead on arrival at Dover. Based Biggin.   Cat 3

101.   Hurricane I, P3401   **32**
off Dover. Shot down into the sea by Lw fighters. Pilot missing. Based Biggin Hill.
                              Cat 3

102.   Lysander II, P1745   **26**
W. Malling a/f (Base). Overshot on landing and crashed. P/O Penny and LAC Griffiths unhurt.   Cat 3

103.   28.6.40   Blenheim, L1397   **600**
Manston (Base). Overshot on landing and hit a dispersal pen.   Cat 3

104.   29.6.40   Spitfire I, P9498   **610**
Gravesend (Base). Hit a tractor on take off and crashed into a pillbox. Sgt Haines killed.
                              Cat 3

105.   30.6.40   Hurricane I, P3787   **151**
Ramsgate. Shot down by enemy aircraft into the Channel. S/L Donaldson was picked up by Ramsgate L.B. Based North Weald.   Cat 3

106.   3.7.40   Do17Z   **2/KG77**
Dover. Shot down by the R.A.F. and ditched. Oblt Kretzschmann and 3 crew missing. Based Laon-Couvron.

107.   Do17Z   **8/KG77**
Horsmonden. Damaged by both R.A.F. and A.A. with the result that it crashed.

108. Do17Z **9/KG77**
off Dover. Shot down into the Channel by A.A. Oblt Kapsch and three crew missing. Based Asche(?) Dover Harbour was the target for the raid.

109. Spitfire I, K9928, JH-N **74**
nr Margate. Was struck by lightning and Sgt White killed. Based Hornchurch. Cat 3

110. 4.7.40 Hurricane I, N2619 **79**
St Margarets Bay. Shot down by Me109's. Sgt Cartwright killed after his aircraft caught fire and he baled out with a burning 'chute. A H.S.L. picked up his body. Based Biggin Hill. Cat 3

111. Me109E **4/LG2**
off Hawkinge in the sea. Was shot down by a 32Sq Hurricane (Smythe) and the pilot Uffz F. Burger killed. Based St Omer-Fort Rouge.

112. Spitfire I, P9450 **64**
Hawkinge. Crash landed after combat with Lw fighters over Rouen. SubLt D. Paul unhurt. Cat 2

113. 5.7.40 He111H, V4+GS, 5387 **8/KG1**
off Dover, Shakespear Cliff. H.E. and incendiary bombs were dropped before the e/a was shot down by 65Sq Spitfires (Hart, Kilner and Proudman). It had been on an armed shipping reconnaissance. Obfw H. Frischmuth and Uffz G. Wagner were made POW's. Uffz R. Marckovitz, Gfr F. Burger and F. Martinek missing. Based Rosieres en Santerre.

SubLt Dawson Paul, R.N.V.R.
This officer was one of a small group from the Fleet Air Arm who volunteered to fly with Fighter Command and most of whom failed to survive the Battle.

He joined 64Sq to fly Spitfires and operated from R.A.F. Church Fenton, Leconfield and Kenley, commencing on the first of July.

He was credited with a shared Do17Z of 2/KG77 south of Beachy Head on his first sortie and nine days later claimed two Me110's of III/ZG26 near Calais. On the 13th in L1035 he shot down a Me109E of 9/JG51 south of Folkestone, followed by a Do215 a week later.

Once again in L1035 on the 25th he was himself shot down by a Me109E off the Kent Coast, and picked up by an E-boat only to die as a P.O.W. on the 30th. A very full month.

114. 6.7.40 Blenheim, L8789, PZ-J **53**
Ramsgate. Carried out a night recce of road and rail traffic in the Dunkirk-Calais-Boulogne area. The aircraft was damaged in bad weather conditions and had to force land at Ramsgate. F/L Bartlett, Sgts Aldridge and Sheldrick safe. Based Detling. Cat ?

115. 7.7.40 Blenheim, R3678 **53**
Detling. Damaged in a night landing after ops. on shipping at Ostende. Based Detling. Cat 2

116. Spitfire I, R6711 **54**
Deal. P/O Campbell was slightly wounded when his aircraft was shot down by a Me109. Based Hornchurch. Cat 3

117. Spitfire I, P9389 **54**
Manston. As above F/O D.A. McMullen safe. Cat 3

118. Spitfire I, P9390 **54**
As above P/O E. Coleman safe. Cat 3

119. Spitfire I, R6615 **65**
Folkestone. Shot down in combat with Me109's. F/O G. Proudman killed. Based Hornchurch. Cat 3

120. Spitfire I, N3129 **65**
As above Sgt Hayes killed. Cat 3

121. Spitfire I, R6609 **65**
Folkestone. As above P/O Brisbane killed. Cat 3

122. Hurricane I, P2756 **79**
Folkestone, Chilverton Elms. Cause of crash not known. S/L Joslin killed. Based Hawkinge. Cat 3

123. 8.7.40 Hurricane I, N2460 **32**
Hawkinge. Force landed after combat damage caused by Me109's over a convoy near Dungeness. F/O Smythe unhurt. Based Biggin Hill. Cat 2

124. Spitfire I, K9907 **65**
off Dover. After being attacked by Me109's S/L Cooke went into cloud and was not seen again. Based Hornchurch. Cat 3

125. Spitfire I, P9465 **74**
Manston. Crash landed but P/O P.C. Stevenson was unhurt. Based Hornchurch. Cat 2

126. Hurricane I, N2384 **79**
Dover. Shot down in flames P/O J.E. Wood baled out but was found dead in the sea. Based Hawkinge. Cat 3

127. Hurricane I, P3461 **79**
Dover, Temple Ewell. As above F/O Mitchell killed.

128. Spitfire I, R6806 **610**
Dover. 6 miles off. Shot down by gunners of a Do17Z. P/O A. Raven was seen in the sea believed drowned. Based Biggin Hill. Cat 3

129. Me109E, 2964 **3/LG2**
nr Sandwich. Shot down by 54Sq (Way). The first one to fall on English soil. Lt Striberny POW. Based Calais-Marck.

130. Me109E, 1162 **4/JG51**
Elham. Shot down by 74Sq (Mould). Lt Boehm unhurt and POW. Based Peuplingne.

131. Me109E **7/JG51**
Dover. 8 miles off. Shot down by 65Sq (F/S Franklin. Uffz Schneiderberger killed.

132. Me109E **III/JG51**
Channel. Shot down by 54Sq (Garton and Way). Pilot killed. Based St Quentin — Clastres.

Incident No. 139. This air/sea rescue He59 was forced down near the Goodwins by aircraft of 54 Squadron.
(Kent Messenger)

133. **9.7.40** Spitfire I, N3183 **54**
Manston. After a collision with a Me109E F/L A. Deere, slightly burnt, had to force land. Based Hornchurch. Cat 3

134. 2 × Me109's
off Dover. Shot down whilst acting as escort for a SeenotflugKdo mission. Pilots missing.

135. Spitfire I, R6705 **54**
nr Manston. P/O Garton killed in combat with Me109's. Based Hornchurch. Cat 3

136. Spitfire I, L1093 **54**
Dover, S of. Shot down by Me09's. P/O Evershed killed. Cat 3

137. Hurricane I, P3806 **151**
Thames Estuary. Shot up whilst on a convoy escort. Mid. A. Wightman baled out and was picked up by a fishing boat which later transferred him to a destroyer. Based North Weald. Cat 3

138. He59 Seenotflkdo, D-ASUO
Goodwins. This Lw A.S.R. aircraft was forced down by 54Sq where the crew were made POW's. Uffz Anders, Bartmann, Maywald and Schiele. Later the seaplane was towed inshore by a trawler from this exposed position. The following day the L.B. continued the tow to Dover Harbour. Shortly after its arrival it was sunk during a Jabo attack. Based Boulogne Harbour.

140. **10.7.40** Me110 **III/ZG26**
Thames Estuary. Crew of this aircraft were missing after it was shot down by 151Sq Hurricanes. Based at St Omer or Barley.

141. Spitfire I, K9863 **74**
Manston. Damaged in combat with Do17Z's and their escort, and had to force land. P/O Freeborn safe. Based Hornchurch. Cat 2

142. Hurricane I, P3671 **111**
off Folkestone. Attacked by Me109's of III/JG51 and collided with a Do17Z of 3/KG3 losing a wing at 6000ft. F/O Higgs' body came ashore at Noordwijk 15.8.40. Based Croydon. Cat 3

143. Me110 **8/ZG26**
Dungeness — Folkestone. Shot down by 56Sq (Gracie and White) over a convoy. Lt Kuhrke and his gunner missing. Based at St Omer or Barley.

144. Hurricane I, P3554 **56**
Manston. Damaged by Me110's over a convoy off Dungeness and its engine seized whilst force landing. F/L E. Gracie unhurt. Based N. Weald. Cat 2

145 Spitfire I, P9399(?) **74**
Lympne. Force landed after combat with a Me109 with a damaged radiator. P/O D. Cobden safe. Based Hornchurch. Cat 2

145A. Me109E **5/JG51**
Thames Estuary. Shot down by fighter escort of a convoy off North Foreland. Uffz Stocker killed. Based Peuplingne.

146. Spitfire I, P9446 **74 or 54(?)**
Manston. Force landed after combat damage during an encounter with a mixed bomber and fighter force over Dover. Sgt Mould unhurt. Based Hornchurh. Cat 2

147. Hurricane I, P3663 **111**
Hawkinge. Sustained a damaged wing in a fight off Folkestone and crash landed. Sgt Carnall unhurt. Based Croydon. Cat 2

148. Spitfire I, L1000 **610**
Hawkinge. Had similar damage to the above also crashed. S/L Smith unhurt. Based North Weald. Cat 2

149. Do17Z **3/KG2**
Channel. Shot down by both R.A.F. and A.A. One of the crew killed others missing, after an attack on a convoy. Based Arras.

150. Do17Z **3/KG2**
nr Dungeness Buoy. Lost a wing in a collision with a 111Sq Hurricane. Hptm Kreiger and Obfw Thalmann POW's. Fw Osinsky and Fw Winkelmann missing. Based Arras.

151. Me110 **8/ZG26**
off Folkestone. Shot down by Combined R.A.F. and A.A. fire. Oblt Siegmund POW but his gunner missing. Based at St Omer or Barley.

152. Me110 **8/ZG26**
Folkestone. Whilst in combat with the R.A.F. was shot down by A.A. Obfw Meyer. POW. Gefr Rhode missing. Based as above.

153. The Coastguards reported three aircraft down in the sea and the Lifeboat made a search, but only scraps of Luftwaffe uniform were found.

The above incidents are typical of the running fights which took place over the coastal convoys at this time.

154. **11.7.40** Ju87B **II/LG1**
Dover. One crew member killed and one missing when this a∕c was shot down by R.A.F. Based Orleans (?)

155. Anson I, N5228, MK-F **500**
Detling (Base). Three Ansons were briefed for a Channel patrol in minimal weather conditions, low temperatures, continuous heavy rain and winds Force 7-8. At 0155hrs two of them were able to take off in a short clearer break. The other did not get clearance until 0205hrs when a very short break in the low cloud occurred. In very poor visibility Sgt J. Wilson became airborne but in a matter of seconds hit trees only half a mile from the perimeter. He and the rest of the crew Sgts L. O'Kelly, W. Shier and Worton were killed and their bodies not found until the following morning. O'Kelly and Shier are buried in the local churchyard. Cat 3

156. **12.7.40** Anson I, MK-R **500**
Detling (Base). After circling the airfield this a/c crashed and burned. P/O's Aston and Chauffey and Sgts Prentice and A/C Hubbard killed.

157. 3 × Me109's **9/JG51**
Folkestone. Lost in the sea. No further details available. Based St Omer or St Quentin.

160. **13.7.40** Spitfire I, R6807 **610**
Tatsfield, Skid House. Crashed whilst on a routine patrol. Sgt W. Parker killed. Based Biggin Hill. Cat 3

161. Hurricane I, P2985 **56**
Rodmersham. Force landed after combat over the Channel. Sgt R. Baker unhurt. Based N. Weald. Cat 2

162. Spitfire I, K9795 **64**
Hawkinge. Hit by A.A. fire during a dogfight and had to belly land. Sgt Binham unhurt. Based Kenley. Cat 2

163. Me109E4 **9/JG51**
Folkestone, south of. Shot down by 64Sq Spitfires (Sublt Paul). Lt Lange killed. Based St Omer or St Quentin.

165. **14.7.40** Hurricane I, P2958 **111**
Hawkinge a∕f. Crashed on take off from this the advanced base. P/O A. Fisher unhurt. Cat 2

166. Ju87B **11/LG1**
east of **Dover.** Shot down by yellow section 615Sq (Collard, Hugo and Gaynor). Oblt Sonnberg killed and his gunner missing. Based Cambrai-Epinoy.

167. Hurricane I, L1584 **615**
St Margarets Bay. Shot down by Me109's of II/JG51 over Dover. P/O M. Mudie baled out badly injured and was picked up from the sea by the R.N. only to die in hospital 15.7.40. Based Kenley. Cat 3

168. **17.7.40** Hurricane I, N2588 **32**
nr Dungeness. Force landed due to loss of oil. F/O J. Humpherson unhurt. Based Biggin Hill. Cat 2

169. **18.7.40** Spitfire I, P9452 **610**
Channel. Shot down by Hptm J. Tietzen (Staffel Kapitan) 5/JG51. P/O Litchfield killed. Based Biggin Hill. Cat 3

170. **19.7.40** Defiant I, L6995 **141**
Dover-Folkestone. Ditched after being attacked by Me109's of III/JG51. P/O R. Howley and Sgt A. Curley missing. Based W. Malling adv. Hawkinge. Cat 3

171. Defiant I, L7015 **141**
Folkestone. As above P/O R. Kidson and Sgt F. Atkins killed. Cat 3

172. Defiant I, L7016 **141**
As above F/O J.R. Gard'ner baled out wounded and picked up. P/O Slatter missing. Gard'ner needed three months treatment before returning to duty. Cat 3

173. Defiant I, L6974 **141**
As above F/O J. Kemp and Sgt R. Crombie missing. Cat 3

174. Defiant I, L7009 **141**
Dover, Elmsvale Road. Shot down by Me109's. F/L Donald and P/O Hamilton killed. Cat 3

175. Defiant I, L6983 **141**
nr Hawkinge. As above P/O I. McDougall unhurt, Sgt J. Wise baled out missing. Cat 3

176. Defiant I, L7001 **141**
nr Dover. As above F/L Loudon and F/O Farnes baled out safely. Cat 3

The Defiant failure

141 Squadron's losses on the 19th serve to illustrate the failure of this type as a day fighter. Just after noon the squadron took off from Hawkinge and rendezvoused with 111Sq Hurrs. Over the Channel they met III/JG51. The Hurricanes were hard pressed to defend themselves against the Me109's and the Defiants were completely outflown. Two of them were shot down almost immediately and were followed by a further five.

After a few initial successes when first operational their lack of speed, ability to manoeuvre and lack of full arc of fire made them especially vulnerable to head on attacks.

Churchill on a visit to H.Q. Fighter Command was given the news that 141Sq had been practically wiped out, and was very concerned about the loss of aircraft, but the AOC in C, Sir Hugh Dowding said his concern was for the four pilots and six gunners missing or killed, and the two pilots in hospital.

177   Me109E
over Dover. Shot down by 74Sq (Malan and Stevenson).

178.   Hurricane I, P3144   **32**
Dover, Hougham. Probably shot down by Uffz Mayer III/JG51, whilst evading the attentions of Dover A.A. F/S Turner baled out badly burnt. Based Biggin Hill.   Cat 3

179.   He115   **KuflGr3/906**
Thames Estuary. Shot down by 64Sq Spitfire (Jeffrey). Oblt Hilderbrandt, Lt Dr Steinert and one other missing. Based ?

180. **20.7.40**   Hurricane I, N2670   **32**
Dover, Lydden. Shot down by Oblt Priller. Sublt G. Bulmer missing whilst on convoy escort with 610Sq. Based Biggin Hill.   Cat 3
(There is some doubt about crash site. It may have been *off* Dover.)

Oblt Josef Priller

Was one of the few Lw aces whose score was entirely against the Western Allies. He became operational in October 1939 as a Staffel Kapitan with JG51 and flew with that unit during the Battle for France and the hardest part of the Battle of Britain.

In November 1940 he was posted to JG26 and flew consistently against the R.A.F. and then the U.S.A.A.F., until as an Oberst he was made Inspector of Fighters. Surely the longest continuous period of ops. in any Air Force during WWII.

He survived the War and worked in his father's Munich Brewery until May 1961 when he died suddenly of a heart attack.

It should be remembered that the Luftwaffe did not subscribe to the policy of rest periods from operational flying after a set period or after a certain number of operational flights, as did the Allied Air Forces, so aircrew flew until medically unfit, promoted to command or killed, with only short leaves. This helps to account in part for some of the high scores of their aces, and in part for the weakness of the training system as experience died and was not handed on.

181.   Hurricane I, N2532   **32**
nr Hawkinge. Had its engine and fuel tank damaged in combat with II/JG51 off Dover, whilst being flown by S/L Worrall who was unhurt. Claimed by Obfw Ilner. Based Biggin Hill.   Cat 3

182.   Spitfire I, N3201   **610**
nr Denton. Had its tail shot off by Obfw Schmidt of I/JG51. P/O Keighley baled out. Based Biggin Hill.   Cat 3

184. **21.7.40**   Ju87B   **II/StG2**
Channel. The fate of this aircraft and crew is not recorded in the Lw Q.M.'s records. Based St Malo or Lannion.

185. **23.7.40**   Ju88A   **4(F)122**
nr Dover. Missing whilst on a recce. mission Lt Forster and crew missing. Based Brussels(?)

186. **24.7.40**   Me109E4   **III/JG26**
Margate, Byron Ave., shot down by 54Sq (Gray?). Lt J. Schauff baled out but his 'chute failed to open and he fell in Deal. Based Caffiers.

188.   Me109E   **7/JG52**
nr Dover. Crashed in the sea after being shot up by 610Sq (Smith). Oblt Fermer dead. Based Coquelles.

189.   Me109E   **III/JG52**
off Margate. Another of 610Sq's victims. Hptm von Houwald killed. Based Coquelles.

190.   Me109E   **7/JG52**
nr Margate. Claimed by 610Sq (Ellis) Gfr Frank killed. Based Coquelles.

191.   Spitfire I, R6812   **54**
Cliftonville, on an electricity sub-stn. Old Charles Inn. Had its engine damaged by III/JG52. (It could also have been the Spitfire claimed by Maj A. Galland over the Estuary of which the pilot baled out.) The a/c is reported as stalling en route to Manston killing P/O Allen J. and Homeguard C. Cuthbert whilst he was attempting a rescue. This incident is far from clear. Based Hornchurch.

                                          Cat 3

Of this period G/C Gray (then a P/O in 54Sq) said: 'My squadron flying from Hornchurch lost half its aircraft and pilots in the 4½ days 24-28th July.'

192.   Me109E   **8/JG52**
off Margate. P/O Gray shot down this aircraft. Oblt Erlich, Staffel Kapt. missing after he baled out. Based Coquelles.

Incident No. 193. A Me109E of III/JG26 force landed at Margate after combat with 65 Squadron.

193.   Me109E, 6296 **III/JG26**
Margate, Northdown. Force landed after being shot up by 65Sq (Sawyer). Oblt W. Bartels Geschwader Tech. Officer had been a civil aviation engineer in Austria pre-war and Priller in his book on JG26 said that his loss was a severe blow for that unit. Based Caffiers.

The standard operating procedure for these free chase operations over S.E. England was to take off from the Pas de Calais or Cotentin Peninsular airfields, assemble over the French coast at 15-18000ft then climb to 21-25000ft, taking roughly 30 minutes to cross the English coast leaving little combat time before the return flight.

194. **25.7.40**   Spitfire I, N3128 **65**
Manston (Adv. base). A section was scrambled only to be recalled after 10mins. On the return flight this battle weary aircraft developed a glycol leak and the cockpit filled with white fumes. On landing it struck a hollow in the airfield surface and crashed with its undercarriage unlocked. P/O B. Finucane was unhurt.   Cat 2

195.   Spitfire I, R6707 **54**
Deal-Dover. Shot down whilst on a convoy escort. F/L B. Way killed. Based Rochford.
                                              Cat 3
196.   2 × Ju87B's **II/StG1**
Channel. Shot down by the R.A.F. Whilst the fate of one crew of two N.C.O.'s is not known; Lt Roden and his gunner in the other were posted as missing.

197.   Hurricane I, P3677 **32**
nr Dover. Was part of a convoy escort at 22000ft over the Channel, when it became separated from the rest of the flight and was attacked by six Me109's and badly shot up. P/O V.G. Daw was slightly wounded in the leg, but managed to cross the coast before force landing. Based Biggin Hill.   Cat 2

198.   Spitfire I, P9387 **54**
nr Dover. Crashed following combat with Me109's. P/O Turley-George unhurt. Based Hornchurch.   Cat 2

199.   Spitfire I, P9421 **64**
off Dover. Shot down by Me109's. P/O A. Jeffrey killed. Based Kenley.   Cat 3

200.   Spitfire I, L1055 **64**
Hawkinge. Force landed with air system damaged by return fire from Ju87's over the Channel. S/L McDonnell unhurt. Based Kenley.   Cat 2

201.   Spitfire I, R6595 **610**
Biggin Hill (Base). Damaged in combat over a convoy. P/O F. Gardiner wounded in the arm. Based Biggin Hill.   Cat 2

202.   Spitfire I, R6693, DW-A **610**
Hawkinge. Crashed and burned after combat with Me109's. S/L A. Smith killed.   Cat 3

203.   Spitfire I, R6816 **54**
Kingsdown (Dover). Was also lost to Me109's whilst on convoy protection off Dover. P/O A. Finnie killed. Based Hornchurch.   Cat 3

204.   Spitfire I, R6700, SH-K **64**
Lympne a/f. After combat over Folkestone landed with supercharger failure. F/L L. Henstock unhurt. Based Kenley.   Cat 2

Incident No. 214. It is possible to decipher the claimed victories on the tail of this Me109E flown by Oblt Muncheberg of III/JG26. This incident is likely to be one of them. (Armée de l'Air)

205. Me109E 7/JG52
off Folkstone. Shot down by 610Sq (Ellis and Wilson). Oblt Keidel (Staffel Kapt.) missing. Based Coquelles.

206. Me109E 9/JG26
Thames Estuary, off the Kent coast. Shot down by a Spitfire 54Sq (Collett) or 65Sq (F/S Franklin). Fw Eberz killed. Based Caffiers.

207. Me109E, 6+ 8/JG52
Deal, Elvington Court. Shot down by 610Sq Spitfires. Uffz Reiss made POW. Based Coquelles.

208. Spitfire I, L1035 64
Channel. Shot down. Sublt D. Paul severely wounded and picked up by Seenoflkdo to die a POW 30.7.40. Based Kenley. Cat 3

209. Me109E 7/JG52
off Dover. Shot down by 610Sq. Oblt Bielefeld killed. Based Coquelles.

210. Me109E 7/JG52
Dover-Folkstone. Shot down by 610Sq (Ellis). Lt Schmidt missing.

On this day JG26 claimed 2 a/c shot down off Margate and 3 off Dover. Not yet identified.

211. **26.7.40** Hurricane I, P3808 501
off Dover. F/L P.A. Cox was shot down by III/JG52 over the Harbour and his body was not found. Based Gravesend. Cat 3

212. **27.7.40**
Blenheim IF, L1119, ND-C 236
nr Detling. Force landed short of fuel. Sgts N. Barron and J. Lowe unhurt. Based Thorney Island. Cat 2

213. **28.7.40** Hurricane I, P3622 257
nr St Margarets Bay. Seriously damaged by Me109's over the Channel and forced to land. Sgt R. Forward slightly injured. Based Northolt. Cat 3

214. Spitfire I, P9547 74
Goodwin Sands. P/O J. Young shot up over Dover and crashed on the sands. This victory was claimed by Oblt Meuncheberg of III/JG26. Based Hornchurch. Cat 3

215. Spitfire I, P9336 74
Dover. This aircraft crashed on the roof of Buckland Mill after Sgt E. Mould had baled out wounded. Based Hornchurch. Cat 3

216. Spitfire I, P6779 74
Manston. P/O P. Stevenson force landed with a seized engine as a result of combat damage inflicted by Oblt Leppla (I/JG51) who attacked him whilst he was himself attacking the famous Major Mölders.

Werner Mölders

First attempted to become a pilot when, as a 22 year old army leutnant, he applied for a flying course, but was rejected on medical grounds. A later application met with success and by 1938 he was a pilot with JG88, part of the Kondor Legion in the Spanish Civil War. He gained a reputation amongst his contemporaries far out of proportion to his age and rank. In the early part of WWII he was a little older than most of the other fighter pilots, but became a brilliant leader, and like Adolf Galland had the ability to teach by example. By 1941 he was Germany's highest scoring fighter ace with 115 successes to his credit.

21

He became Inspector of Fighters with the rank of Major General. Whilst carrying out an inspection of units in the Ukraine General Udet committed suicide and Mölders was flying as a passenger in a He111 to Berlin when it crashed and he was killed.

His claims for 1940/41 were:

6.9.40	Spitfire	Folkestone
11.9.40	Hurricane	SE London
20.9.40	2 × Spitfires	Dungeness
27.9.40	Spitfire	Maidstone
28.9.40	Spitfire	Littlestone
11.10.40	Spitfire	Folkestone
12.10.40	Hurricane	Dungeness
22.10.40	3 × Hurricanes	Maidstone
25.10.40	Spitfire	Dover and 1 at Margate
29.10.40	Hurricane	Dungeness
1.12.40	Hurricane	Ashford
26.2.41	Spitfire	Dungeness
16.4.41	Hurricane	Dungeness
4.5.41	Hurricane	Canterbury
6.6.41	Hurricane	Dover
8.5.41	Spitfire	Dover

If only half of these claims proved to be correct it would be an impressive performance in eight months.

218. Spitfire I, P9429 **41**
Manston. Shot up by Maj Mölders. F/O .A.D. Lovell had to crash land wounded. Based Manston. Cat 2

219. Me109E **2/JG51**
off Dover. This aircraft was credited to P/O Bennion (41Sq), but was also claimed by S/L A. Malan. Gfr Gebhardt missing. Based St Omer(?)

The 28th was a day of considerable Lw activity, with a sweep across Kent by at least 35 Me109's of JG26 and JG51. It was intercepted by 41 and 74 Sq Spitfires and 257Sq Hurricanes. Claims made by both sides proved to be excessive.

220. 29.7.80 Spitfire I, R6645 **64**
St Margarets Bay. Damaged by fire from a Ju87's gunner over the Channel. Sgt A. Binham had to be escorted to the Coast by 504Sq (Gibson) where he force landed. Based Kenley. Cat 2

221. Ju87B **II/LG1**
off Dover. Shot down by a Spitfire of 41Sq. Lt Furnwagner and gunner missing. Based Cambrai or Orleans.

222. Ju87B **II/LG1**
As above Oblt Kothe and gunner missing.

223. Hurricane I, P3879 **56**
off Dover. Whilst in combat with the Stukas and escort was shot down into the sea. F/S C. Cooney missing. Based North Weald. Cat 3

224. Hurricane I, L1865 **501**
Gravesend (Base). In combat with Ju87's was damaged in port wing. P/O J. Bland unhurt just managed to reach base and force land. Cat 2

225. Spitfire I, N3038 **41**
off Dover. Failed to return after combat. Believed crashed in sea. F/O D. Gamblen missing. Based Manston. Cat 3

226. Spitfire I, N3100 **41**
Manston (Base). Damaged in action over Dover. Undercarriage collapsed on landing. P/O Scott escaped unhurt. Cat 3

227. Me109E1 **6/JG51**
off Dover. Shot down whilst escorting Ju87's. Fw Hemmerling missing.

230. Spitfire I, N3264 **41**
Manston (Base). Had flaps damaged in combat and crash landed base. P/O Bennions unhurt. Cat 2

231. Spitfire I, N3113 **41**
Manston (Base). Damaged attempting a force landing. F/L Webster unhurt. Cat 2

232. Spitfire I, N3112 **41**
Deal, Ringwould. Was unable to make base crashing en route as a result of damage caused when F/O McKenzie intercepted an escorted bomber formation over Dover. His cockpit filled with fumes and his canopy jammed, so that he had to force land. He was unhurt. Based Manston. Cat 2

233. Hurricane I, L1955 **43**
Ashford, Brabourne Lees. Suffered an engine failure. P/O K.C. Campbell attempted a force landing but crashed and burned and he was killed. Based Northolt. Cat 3

A bad day for 41Sq.

234. Spitfire I, P9503 **610**
Gravesend (Base). Had a tyre burst by fire from a Do17Z (Stab/KG2) off Dungeness and crash landed at base. P/O Norris unhurt. Cat 2

235. 31.7.40 Spitfire I, P9398 **74**
Folkestone Harbour, 100yds from Victoria Pier. Whilst patrolling over Manston at 18000ft was shot up by Hptm Tietzen (4/JG51) and fell in flames into the harbour. Sgt Eley killed. Based Hornchurch. Cat 3

236. Spitfire I, P9379 **74**
Folkestone. Believed shot down by Oblt Föcö. P/O Gunn killed. Based Hornchurch. Cat 3

237. Spitfire I, R6983 **74**
Manston. F/L Kelly leading 'A' and 'B' Flights was over Manston when they sighted 15 × Me109's. In the ensuing dogfight this aircraft took a 20mm shell in the fuel tank and the cockpit filled with fuel and fumes. Although it was only just controllable Kelly continued to fight until at last he was forced to dive away. He failed to reach base and force landed. It was known later than his opponent had been Lt Hohagen of JG51. Based Hornchurch. Cat 2

238. Blenheim, PZ-K **53**
Detling. Crashed in bad weather. P/O
Mallon, Sgt Wilcox and Shackleford safe.
Cat 2

239. Hurricane I, P3646 **501**
Lydden Marsh. Crashed and burned after
combat against a raid over Dover. P/O R.S.
Don baled out injured. Based Gravesend.
Cat 3

239A. Hurricane I, P3349 **501**
Gravesend (Base). As above. Undershot run-
way and crashed. P/O E.G. Parkin injured.
Cat 2

240. **1.8.40** Avro504, AX871 exG-ADBM
SD Flt (Station Flt?) Hit a hut on take off and
crashed. Cat 3
It has not been possible to clarify this
incident. What was an aircraft of this obso-
lete type doing at **R.A.F. Hawkinge?** Why
was it flying?

241. **4.8.40** Magister I **16Gp Comm Flt**
Chatham, Luton. Crashed on an overshoot at
Rochester a/f. Based Rochester (?) Cat 3

242. **5.8.40** Me109E4 **1/JG51**
Channel. Shot up by the R.A.F. over Dover.
Obfw Schmid killed. Based St Omer.

243. Spitfire I, N3234 **41**
Manston. Crashed on take off, cause not
known. Pilot unhurt. Based Hornchurch.
Cat 3

244. Spitfire I, L1029 **64**
Folkestone, in shallows. Shot down by
Me110's. Sgt Isaac missing. Based Kenley.
Cat 3

245. Spitfire I, K9991 **64**
Hawkinge. Seriously damaged during
combat by 20mm cannon shell. F/O Donahue just reached the airfield and force
landed unhurt. Based Kenley. Cat 2

246. Spitfire I, P9436 **65**
Manston. Received strikes from Me109's fire
and was hit in the fuel tank, causing a mid-
air fire. Despite this and being slightly wounded Sgt Walker managed to force land. His
opponent was thought to be an Oblt Seiler.
Based Hornchurch. Cat 3

247. Me109E **I/JG54**
off Dover. After the above combat Oblt
Seiler was shot down by 151Sq (Blair or
Orchard) to be picked up from the sea
slightly wounded. Based Guines or Yvrench.

249. **6.8.40** Me110 **V/LG1**
Channel. Shot down by the R.A.F. Names of
crew not in Lw Q.M.'s records, and it is not
confirmed by any other source. Based Caen.

250. Hurricane I, V7205 **32**
Biggin Hill (Base). Force landed. Causes not
known, but not in unit's F541 so may have
been a non-op. flight. Cat 3

251. **7.8.40** Hurricane I, P3041 **501**
Gravesend (Base). Collided with another
Hurricane during approach to base in poor
weather. Sgt E. Howarth unhurt. Cat 2

252. Hurricane I, P3083 **501**
Involved in the above incident. Sgt Wilkinson unhurt. Cat 2

253. **8.8.40** Spitfire I, P9369 **64**
Capel le Ferne, Gt Couldham. Believed to
have been attacked by Hptm Trautloft of
III/JG51. Sgt J. Squier force landed injured.
Based Kenley. Cat 3

254. Spitfire I, L1045 **610**
Wittersham. Force landed after combat with
aircraft of JG51 over Hawkinge. Pilot believed hurt. Based Biggin Hill. Cat 2

255. Spitfire I, R6765 **610**
Hawkinge. Severely damaged in above
attack. Pilot unhurt. Based Biggin Hill. Cat 2

256. Spitfire I, K9911 **65**
Ramsgate area. Sgt D.I. Kirton, an inexperi-
enced pilot who had flown his first
operational sortie only a week before was
shot down and killed by Oblt Fronhofer of
9/JG26. Based Kenley. Cat 3

257. Me109E4 **8/JG26**
off Dover. Shot down by 64Sq Spitfires (Mcdonnell and Mann). Oblt Oehm missing.
Based Caffiers.
(In this combat Sgt Mann's aircraft was hit
by a 20mm round and so badly damaged
that, although he was able to reach Kenley
and force landed the Spitfire was a complete write-off.)

258. Spitfire I, K9905 **65**
Manston. Claimed as shot down by Oblt
Meuncheberg of III/JG26. Sgt N.T. Phillips
killed. Based Kenley. Cat 3

259. Blenheim II, L8665 **600**
off Ramsgate. Was on practice interceptions
with another Blenheim when it was shot
down by Oblt Sprick of III/JG26, crashing in
flames. F/O Grice is reported as pulling it
out of a dive to crash in the sea. Sgt Keast
and A/C J.B. Warren also killed. Based Man
ston. Cat 3

260. Spitfire I, L1039 **64**
Dover, W. Langdon. Caught fire in combat
with JG51 and crashed. P/O F. Kennard-
Davis baled out but died of injuries. Based
Kenley. Cat 3

261. **9.8.40** Spitfire I, R6639 **64**
Hawkinge. Forced landing after being dam-
aged in combat. P/O Andreae was unhurt.
Based Kenley. Cat 2

262. Spitfire I, R6992 **64**
As above, pilot P/O A.G. Donahue.

263. **15.8.40** 6 × Stirlings
Rochester. Aircraft Nos. N3645, 3647, 3648,
3649, 3650 and 3651 all destroyed during a
raid on Short's plant, by the Lw.

23

264.   Blenheim I, L8679 **600**
Westgate, nr Margate. Crew baled out after
an engine failure on night ops. F/O le Rougetel picked up by lifeboat whilst Sgt E.C.
Smith swam ashore. Based Manston.   Cat 3

265. **11.8.40**   Me109E1 **3/JG3**
off Margate. Shot down by the R.A.F. whilst
on an escort mission for Ju87's. Fw Heise
killed. Based Samer.

266.   Me109E1 **3/JG3**
Margate. S/L Malan and part of 74Sq took
off to patrol Manston at 10000ft, sighted 30
× Ju87's 2000ft lower and attacked. In turn
they were bounced by the Me109 top cover.
Malan shot down a fighter which crashed at
Margate. Fw Hofelich was killed and his
body washed up at Escalles (nr Calais) on
the 29th.

268.   Me110 **I/ZG26**
Thames Estuary. Shot down by a Spitfire of
74Sq (?Freeborn). Fw Puschnerus and another N.C.O. missing. Based St Omer or
Yvrench.

269.   Do17Z **9/KG4**
off Folkestone. Shot down by the R.A.F. One
of the crew wounded and all POW's. Based
Schipol.

270.   Ju87B **IV/LG1**
Thames Estuary. Possibly shot down by
151Sq. Both crew members missing. Based
Tramecourt.

271.   Ju87B **II/StG1**
Thames Estuary. Believed shot down by
74Sq Spitfires. One of crew killed and the
other missing. One of these was a Sonderfuhrer. Based Angers.

272.   Me109E **5/JG27**
Channel. Shot down by the R.A.F. Pilot
baled out and was picked up by Seenot
flkdo. Likely to have been Uffz Lackner.
Based Montreuil (?)

273.   Spitfire I, P9393 **74**
Dover. P/O P.C. Stevenson took off at
0750hrs and at 15000ft attacked a formation
of Me109's with a 2 sec. burst causing one to
dive straight into the sea. He then climbed
to 23000ft and saw another enemy aircraft
2000ft below. Whilst in a shallow dive to
attack his aircraft was hit by cannon and
m.g. fire causing the diving speed to
increase. With difficulty he managed to
slide back the canopy and to force his head
into the slipstream, which in turn pulled out
the rest of his body. It took several minutes
to reach the sea surface and during this time
he was blown out to sea. His leg had
become entangled with the 'chute's shrouds
in such a way that he was towed mostly with
his head under water for three or four
minutes. When he finally extricated himself
he was in the water another hour before
being picked up by an M.T.B. Based Hornchurch.   Cat 3

P.C.P. Stevenson
Was born in Lincolnshire. By 1940 he had
been granted a commission in the R.A.F. and
was serving with 74Sq.
   During the Battle of Britain he frequently
flew as No.2 to S/L A. Malan, and had his
first confirmed success on 25.5.40. His win-
ning streak continued during the following
three months.
   After eight confirmed victories and being
awarded the D.F.C. he was killed in action.

274.   Me110 **I/ZG26**
Thames Estuary. Shot down by a Spitfire of
74Sq (Park) over Convoy 'Booty'. Hptm
Kogler and his gunner were both wounded
but picked up and made P.O.W.'s. Based St
Omer or Yvrench.

275.   Me109E4 **8/JG27**
Channel. Failed to return from a sortie. Uffz
Menz missing. (This may have been in the
Western Channel.) Based Carquebut (?)

276.   Hurricane I, N2667 **56**
Thames Estuary. Shot down as a result of
bad aircraft recognition by the pilot of a
74Sq Spitfire. Sgt R. Baker baled out but was
picked up dead by a H.S.L. (This incident is
also reported as taking place off the Naze.)
Based North Weald.   Cat 3

277.   Hurricane I, P3105 **111**
North Foreland. Crashed after being shot up
by Me109's off Margate. P/O J.H. Copeman
killed. Based Croydon.   Cat 3

278.   Hurricane I, P3922 **111**
off Margate. Believed to have suffered the
same fate as P3105. P/O J.W. McKenzie
missing. Based Croydon.   Cat 3

279.   Hurricane I, P3595(?) **111**
off Margate. Thought to have been badly
damaged in combat with Do17's and
Me109's. P/O R.R. Wilson missing. Based
Croydon.   Cat 3

280.   Hurricane I, P3942 **111**
As above Sgt R.B. Sim missing.   Cat 3

280A.   Me109E1 **I/JG27**
Channel. Shot down by the R.A.F. Pilot un-
hurt and picked up by Seenotflkdo. Based
Guines (?)

281.   Hurricane I, N2328(?) **615**
Hawkinge. Overturned on landing after hit-
ting a fence on an undershoot. P/O J.A. Mc-
Clintock unhurt. Based Kenley.   Cat 2

282.   Me109E3 **5/JG51**
off Dover. Thought to have been shot down
by 54Sq Spitfire (Deere). Fw Walz missing.
Based St Omer-Longuenesse.

283.   Blenheim, R3911, PZ-N **53**
Manston. Thirteen Blenheims were despatched on an offensive recce. over the
Channel ports in France. This one crashed
on landing due to serious combat damage
caused by Me109's. F/L Stevenson, Sgts
Clayton and Roberts (?) safe. Based Detling.
                                    Cat 2(?)

284. **12.8.40** Spitfire I, L1044 or K9818 **610** **off New Romney.** Shot down in flames. F/O E.B. Smith baled out and was picked up from the Channel and hospitalised. (Also reported off Dover.)

285. Me109E1 **II/JG52** **New Romney.** Shot down in the above action by 610Sq. Uffz Kern killed. Based Pauplingne.

286. Spitfire I, R6806 or 6891 **610** **Biggin Hill** (Base). Sustained a damaged port wing and fuel tank in the above action. Further damaged in heavy landing. F/O F.T. Gardiner wounded in the leg. Cat 2

287. Spitfire I, P9495 **610** **Hawkinge.** Crashed battle damaged. Sgt Arnfield unhurt. Cat 3

288. Spitfire I, R6621 **610** **Hawkinge** As above. Pilot not known, unhurt. Cat 2

(This incident not in unit's F.541.)

289. Spitfire I, R6815 **54** **Lympne.** Damaged over Dover. P/O J.L. Kemp injured and had to force land. Cat 2

290. Spitfire I, R6914 **54** **Denton.** Crash landed after being damaged by Me109's. P/O Turley-George had head injuries. Based Hornchurch. Cat 2

291. Spitfire I, N3160 **54** **Dartford.** Damaged by Lw fighters during a front gun action on a Lw pilot who had ditched in mid-Channel, and had to force land. P/O E.F. Edsall unhurt. Based Hornchurch. Cat 2

292. Hurricane I, P3803 **501** **Ramsgate**-Dover. Shot down by Me109's escorting Ju87's. F/O V. Lukaszewicz missing. Based Gravesend. Cat 3

293. Hurricane I, P3304 **151** **off Ramsgate.** After being shot down into the sea P/O R.W. Beley was picked up dead. Based North Weald. Cat 3

294. Hurricane I, P3302 **151** **off N. Foreland.** Shot up by Lw fighters off Margate and ditched. F/O Tucker was picked up by H.S.L. and hospitalised with back injuries. Based North Weald. Cat 3

295. Hurricane I, P3397 **501** **nr Dover.** Force landed following combat with Me109's off Westgate. S/L A. Holland unhurt. Based Gravesend. Cat 2

296. Me109E1 **3/JG3** **Channel.** Shot down by 54Sq Spitfire (Gray). Based Samer.

297. Me109E1 **3/JG3** As above but shot down by F/O H.K. Matthews (54Sq).

298. 2 × Blenheims **600** **Manston** (Base). Damaged on the ground during a raid by Do17's of KG2 and Me110's of EproGr 210.

299. Hurricane I, N2329 **501** **Hawkinge.** The undercarriage of this a/c collapsed as a result of damage to r/w caused by the large number of H.E. bombs dropped during the day. Sgt J. Lacey unhurt. Based Gravesend. Cat 2

300. Me109E4 **III/JG54** **Deal**-Dover. 32Sq were ordered to patrol Hawkinge at 15000ft and then Deal at 20000ft. 30-40 × Do17Z's and 9 × Me109's were sighted. P/O A.R. Barton fired at one of the fighters and saw a large piece break off. Its destruction was confirmed by a searchlight unit. It may have been flown by Gfr Stabner who was reported missing, although two more Me109's were also lost in the Channel. Based Guines or Yvrench.

301. Hurricane I, N2596 **32** **nr Hawkinge.** Involved in the above action and crash landed. P/O A.R. Barton unhurt. Based Biggin Hill. Cat 3

302. Hurricane I, P2986 **501** **Hawkinge.** Nosed over on landing due to runway damage. F/L J.A. Gibson unhurt. Based Gravesend. Cat 3

303. Me109E1 **I/JG26** **off Folkestone.** Shot down by 64Sq Spitfire (Woodward). Lt Regenhauer made POW. Based Audembert.

304. Spitfire I, X4018 **64** **Sellindge.** Shot down by Me109's, crashing and burning. P/O A.G. Donahue baled out burnt. Based Kenley. Cat 3

305. **12.8.40** Me109E1 **III/JG54** **Margate,** Hengrove. Force landed after combat with 32Sq Hurricane (Crossley) near Dover. Oblt Drehs missing. Based Guines.

306. Hurricane I **56** **Manston.** Was hit in the coolant tank when 10 miles N. of Manston, by return fire from a Do17Z of KG2 and had to force land. P/O F.B. Sutton unhurt. Based N. Weald Cat 2

307. Spitfire I, X4060, SH-N **64** **Hawkinge.** Force landed after being damaged by Me109's over Dover. F/L L.F. Henstock unhurt. Based Kenley. Cat 2

309. 2 × Me109E4's **3/JG54** **Channel.** Shot down in combat. It is possible that these are the two aircraft mentioned in Incident 300. Based Guines or Yvrench. (This may be the aircraft claimed by F/O B. Finucane of 56Sq.)

310. Me109E1 **I/JG26** **Elham,** Standard Hill Fm. Probably shot down by 54Sq (Deere). Oblt Butterweck killed. (Parts of this a/c are on show at Brenzett Aero. Museum). Based Audembert.

311. Me110D **EproGr210** **nr Manston.** Probably shot down by 54Sq Spitfire (Deere), but there is another report that it crashed near Calais. One of the crew was wounded. Based Calais-Marck.

It will be seen from this day's incidents that it is difficult to match claims and losses. The Intelligence branches of both the R.A.F. and the Lw relied on the de-briefing of crews who, in the heat of battle, thought they saw their own or enemy a/c crashing. Often, due to poor visibility, uncertainty of their own position, and excitement their reports were at best inexact and incomplete. Claims by more than one pilot also exaggerated the results.

312. Hurricane I, P2970 **56**
Margate, 2 miles N. P/O A. Page baled out and was rescued slightly burnt. Based North Weald. Cat 3

313. Me109E **II/JG52**
New Romney. Shot down by 610Sq Spitfires. Lt Gehlhaar (or Gehalsis) was missing. Based Peuplingne.

314. 13.8.40 Spitfire I, R6759 **74**
Manston. F/L P. Kelly was hit by return fire from one of a number of Do17s dropping bombs in the Herne Bay area and had his coolant tank punctured. He force landed safely, unable to reach base. Based Hornchurch. Cat 2

315. 3 × Do17Z's
St Nicolas-Barham-Stodmarsh. This was one of twelve Hurricanes intercepting 20 × Do17's. P/O McIntyre shot down one Do17, in a 111Sq Hurricane P3520; S/L J.M. Thompson another and P/O J.A. Walker a third. Wreckage of a/c was found in each of the locations. It is not possible to decide which pilot claims which victory. 111Sq were based at Croydon.

316. Blenheim, T1937 **53**
Hawkhurst, Conghurst Fm. Became lost and F/O Jameson, Sgt's Andrews and Butler baled out. Based Detling. Cat 3

317. 22 a/c mostly Ansons **500**
Detling. Were destroyed when the airfield was attacked by 40 × Ju87's of LG1 escorted by 90 × Me109's of JG26 led by Major Handrich, the Stukas by Hptm von Brauschitsch.Most of the a/f buildings were destroyed and over 60 R.A.F. and W.A.A.F personnel killed includng the Station Commander, G/C E. Davis. Despite the intensity of the raid the a/f was operational again in 24 hours. There appear to have been no Lw losses.

318. 5 Blenheims, L9460, R3677, R3819
R3849, T1938 **53**
Detling. These were also destroyed together with another Blenheim R3632 of R.A.F. Andover Station Flight.

319. Do17P **3(F)22**
off Kent Coast. Was attacked by 74Sq Spitfires (S/L Malan) whilst it was on a long range reconnaissance. Lt Pannhas was killed and two other crew members missing. Based Stavanger-Sola. Advanced Base (?) Brussels

320. Spitfire I, K9871 **74**
W. Malling. P/O Szczesny found he could not lower his undercarriage after a successful combat with a Do17Z off Whitstable and crashed. He was unhurt. Based Hornchurch. Cat 2

321. Spitfire I, N3091 **74**
Thames Estuary. Do17Z's gunners shot down this aircraft flown by F/L Brzezina who baled out unhurt. Based Hornchurch. Cat 3

322. Spitfire I, N3178 **266**
Eastchurch. Damaged during an air raid. No flying personnel involved. Based Tangmere. Cat 2

323. Do17Z **Stab/KG2**
nr Barham. Oberst J. Fink (Geschw. Kmde) led a force of 84 Do17Z's from Arras to attack Eastchurch. Whilst flying westward over the Estuary they were intercepted by 74Sq Spitfires, whilst without their own escort. Oblt H. Schlegel, whilst in sight of the target received hits in the starboard engine which stopped. With the port one also damaged he turned south. Uncertain of his position he broke cloud and landed in an obstructed field. The crew barely had time to escape from the wreck before they were surrounded by Army personnel. Oblt Schlegel and Oswald, Obfw Babbe and Holz were all made POWs. Based St Trond. Over 250 H.E. bombs were dropped on the Isle of Sheppey during this raid.

324. Do17Z **7/KG2**
Margate. St Nicolas at Wade. Involved in the above raid. Oblt von Groben and 3 crew members killed. Based Caen or Cambrai-Epinoy.

325. Do17Z **7/KG2**
Seasalter, mudflats. As above. This aircraft was shot down by F/O H. Ferris of 111Sq, who reported as follows:
'At about 0710hrs a formation of bombers was sighted and a head on attack commenced . . . the enemy dived through lower cloud.' F/O Ferris was able to relocate them when they dropped their bombs.
'Again in a head on attack I fired a 5-10 seconds burst, but was hit by return fire.'
He then chased what he took to be a Do215 finally firing from 100yds astern. He saw it start to burn over the Estuary. 4 crewmen baled out but one became entangled on the tail plane before it fell into the sea. Oblt Morch and Muller were made POWs. Obfw Langer killed.

326. Do17 **7/KG2**
Stodmarsh, Paxton Fm. Shot down by the R.A.F. during the above raid and force landed. Uffz Vogel, Arndt, Mahringer and Gfr Bahr all POWs. Based Caen or Cambrai-Epinoy.

327. Do17Z, U5+FR **7/KG2**
Birchington. Shot down by 111Sq Hurricanes. Fw Dannisch and Schwertfeger, Obgfr Nitsche, Gfr Beck all killed. Based as above.

Incident No. 326. This Do17Z which crashed at Stodmarsh was reported as being with KG3 but the identification letters are those of KG2. (SE Press)

328.   Me110, 3526(?) **3/ZG26**
Sheppey, Warden Bay. Shot down into the sea by a 56Sq Spitfire (F/O Weaver). Oblt Fuchs and Uffz Ebben killed. (The remains of this a/c are in the Kent Battle of Britain Museum at Hawkinge. Based St Omer or Yvrench.

329.   Me109E **5/JG26**
Barham, Denton. Shot up over Folkestone by the R.A.F. Uffz Wemhoner made POW. Based Porte le Grand.

330.   Hurricane I, N2429 **56**
Whitstable, Seasalter. Shot down in combat with Me110's of EproGr210. P/O P.F. Davies badly burnt and had to bale out. Based N. Weald.   Cat 3

331.   Hurricane I, P3479 **56**
off Leysdown. The radiator exploded after an attack on a Me110. P/O C.C. Joubert baled out slightly injured, landing at Copton Fm, Faversham. Based N. Weald.   Cat 3

332.   Hurricane I, R4093 **56**
off Sheerness. Shot down by a Me110 in head on attack. Sgt P. Hillwood baled out into the sea and swam 2 miles to Sheppey. Based N. Weald.   Cat 3

333.   Hurricane I, P3587 **56**
Hawkinge a/f. Wrecked in a forced landing after combat over the Estuary. F/O R.E. Brooker unhurt. Based N. Weald.   Cat 3

334.   Spitfire I, R6766 **65**
Eastry. Crashed during a night flying practice, cause unknown (Spitfires were difficult to land in darkness). P/O F.S. Gregory baled out too low and was killed. Based Hornchurch.   Cat 3

335. **14.8.40**   Whitley V, P4965 **10**
Dymchurch, 1 mile off. Ditched. The crash

was found by a fishing boat which picked up two of the crew, another survived as the result of the efforts of Miss P. Price who put to sea in a small canoe. (She was later awarded the O.B.E.) P/O Parsons and Sgt Campion were missing, Sgts Chamberlain, Marshall and Sharpe survived. They attacked Turin and Milan. Based Leeming.
                                                    Cat 3

336.   Me109E1 **6/JG3**
Channel. Failed to return after combat over Dover. Obfw Dabusga missing. Based Samer(?)

337.   Me109E1 **8/JG3**
As above Uffz Flebbe killed. Based Desevres(?)

338.   Me109E **I/JG26**
off Dover. Shot down in flames from 19000ft by F/B B. Finucane of 65Sq who also claimed another Me109 as a probable. Based Audembert.

339.   2 × Me109E **4/JG52**
Failed to return from a sortie over the Canterbury area. The one flown by Fw Ruttinger may have been shot down by 151Sq (Gordon). The other flown by Obfw Weiss shot down by Sublt Beggs of 151Sq and pilot killed. Both Lw pilots were posted missing. Based Peuplingne.

340.   Blenheim, L1521 **600**
Manston. Bombed on the ground by Me110's of EproGr210.   Cat ?

341.   2 × Blenheims **600**
Manston. Also destroyed by bombing.

342.   Ju87B **10/LG1**
off Folkestone. Shot down in combat with a Hurricane of 615Sq (Lofts). Oblt Gramling and his gunner killed. Based Tramecourt.

343.   Me110D2, S9 + NK   **2/EproGr210**
Manston. Was shot down by A.A. crashing
and burning. Lt Brinkmann and Uffz R.
Mayer were killed. Based Calais-Marck.

344.   Ju87B   **10/LG1**
off Folkestone. Shot down by a Spitfire of
610Sq. Both crew members missing. Based
Tramecourt.

345.   Ju87B
As above.

346.   Me109E3   **5/JG52**
Canterbury. Missing following ops. over the
city. May have been shot down by Spitfires
of 65Sq. Obfw Potthast was missing. Based
Peuplingne.

347.   Hurricane I, P3109   **615**
off Dover. Failed to return from combat.
May have been shot down by a Me110. F/O
Collard missing. Based Kenley.   Cat 3

348.   Spitfire I, X4166 or L1009   **610**
nr Folkestone. Severely damaged in combat
over the town. P/O Gray slightly hurt. Based
Biggin Hill.   Cat 2

349.   Spitfire I, K9947   **610**
Wye. Force landed following the destruction
of a Me109 off Folkestone. Sgt B.G.
Gardner hospitalised with wounded arms.
Based Biggin Hill.   Cat 2

350.   Spitfire I, R6602   **65**
Manston. Severely damaged and forced to
land after combat with Me109's over the
Channel. P/O L.L. Pyman unhurt. Based
Hornchurch.   Cat 2

351.   Me109E1, 4827, 8 +   **I/JG26**
Dover, Coldred. Possibly shot down by a
Hurricane of 32Sq (Smythe). Uffz G. Kemen
was made a POW. (Some items from this a/c
in the Kent B of B Museum.) Based Audembert.

352.   Hurricane I, P3160   **615**
off Dover. Shot down by Me109's over the
Channel. P/O C.R. Montgomery killed. Based
Kenley.   Cat 3

353.   Hurricane I, L1983   **615**
Hawkinge. The undercarriage collapsed fol-
lowing combat. P/O E.B. Rogers unhurt.
Based Kenley.   Cat 2

(Hptm Ebbinghausen and Lt Krug of II/JG26
each claimed a victory on the 14th. These
may have been Incidents 347 and 352, but it
has not been possible to verify this.)

354.   Hurricane I, P3171   **32**
Hawkinge. Force landed after hits in the glycol tank during combat at 16000ft between
six Hurricanes and nine Me109's P/O R.F.
Smythe unhurt. Based Biggin Hill.   Cat 3

355.   Me110, S9 + MK   **2/EproGr210**
Manston. 16 × Me110's of this Gruppe were
involved in bombing the airfield. This aircraft was hit by a 40mm Bofors round which
removed its tailplane, causing it to collide

with another. It then dived into the ground
and cartwheeled across the airfield, finish-
ing on its back. Uffz H. Steding was killed,
but Gfr A. Schank baled out from 500ft to
be dragged along the ground by his 'chute,
whilst his own unit's bombs fell around him.
He was rescued by F/L C. Pritchard who ran
from a shelter and dragged him back. Based
Denain-Prouvy.

356.   Hurricane I, P3146   **32**
Hawkinge. Force landed after receiving
damage in combat. P/O A.R. Barton unhurt.
Based Biggin Hill.   Cat 2(?)

357.   Hurricane I, V7223   **32**
As above P/O Wlasnowolski unhurt.

358.   Me109E4   **3/JG54**
Sandwich Bay. The aircraft fell in the sea,
but the pilot was picked up and became a
POW. Based Guines or Yvrench.

359.   **15.8.40**   Spitfire I, R6981   **54**
Godmersham, Pope Street. F/L A. Deere
baled out at 1500ft and was unhurt apart
from a sprained wrist. He had been chased
across the Channel after an offensive action
over Calais-Marck a/f. Based Hornchurch.
    Cat 3

360.   Spitfire I, R7019   **54**
Maidstone - West Malling. After being dam-
aged by a Me109E had to force land. P/O
H.K. Matthews was unhurt. Based
Hornchurch.   Cat 2

361.   Spitfire I, N3097   **54**
off Dover. A successful attack on a Ju87B
was made before this a/c was shot down by
one of the Me109 escort. Sgt N.A. Lawrence
was picked up by the R.N. and later hospitalised. Based Hornchurch.   Cat 3

362.   Spitfire I, R7015   **54**
Hythe. Crashed after a dogfight over Dover.
Sgt W. Klozinsky was injured and hospital-
ised. Based Hornchurch.   Cat 3

363.   Ju88A1   **5(F)122**
Thames Estuary. Missing after a recce. over
Rochester. Cause not known. Based Haute-
Fontaine (?)

364.   Me109E   **5/JG54**
off Dover. Shot down in combat by the
R.A.F. Uffz Hautkappe probably a POW.
Based Hermalinghen.

365.   Ju87B   **1/StG1**
Lympne Hawkinge. Shot down by fighters
into the sea. Crew baled out but were missing. Based Lannion or Lanveoc.

366.   Me109E4   **2/JG54**
off Folkestone. Shot down by 615Sq Hurricanes (Eyres and Lofts) or 266Sq (SubLt
Greenshield). Lt Gerlach missing. Based
Guines or Yvrench.

367.   Hurricane I, V7230   **501**
Gravesend (Base). Damaged following an
attack on Ju87's over Hawkinge. F/O Witorzenc unhurt.   Cat 2(?)

28

368. Hurricane I, P3040 **501**
off Folkestone. As above F/L A.R. Putt unhurt. Based Gravesend. Cat 3

369. Hurricane I, P3582 **501**
Dover, Alkham. As above F/L J.A. Gibson
baled out unhurt. Based Gravesend. Cat 3

370. Ju87B **II/StG2**
Channel. Shot down by a Spitfire of 54Sq
whilst it was attacking Hawkinge. Lt von
Rosen and his gunner missing. Based St
Malo or Lannion.

371. Ju87B **II/StG2**
off Folkestone. Shot down by 54Sq (Lawrence). The crew of two N.C.O.'s missing.

373. He111H2 **II/KG53**
Channel. Ditched after combat with the
R.A.F. No further details in the Lw Q.M.'s
returns. Based Lille-Vendeville.

374. Ju87B **II/StG2**
off Folkestone. Shot down by a Spitfire of
54Sq during the attack on Hawkinge. The
pilot became a POW but as so often happened the gunner was lost. Based St Malo or
Lannion.

375. Spitfire I, N3245 **266**
Manston (Base). Me110's made a strafing
run across the airfield and this aircraft was
damaged but no aircrew loss. Cat 2

376. Hurricane I, P3161 **615**
Hawkinge. The air battle that took place at
this time also resulted in this Hurricane
having to attempt a force landing, but it
crashed in the attempt. P/O D. Evans unhurt.
Based Kenley. Cat 2

377. Hurricane I, P2801 **615**
Sevenoaks, Seal. Crashed and burned after
combat with enemy fighers. Sgt D. Halton
missing. Based Kenley. Cat 3

378. Hurricane I, P3961 **111**
Hawkinge. Had a damaged coolant system
as a result of return fire from a Do17Z over
the Estuary and had to make a dead engine
landing. F/O Ferris unhurt. Based Croydon.
Cat 2

379. Hurricane I, R4195 **111**
W. Malling a/f. As above. Sgt W. Dymond
unhurt. Based Croydon. Cat 2

380. Spitfire I, N3230 **64**
Hawkinge. Another example of an aircraft
having to force land as a result of a damaged coolant system. This was sustained
over Dungeness. P/O E.G. Gilbert unhurt.
Based Kenley. Cat 2

381. Spitfire I, R6990 **64**
off Dungeness. F/O C.J. Andreae shot down
and missing after combat. There is no record
of a lifeboat or A.S.R. search. Based Kenley.
Cat 3

The use of Lifeboats for A.S.R.
During the early part of 1940 in particular
there was a strict control on the launching
of these boats in the South-East. Permission
had to be obtained on each occasion from
the Senior Naval Officer in the area.

The coxswain of one of the Kent boats at
the time said that on a number of occasions
he had seen aircraft fall into the sea, not far
off shore but the boat was not allowed to
launch. It has not been possible to trace a
record of these instructions but it seems
likely that was to do with the avoidance of
false invasion alarms.

382. Me109E4, 2 + **5/JG51**
off Margate. Shot down by the R.A.F. Fw
Steigenberger was rescued from the sea by
the Margate L.B. and made a POW. Based St
Omer.

383. Do17Z3 **6/KG3**
Reculver, 1 mile E. Whilst on a bombing
mission over the Estuary was shot down by
the R.A.F. or A.A. Lt Kringler, Uffz Depenheuer and Gfr Rohleder killed. Obgfr Duda
POW. Based Antwerp-Deurne.

384. Do17Z3 **6/KG3**
off Ramsgate. As above Lt Walter, Fw
Schauer, Uffz Kirchubel and Pieronczyk all
POWs.

385. Spitfire I, X4060 **64**
Hawkinge. Force landed for unknown
reason. Sgt Hawke was unhurt. Based
Kenley. Cat 2(?)

KG3 lost a further 5 a/c on this day, 1 near
Dover and 4 in the Estuary. It was not
possible to identify these. H/E bombs were
dropped on Faversham and Sheppey and
around the Medway.

386. Hurricane I, L1975 **151**
Ashford, Eastwell Park. Force landed after
engine trouble resulting from excessive use
of boost during combat. P/O J.L. Ellacombe
slightly injured. Based N. Weald. Cat 2

387. Hurricane I, V7410 **151**
off Dover. Failed to return from combat
over the Channel. P/O M. Rozwadowski
missing. Based N. Weald. Cat 3

388. Hurricane I, P3941 **151**
off Dymchurch. After an attack by Me109's
P/O J. Johnston was picked up dead from
the sea. Based N. Weald. Cat 3

389. Whitley V **10**
off Dover. After re-fuelling at R.A.F. Abing-
don took off with others to attack Torino.
Due to combat damage (?flak) crew were
ordered to bale out over Italy (later known
to be POWs). Sgt Green then flew the aircraft, alone, to ditch off Dover out of fuel.
Based Leeming. Cat 3

390. Hurricane I, P3065 **151**
Shorncliffe. Shot down by Me109's over
Dover. Sublt H.W. Beggs wounded. Based
N. Weald. Cat 3

Incident No. 400. Two photographs of Do17Z of 3/KG76 was shot down by F/O Ferris of 111 Squadron crashing near Brenchley. (SE Press)

Sublt H.W. Beggs, R.N.
Joined 151Sq flying Hurricanes from R.A.F. North Weald and Stapleford Tawney. He shot down a Me109 of 4/JG52, over Kent, on 15.8.40. He flew with the R.A.F. until 28.1.42 when he re-joined the Fleet Air Arm and was lost when HMS Avenger was sunk 15.11.42.

391. Ju87B **10/LG1**
Folkestone, Morehall. This Stuka burst into flames when it hit H.T. cables. Uffz Weber and Uffz Kraus were killed and a third (?) is reported as baling out to die later. If this is correct then the aircraft, from a Lehrgeschwader may have been specially modified. A more likely explanation is that the third man was from another incident entirely. Based Tramecourt.

392. Ju87B **10/LG1**
off Folkestone. Another sitting duck for R.A.F. fighters shot down into the Channel. Hptm Münchenhagen was picked up wounded and made a POW, but his gunner Obfw Heyse was killed.

393. Spitfire, N3168 **266**
Teston, on the bank of the River Medway. After combat over Kent P/O F.W. Cale baled out and was found dead. Based N. Weald.
Cat 3

394. Me110D **EproGr210**
Ightham. S/L Worrall and F/L Crossley (32Sq) shot down this aircraft whilst it was on its way to attack Croydon. Lt Ortner baled out wounded but his gunner Obgfr Lohmann was killed. Based Calais-Marck.

395. Me110D, 3341 **2/EproGr210**
Hawkhurst. On the above attack was shot down by 111Sq (Dymond). Oblt Habisch and Uffz Elfner both POWs. Based Calais-Marck.

396. Me109E **9/JG54**
Cranbrook, Bullwood Fm, Hartley. Shot down whilst escorting the above Me110's. Uffz Neidermaier killed. Based Guines or Yvrench.

397. Me109E4 **2/EproGr210**
nr Frant. During a mission to attack Croydon Lt Marx (Staffel Kapt) baled out after an attack by 32Sq Hurricanes to become a POW. (Some items from this crash are in Robertsbridge Air Mus.) (This crash was on the border of Kent and E. Sussex.)

398. 16.8.40 Lysander II, L6854 **26**
W. Malling (Base). Destroyed during a raid on the airfield, two others were damaged. No air crew involved. Cat 3

399. Hurricane I, V7368 **56**
Manston area. Set on fire whilst on a section patrol, by a surprise attack. P/O L.W. Graham baled out slightly wounded. Based N. Weald. Adv. Rochford. Cat 3

400. Do17Z3 **7/KG76**
Brenchley, Moatlands. Collided with a Hurricane of 111Sq (Ferris) over Marden

after an attack on Hornchurch. Obfw Wachter, Riedel and Brauer + Fw Klumb missing. Based Cormeilles en Vexin.

401. Do17Z3 **3/KG2**
Canterbury, Stodmarsh. 111Sq Hurricanes shot down this aircraft. Lt Moellenbrok, Uffz Hess missing; Gfr Reinicke and Golob dead. Based Arras.

402. Do17Z3 **3/KG2**
N. Kent Coast. In the attack on Hornchurch was shot down by the R.A.F. Oblt H. Brandenburg missing Gfr E. Genter and K. Hirsch + Flgr H. Koch killed. Based Arras.

403. Me109E **6/JG51**
Woodnesborough-Goodnestone, Summerfield, Staple. Crashed. No further details. Based St Omer.

403A. Me109E4 **3/JG54**
Channel. Failed to return from a sortie over S.E. England. Fw Knedler missing. Based Guines or Yvrench.

404. Me109E3 **4/JG51**
Whitstable. Crashed. Uffz Bruder was made a POW. Based St Omer (?)

405. Hurricane I, P3029 **111**
Brenchley, Palmers Green Fm. Shot down in combat. Sgt R. Carnall baled out slightly wounded and landed at Trottenden Fm, Goudhurst. Based Croydon, Adv. Hawkinge.
Cat 3

406. Spitfire I, R6768 **266**
Deal, Eastry Court. Me109's shot down this aircraft which crashed and burned. Sqdn Ldr R.L. Wilkinson was killed. Based Hornchurch.
Cat 3

407. Spitfire I, N3095 **266**
Canterbury, Adisham. Shot down in flames by enemy fighters. P/O N.G. Bowen killed. Based Hornchurch. Cat 3

408. Spitfire I, P9312 **266**
nr Wickhambreux. Was on fire after combat. F/L S.H. Bazley baled out burnt. Based Hornchurch. Cat 3

SubLt H.L. Greenshield
Joined 266Sq from the F.A.A. 1st July to fly Spitfires from Wittering and Tangmere. He was credited with a Me109E4 on the 15th S.E. of Dover, but was killed on the 16th. The unit had been scrambled from Hornchurch when Greenfield in N3240 was shot down by enemy fighters, crashing near Calais. He is buried in a cemetery in the town.

409. Spitfire I, L1038 **64**
Hawkinge a/f. Damaged by Me109's over the Channel and had to force land. Sgt J. Mann slightly injured. Based Kenley. Cat 2

410. Hurricane I, R4193 **111**
Marden, Sheephurst Fm. Collided with a Do17Z of 7/KG76 during a head on attack. F/L H.M. Ferris was killed. He had been in the thick of the Battle and appears in this

31

log several times. One H.E. bomb was dropped on Marden. Based Croydon. Cat 3

411. Spitfire I, K9864 **266**
Nr Oare. Severely damaged in combat over Canterbury and had to force land. P/O S.F. Soden slightly wounded in the legs. Based Hornchurch. Cat 2

412. Me109E4 **StabII/JG26**
Dover, 6 miles off. Shot down by 266Sq over the Channel. Hptm Ebbinghausen missing. He was Gruppe Kdr of II Gruppe. Based Marquise.

413. Spitfire I, R6802, DW-Z **610**
off Dungeness. Shot down in combat by Me109's. F/L W.H. Warner killed. The Dungeness L.B. picked up his body complete with 'chute. It was thought that a heavy impact with the sea had caused fatal injuries. Based Biggin Hill. Cat3

414. Hurricane I, P3547, US - A **56**
Whitstable, south of. Hit by return fire from a Do17Z off Eastchurch and had to force land. F/S F.W. Higginson was slightly wounded. 40 H.E. bombs were dropped on Northfleet. Based N. Weald Adv. Rochford. Cat 3

415. Spitfire I, X4065, DW - D **610**
Biggin Hill (Base). Sustained damage to R/T through fire from a Me109 over Dungeness. P/O McI Gray uninjured. Cat 2

416. Spitfire I, K9915 **65**
off Deal. Failed to return from combat over the Channel. P/O L.L. Pyman killed. Based Hornchurch. Cat 3

417. Spitfire I, R6618 **65**
Manston a/f. Destroyed by strafing aircraft. No aircrew involved. Cat 3

418. 2 × Blenheims **600**
Manston. L1295 damaged in above raid, L6608 destroyed. No aircrew involved.

419. **18.8.40** Me110 **7/LG2**
Thames Estuary. Shot up by Spitfires of 54Sq at 31000ft over Manston. Oblt Werdin and his gunner killed. Based St Omer Fort Rouge.

420. Hurricane I, R4219 **501**
East Seal, Cronks Fm. Shot up by Me109's over Biggin Hill. F/O R.C. Dafforn baled out unhurt. Based Gravesend. Cat 3

421. Hurricane I, L1921 **17**
off Dover. Missing following an engagement with Me109's. P/O N.D. Solomon killed. Based Debden. Cat 3

422. Hurricane I, R4221, KW-J **615**
Sidcup, Midfield Way. Shot up by JG3 aircraft resulting in a cockpit flooded with fuel and a dead engine. P/O P.H. Hugo attempted to bale out from an inverted aircraft at 10000ft but caught his harness leg strap on a projection in the cockpit. He then abandoned his attempt to leave and regained control of the Hurricane. Despite many attacks by enemy a/c he managed to

force land slightly injured, and was admitted to hospital. Based Kenley. Cat 3

423. Hurricane I, P3943 **111**
Tatsfield, Botley Hill Fm. Was caught by return fire from a Do17Z during a low level raid on Kenley, and started to burn. Sgt H.S. Newton baled out unhurt. Based Croydon. Cat 3

424. He111H3, V4 + GK **2/KG1**
Snargate - Dymchurch. Battle damaged whilst attacking Kenley and lost one engine. Near Ashford it was again attacked by 32Sq (S/L M. Crosley) whose fire caused oxygen bottles to explode, wounding one of the crew and causing further damage to the cockpit. The other engine was also hit and had to be shut down. The aircraft crashed and Lt R Ahrens and his crew climbed out of the wreckage carrying the injured flight engineer, then ignited an incendiary device. Uffz Gericke later died in hospital. Obfw Katzmarski, Flg Natzke, Uffz Schneider and the pilot were made POWs. Based Rosieres en Santerre.

425. Hurricane I, P3059 **501**
Whitstable. Shot down by Oblt Schöpel of JG26 over Canterbury. P/O K.N. Lee was seriously wounded. Based Gravesend. Cat 3

426. Do17Z, F1 + DT **9/KG76**
Biggin Hill, Leaves Green. Shot down by A.A. and 111Sq Hurricanes. Hptm Roth (Staffel Kapt), Hptm Peters, Oblt Lamberty, Fw Geier and Eberhard all POW's. Based Cormeilles en Vexin.

427. Ju88A **5/KG76**
Sevenoaks Weald, Ide Hill. Shot down by 32Sq Spitfires. Obfw Eichorn and Vetter and Gfr Skuthan killed. High explosive bombs were dropped on the Gasworks and three civilians killed and six injured in this raid. Based Creil.

428 Spitfire I, R6713 **65**
Canterbury, Westbere. Crashed during a patrol from Rochford. F/O F. Gruska killed. Based Hornchurch, Adv. Rochford. Cat 3

429. Hurricane I, N2617 **501**
Lenham. Shot up by Oblt Schöpfel of JG54 over Canterbury. Sgt D.A. Mackay baled out over Dargate, slightly injured. Based Gravesend. Cat 3

430. Hurricane I, P3208 **501**
Canterbury, Sturry. Crashed following an attack by Oblt Schöpfel. F/O J.W. Bland killed. Based Gravesend. Cat 3

431. Me110C, 3U + EP **6/ZG26**
Newchurch, St Mary's. Force landed following an engagement with the R.A.F., claimed by 56Sq (Down). Lt Kastner and Uffz Kaffenburger POW's. Based Crecy.

432. Ju88A **6/KG76**
Aylesford, Church Fm. Shot down by 111Sq (Dymond), Fw Krebs killed; Fw Waterman,

Uffz Loeffler and Sonderfuhrer Buchmeier all POW's. Based Creil.

433. Me110C, 3060, 3U + IP **6/ZG26**
Pluckley. Crashed and burned after being shot up by 56Sq (Sgt Robinson). Obfw Keifel and Uffz Hemmersbach killed. Based Crecy.

434. Me110C **6/ZG26**
Lenham, Platts Heath. As above but shot down by P/O Mounsdon. Oblt Hellmuth and Fw Winter killed.

435. Me109E4 **III/JG3**
Sittingbourne, Bredhurst. Shot down by the R.A.F. Lt von Fonderen killed. Based Desevres.

436. Do17Z **8/KG76**
off Dungeness. Damaged over Kenley at 1325hrs by 32 or 64Sq and finished off by 1Sq (F/L H. Hillcoat, P/O C. Stavert and G. Goodman) when it dived into the sea. Lt H. Leder, Uffz Disch and Szyminski killed; Gfr Ulbrich and Uffz Rudolf missing. Based Creil.

437. Me110C2 **1/ZG26**
Canterbury, Harbledown. 32Sq (Flinders) and A.A. claimed this kill. It crashed and exploded. Uffz J. Gebauer and Mai missing. Based at St Omer or Yvrench.

This Me110 flew east from Kenley passing north of R.A.F. West Malling and Detling pursued by three fighters of 32Sq, then it was seen to dive to 300ft in an endeavour to escape. As the chase continued it was further hit by fire from a Bofors of a detachment of 12th LAA Regiment, to be finally shot down in flames by P/O Flinders.

438. 2 × Lysanders, N1306, P9080 **26**
W. Malling (Base). Were destroyed on the ground by enemy bombing. No aircrews involved.   Cat 3

439. Me110C2 **3/ZG26**
Bonnington. Shot up by 56Sq (Weaver) over Ashford. Obfw Stange and Uffz Hesse missing. Based St Omer or Yvrench.

Views of aerial tactics of the time from both sides
Me110 tactics. These were a direct result of this type's lack of speed and manoeuvrability.
F/O P. Weaver, 56Sq.
'I was leading No.2 Section as the squadron was put into line astern by the squadron leader. I observed five Me110's below in a defensive circle and singled one out for attack. I fired for about 6 sec. and it broke away with smoke and bits pouring from the starboard engine. I then saw another below me and chased it closing to about 200yds and fired a short burst without deflection. My guns ceased firing and the enemy went into a steep right turn and dived vertically into the ground bursting into flames about 8 miles South of Ashford on the north bank of the canal.'

On R.A.F. tactical formations, Oblt G. Schöpfel of III/JG26 said:
'Suddenly I noticed a Staffel of Hurricanes below me (501Sq). They were using the English tactics of flying in close formation of three and climbing in a wide spiral about 1000 metres above. I turned with them and managed to get behind two covering aircraft ('weavers'). I waited until they were once more heading away from Folkestone and then pulled round out of the sun, and attacked from below.'
As a result of this attack he shot down both 'weavers' and one other aircraft.
'The Englishmen continued on having noticed nothing so I pulled in behind the fourth machine and took care of him, but this time I was too close. When I fired pieces of wreckage hit my 'windmill' and oil from the Hurricane splattered over my windscreen so that I could not see anything and had to break off the action.'
As a result of this action 504Sq lost four aircraft, one pilot killed, and 3 pilots wounded.

440. Hurricane I, P3147 **32**
Brenchley, Hatmill Lane. Set on fire by Me110's over Biggin Hill. P/O Pain baled out slightly wounded. Based Biggin Hill.   Cat 3

441. Hurricane I, R4081 **32**
Biggin Hill (Base). Force landed after combat with enemy aircraft. The pilot, who was unhurt being P/O B. Wlasnowolski.   Cat 3

442. Hurricane I, V7363 **32**
Edenbridge, Skeynes, Park Fm. A 20mm cannon shell exploded in the cockpit of this aircraft during the defence of base. F/L H. Russell baled out seriously wounded and applied a tourniquet whilst descending.
Cat 3

443. Spitfire I, N3040 **92**
Tonbridge, Horsmonden. F/L S. Tuck was unofficially operational over Beachy Head when he intercepted a Me110 and shot it down into the sea and then attacked a second only to get a head on hit from a cannon shell. He managed to regain control, but near Tonbridge had to bale out when the engine finally failed. He landed near Plovers, Horsmonden, injuring his leg. Based Pembrey.   Cat 3

444. Hurricane I, V6536 **32**
Otford, Shoreham. Hit by return fire from an enemy bomber in the fuel tank, whilst over base, and had to force land. Sgt B. Henson was slightly wounded. Based Biggin.   Cat 2

445. Me110C **6/ZG26**
off Folkestone. Damaged in combat with 56Sq Hurricanes over S.E. England and finally shot down by 1Sq (P/O G.E. Goodman). Uffz Wollin killed and Fw Stange POW. Based Crecy.

Incident No. 434. Me110C of 6/ZG26 which crashed near Lenham. Both of the crew were killed. (SE Press)

446. Me110C4, 3102, U8+BB **I/ZG26 Lydd,** Dering Fm. Crashed following an attack by 64Sq (S/L McDonnell). This a/c had two damaged engines sustained over Kenley. Oblt Proske and Uffz Mobius both POW's. The pilot had managed to avoid further attacks and reached Dungeness when first one and then the other engine packed up. He was uninjured but Mobius seriously so. Based St Omer or Yvrench.

447. Spitfire I, R6694, DW-F **610 Biggin Hill** (Base). Hit by fire from a Me109 during the return journey to base and then struck a bomb crater when landing. Pilot P/O Pegge. Cat 2

448. Me109E4, 1990, 13+ **2/JG3 Leeds,** Broomfield. In open country. Had engine damaged by 54Sq (Tew), resulting in the loss of coolant and engine seizure. Oblt H. Tiedmann force landed and evaded capture for 12 hours. Based Samer.

449. Spitfire I, R6993, DW-W **610 Biggin Hill** (Base). Returned to base damaged by return fire from a He111 over Dungeness. F/L J. Ellis unhurt. Cat 2

450. Hurricane I, P3815 **501 Whitstable,** Rayhams Fm. P/O Kozlowski seriously wounded after being shot down by Oblt Schöpfel over Canterbury. Based Gravesend. Cat 3

451. Hurricane I, P3209 **17 Manston.** After combat over Dover was caught in a strafing attack on the airfield. Sgt G. Griffiths uninjured. Based Debden. Cat 2

452. Spitfire I, X4061 **266 Manston.** Landed to refuel and was caught as above and burned out. Based Hornchurch. Cat 3

453. Spitfire I, X4066 **266** As above. Cat 3

454. Hurricane I, P2966 **615 Sevenoaks,** Robsack Wood. Shot down by Me109's. F/L L. Gaunce baled out with slight burns and was admitted to hospital. Based Kenley. Cat 3

455. Hurricane I, R4106 **32 Canterbury,** Chartham Hatch. Shot down over the town by Me109's. Sgt L.H. Pearce baled out slightly injured. Based Biggin Hill. Cat 3

456. Hurricane I, N2461, GZ-F **32 Gillingham,** Wigmore. S/L M.N. Crossley baled out unhurt after being shot up by II/JG26. Based Biggin Hill. Cat 3

457. Me110C, 3U+AM **4/ZG26 Eastchurch.** 2 miles East. A.A. shot down this aircraft after it had been attacked by the R.A.F. off the East Coast. Uffz Jaekel killed and Rutters made POW. Based Crecy.

458. Me110C, 3U+CM **4/ZG26 off N. Foreland.** 32Sq Hurricanes on an operational patrol shot down this aircraft. Uffz Baar killed, Fw Gierga picked up from the sea. Based Crecy.

459. Me109E1 **7/JG26 Chilham,** in a wood. Crashed inverted after combat with 32Sq (Brothers and Wlasnowolski) or 54Sq (Campbell). Lt G. Muller-Duhe killed. Based St Omer.

460. Me109E4 **7/JG26**
Kingston, Barham. Shot down over Canterbury by 32Sq aircraft (P/O Eckford, Pniak and S/L Crossley). Oblt W. Blume wounded and POW. Based as above.

P/O K. Pniak
Was a serving Polish Air Force officer in 1939, and during the Campaign of that year was credited with 2½ successes against the Luftwaffe, whilst flying very inferior aircraft.

He arrived in the U.K. after a spell of flying with the Armée de l'Air in France, and joining the R.A.F. was posted to 32Sq. With this unit he had considerable success. In November he was again posted to 257Sq and shortly after was credited with a CR42 Fiat (of 18° Gruppo C.T.) then based in Belgium, and a share in another.

A further move and promotion came when he was posted to 306 (Polish) Squadron for six months and then to 56Sq and conversion to Typhoons.

Later he went to N. Africa with the Polish Fighting Team before a final spell of operations with 308Sq.

461. Me110 D/O **3/ZG26**
Channel, off the French Coast (?). The aircraft had been on an A.A. research flight over S.E. England when it was shot up by the R.A.F. and then crashed in the sea. Oblt Kirchoff with Lt Mader of I/LN Regt 32, as observer, both killed. Based St Omer.

461A. Hurrricane I, V6535 **32**
Ruckinge. Shot down by Me109's. P/O R. de Grunne was badly burnt. Based Biggin Hill.
Cat 3

462. Me109E **5/JG51**
off Whitstable. Believed to have been shot down by 501Sq (P/O P. Zenker). Hptm Tietzen (Staffel Kapt) killed. Based St Omer (?)

463. Me109E **5/JG51**
As above. Believed shot down by 501Sq (Witorzenc). Lt Lessing killed.

464. Hurricane I, P2549 **501**
Chilham, Stile Fm. Shot up by Me110's over Estuary. F/L G.E. Stoney killed. Based Gravesend.
Cat 3

465. He111H3, A1+FR **7/KG53**
off Foreness. Attacked by various fighters over Essex, ditching after a final attack by 85Sq (F/L Hamilton). Oblt Zipse, Uffz Grasser, Gfr Reinhardt, Mailander and Worsch all POW's. Ramsgate L.B. rescued the crew after they been in their dinghy and clinging to the wreck of S.S. Harcola for 24 hours. Based Lille-Vendeville.

466. Me109E4, 2755 **8/JG3**
Marden, Staplehurst, Blue House Fm. Crashed and burned after an attack by S/L Pemberton of 1Sq. Obgfr Basell killed. Based Desevres.

467. 20.8.40 Me109E **1/JG51**
Faversham area. Shot down by 615Sq Hurricanes (Lofts). Fw Maul missing. One source suggests that he may have been picked up by a He59 of3/SeenotFlKdo. Based St Omer (?).

468. Blenheim **600**
Manston (Base). Damaged on the ground during an air-raid.
Cat 2

469. Do17Z3 **9/KG2**
off Leysdown. Shot down by Spitfires of 65Sq and Hurricanes of 615Sq. 2 of the crew missing and 2 POW's. Based Arras.

470. Do17Z, 5K+FT **9/KG3**
Leysdown, Newhouse Fm. Shot down by 615Sq (Kayll and Young) over Eastchurch. Fw Rudinger killed and remainder of crew POW's. Based St Trond.

471. 22.8.40 Hurricane I, P3205 **32**
Hawkinge. Crashed on landing. P/O J. Pfeiffer unhurt. Based Biggin Hill.
Cat 2

472. Spitfire I, R6708 **54**
off Deal. Shot down in combat with Lw fighters. Sgt G.R. Collett killed. Based Hornchurch.
Cat 3

473. Hurricane I, P3901 **615**
nr Deal. Damaged after an attack by another Hurricane and had to force land. P/O D.H. Hone unhurt. Based Kenley.
Cat 2

474. Spitfire I, R6695 **610**
nr Hawkinge. Crashed and burned out after combat with Me109's over Folkestone. Sgt D.F. Corfe unhurt. Based Hawkinge.
Cat 3

475. Spitfire I **65**
Manston. Landed with damage sustained in combat with a Me109E over Dover. Pilot unhurt. Based Hornchurch.
Cat 2
(It is possible that this is the same incident as No.477.)

476. Spitfire I, R6926 **616**
Elham, Adam & Eve Hill. Attacked over Dover by Me109's and caught fire. F/O H.S. Dundas baled out and was hospitalised with arm and leg injuries. Based Kenley.
Cat 3

477. Spitfire I, L1094 **65**
Manston. Landed severely damaged after an engagement over the Channel, possibly with Fw Phillip of II/JG26. Sgt H.C. Orchard safe. Based Hornchurch.
Cat 2

478. Spitfire I, K9909 **65**
off Dover. Shot down by a Me109 possibly flown by Lt Krug. Sgt M. Keymer killed. Based Hornchurch.
Cat 3

479. 23.8.40 Hurricane I, P3900 **32**
Hawkinge. Force landed for unknown reasons. P/O J. Rose unhurt. Based Biggin Hill.
Cat 2

480. Hurricane I, P2795 **32**
Hawkinge. Crash landed with one main wheel only, as a result of combat damage. P/O J. Pfeiffer safe. His second crash at this a/f in two days,
Cat 2

481.　24.8.40　　　2 × Me109E1　8/JG51
off Ramsgate. Collided with another Me of
the same unit. Both Fw Busch and Uffz Harheim missing in the sea. Based St Omer or St
Quentin.

482.　　　　　Hurricane I, L1659　501
Hawkinge. Crashed after combat with
Me109's attacking Manston. A/c finished on
its nose. Sgt W.J. Green unhurt. Based
Gravesend.　　　　　　　　　　　Cat 2

483.　　　　　　　Defiant I　264
Manston. Force landed with combat damaged tail. P/O D. Whitley and gunner
unhurt. Based Rochford.　　　　　Cat 2

484.　　　　　　　Defiant I　264
Manston. Damaged during a collision with
another aircraft during a scramble. F/O B.K.
O'Malley and P/O A. O'Connell unhurt.
　　　　　　　　　　　　　　　　　　Cat 2

485.　　　　　Defiant I, L7013　264
Manston. Attacked by Me109's over Thanet
and badly damaged. Including Verey car-
tridges exploding in the cockpit. F/L Campbell Colquhuon and P/O Robinson unhurt.
　　　　　　　　　　　　　　　　　　Cat 2

486.　　　　　Me109E4　7/JG26
off Margate. Shot down by a Hurricane of
85Sq (Allard). The pilot was wounded but
was picked up by Seenotflkdo. Based
Caffiers.

P/O G. Allard
Was born in York in 1912 and entered the
R.A.F. as an apprentice in 1929. By the time
War broke out he had become a Sgt Pilot.
　He flew with 85Sq in France during 1939
and was credited with nine successes, being
awarded the D.F.M. on return to the U.K.
　Very quickly he increased his score to
twelve receiving a bar to the D.F.M. and
after commissioning, a D.F.C.
　On 1st September he shot down a Do17Z
and a Me109E so that, when the squadron
moved North for a rest, his total was twenty-
three.
　The squadron was converted to Havoc
night fighters before returning to operations.
He had flown down to Debden to pick up
one of the new aircraft, but was killed
taking off.
　A Court of Enquiry established later that
an untightened nut and bolt had caused the
controls to lock.

487.　　　　　Hurricane I, L1933　85
Hawkinge. Believed shot down by Dover
A.A. and had to force land, over-running the
runway due to lack of flaps. P/O J. Lockhart
was slightly wounded. Based Croydon. Cat 3

488.
　Spitfire I, R6686 or K9975(?), DW-S　**610**
Eastry, Ham Mill, Woodnesborough.
Crashed in flames after being attacked by
Hptm Föcö off Ramsgate. Sgt S.J. Arnfield
baled out fracturing his ankle in landing.
Based Biggin Hill.　　　　　　　Cat 3

489.　　　　　Hurricane I, P3141　501
Dover. 4 miles N.W. P/O F. Zenker missing
after combat with Do17Z's and Me109's.
Based Gravesend.　　　　　　　　Cat 3

490.　　　　　　Me109E1　I/LG2
nr Manston. Shot down by 54Sq Spitfire
(Gray). The pilot was killed. Based Calais-
Marck.

491.　　　　　　Me109E4　I/LG2
Manston. Shot down by 54Sq (Robbins).
Pilot missing. Based Calais-Marck.

492.　　　　　Spitfire I, X4102　610
Dover, Eastry, Shepherdswell. Crash landed
after being shot up by Me109's over Dover.
P/O D.M. Gray wounded. Based Biggin Hill.
　　　　　　　　　　　　　　　　　　Cat 3

493.　　　　Spitfire I, R6641, DW-X　610
Hawkinge. Involved in the above action.
P/O E.S. Aldous unhurt.　　　　　Cat 2

494.　　　　Hurricane I, R4183(?)　151
Eastry, east of Acol. Shot down in combat
with Me109's over Ramsgate, crashing and
burning. P/O K.B. Debenham wounded and
to hospital. Based North Weald.　Cat 3

495.　　　　Hurricane I, P3273　151
Faversham, Plumford Fm, Ospringe. Shot
down by Lw fighters over Ramsgate and
crashed. Sgt G.T. Clarke wounded.　Cat 3

496.　　　Defiant I, N1535, PS-A　264
off Margate. Last seen pursuing a Ju88A
after a raid on Manston. S/L Hunter and P/O
F.H. King missing. Based Hornchurch. Cat 3

497.　　　　Defiant I, L6966　264
off Ramsgate - Margate. Lost following a
dogfight with Me109's and Ju88A's off
Thanet. P/O's J.T. Jones and W.A. Ponting
missing.　　　　　　　　　　　　Cat 3

497A.　　　　Defiant, L7027　264
off Ramsgate. F/O I.G. Shaw and Sgt A.
Berry missing.

498.　　　　　　Defiant I　264
Manston. Shot down by JG51's Me109's and
had to crash land. P/O R.S. Gaskell slightly
injured. Sgt W.H. Mechin died of injuries.
　　　　　　　　　　　　　　　　　　Cat 3

499.　　　　Me109E4, 5587　6/JG51
East Langdon, Salton Close Fm. Force
landed due to engine failure after combat
with R.A.F. fighters over Manston. Obfw F.
Beeck may have been shot down by 56Sq
(Wicks) to be a POW. Based Desevres.

500.　　　　　Me109E4　1/JG51
Channel. Collided with a Spitfire and both
crashed into the sea. Fw Oglodek killed.
Based St Omer (?).

501.　　　　　　Ju88A　II/KG76
off Manston. A Defiant of 264Sq (Banham
and Baker) shot this enemy aircraft down
into the sea. Maj Moricke (Gruppe Kdr) and
Oblt Schulte's bodies were washed up on
6th September. Sonderfuhrer Wagner was
killed and the other crew member missing.
Based Creil.
　This aircraft was on a special flight for

LwKrBerkp 4, a unit concerned with the collection of information. It is not known whether this was for operational intelligence or for propaganda.

The rank of Sonderfuhrer and the wearing of a uniform was intended to be a protection for civilians such as War Correspondents, Flight Surgeons or engineering specialists flying on operations. Unlike our war correspondents they were often expected to act as crew members. There is no exact R.A.F. equivalent.

502. Ju88A **StabII/KG76**
off Ramsgate. Shot down by 264Sq Defiant (Garvin and Ash). Uffz Meier, Fw Flessner and Vetter missing; Fw Meyer killed. Based Creil.

503. Ju88A **5(F)122**
Kent Coast. Shot down by 501Sq Hurricanes, Lt Hellermann and Hurck + one other crew member missing. Based Haute Fontaine.

504. Ju88A **4/KG76**
off Manston. Possibly shot down by 264Sq Defiant (Barker and Thorn). Uffz Dubs, Freimann and Froba missing; Uffz Kruell killed. Based Creil.

505. Ju88A **4/KG76**
As above. Claimed by Whitley and Turner. Lt Grell, Uffz Wetzker and Fw Thomas missing; Uffz Henneberg killed.

506. Ju88A1 **III/KG51**
off Kent Coast. Shot down by 501Sq, one crew member killed, two missing, one picked up unhurt. Based Etaples.

507. Me109E1 **III/JG3**
off Dover. Shot down by 32Sq Hurricane (F/L Brothers). Pilot missing. Based Colombert (?)

508. Hurricane I **32**
Dover Harbour. Shot down when attacked by twelve Me109's. P/O Pniak baled out safely. Adv. base Hawkinge.   Cat 3
(Form 540 is ambiguous)

509. Spitfire I, R6884 **65**
Manston. Force landed after being shot up in combat. Sgt Hill uninjured. Based Hornchurch.   Cat 2

510. Me109E1, 9+ **I/JG52**
Margate, Minster Road, Westgate. Force landed due to engine failure during a mission. Fw Bischoff unhurt and POW. Based Coquelles.

511. Spitfire I, P9389 **54**
Deal, Kingsdown, School Lane. Following combat P/O Stewart baled out and was picked up from the sea by the R.N. Based Hornchurch.   Cat 3

512. Me109E1 **2/LG2**
Sittingbourne, Mackledons Farm, Bobbing. Shot up over the Estuary after a low level chase. Ufz H. Moeller killed. Based Calais-Marck.

514. Me110 **AufKlGrob de Lw**
off Sheppey. Shot down by a 151Sq aircraft flown by G/C V. Beamish. Lt Hofer and two crew members missing. This was a 'special' with a crew of three, belonging to the High Command Recce. Group. Although the unit was based at Berlin-Staaken they operated, usually as single aircraft from any German controlled airfield and were operated directly by the High Command.

515. Me109E4 **9/JG3**
off Herne Bay. Crashed into the sea after combat with the R.A.F. Lt H. Achleitner baled out and was picked up by the Lifeboat. Based Desevres.

516. Hurricane I, V7318 **615**
Dartford, Longfield. Engine damaged during an engagement with Me109's over the Estuary, and had to force land. P/O D.H. Hone unhurt. Based Kenley.   Cat 2

517. Hurricane I, V6568 **32**
Lyminge. Crashed after combat over Folkestone. P/O R.F. Smythe wounded and to hospital. Based Biggin Hill.   Cat 3

P/O R.F. Smythe
Was born in Southern Ireland and became a pilot before the outbreak of War.

In 1939 he was posted to 504Sq and in 1940 to 32Sq.

He flew cover for the Dunkerque Evacuation scoring his first success when he shot down a Ju88A. By early August his score had risen to six and he had been awarded the D.F.C. On the 24th he was shot down and wounded and after a period in hospital did not return to operational flying.

518. Hurricane I, V6572 **32**
Rhodes Minnis (also reported Dover). P/O K. Pniak baled out and injured his ankle. Was this the second time he was shot down on the 24th? The unit's Form 541 is ambiguous on this day.

519. Hurricane I, V6567 **32**
Elham, Tedders Leas. Shot down in combat with Me109's. P/O E.G. Seghers baled out unhurt. Based Biggin Hill.   Cat 3

520. Hurricane I, L1865 **501**
W. Kingsdown, Pells Fm. P/O K.R. Aldridge baled out over Ryarsh after a dogfight and broke his arm. Based Gravesend.   Cat 3

521. Hurricane I, P3481 **32**
Lyminge - Hawkinge. Crashed following combat over Folkestone. S/L Crossley unhurt. Adv. base Hawkinge.   Cat 3

522. Me109E **9/JG51**
off Folkestone. Shot down by 32Sq (Higgins). Uffz Kroll killed. Based St Omer or St Quentin.

523. Blenheim IV, T2035 **53**
Dover, Elms Vale. Returning from ops. when it crashed on a house. Police Constable Maycock was just leaving to go on duty and he and his wife were killed, as were F/O Rochford and Sgt Briggs and Brooks. Based Detling.   Cat 3

524.　**25.8.40**　　　Hurricane I, N2433 **32**
nr Dover. Me109's shot down this a/c, but
S/L Crossley survived. Based Biggin Hill.
　　　　　　　　　　　　　　　　　Cat 3

525.　　　　　　　Hurricane I, P2755 **32**
off Dover. Failed to return from the above
combat. P/O K.R. Gillman missing.　　Cat 3

(There is confusion over the a/c Nos. in the
above two incidents and if N2433 was
written off or not.)

526.　　　　　　　Hurricane I, P3402 **85**
Gravesend a/f. Had to force land, reasons
not recorded, nor is the pilot's name. Based
Croydon.　　　　　　　　　　　　Cat 2

527.　　　　　　　Hurricane I, V6547 **32**
off Dover. Shot down by a Me109 into the
sea. P/O J. Rose baled out and was picked
up by a shore boat in 90 minutes. Based Biggin Hill.　　　　　　　　　　　　Cat 3

528.　　　　　　　Spitfire I, R6966 **616**
nr Whitstable. Shot down in flames over
Canterbury. Sgt T.E. Westmoreland missing.
Based Kenley.　　　　　　　　　　Cat 3

529.　　　　　　　Spitfire I, R6969 **54**
Birchington, Brook End. After being
damaged in combat with the Luftwaffe over
Dover, P/O M.M. Shand had to force land
with a nerve in his arm severed by a shell
splinter.
　He was admitted to hospital and did not
return to flying operationally until 25th May
1941. Based Hornchurch.　　　　　Cat 2

530.　　　　　　　Spitfire I, K9931 **610**
Deal, Stoneheap Fm, Northbourne. P/O F.T.
Gardiner baled out slightly wounded. Based
Biggin Hill.

531.　　　　　　　Me109E4 **I/JG54**
St Nicholas at Wade. Shot down in combat
with 54Sq (P/O Gray). Oblt H. Held dead.
Based Guines or Yvrench.

532.　**26.8.40**　　　Battle, L5507 **142**
Eastchurch (Base). Crashed during a night
landing. Crew state not known. (This
squadron had moved from Binbrook
specifically to attack invasion barges in the
Channel ports.)　　　　　　　　　Cat 3

533.　　　　　　　Anson I, N5229 **500**
Detling (Base). Crashed on take off. No
details as to cause or crew state, in Form
541.　　　　　　　　　　　　　　Cat 3

534.　　　　　　　Anson I, N5317 **500**
As above.
The crew of the above Anson was F/O
Peters, Sgts Stanley, Collorossi and Newton.

535.　　　　　　　Me109E1, 6221 **4/JG3**
Hoath, Knaves Ash. Shot down during a
sortie over Canterbury by Hurricanes of
615Sq. Uffz Muller missing. Based Colombert or Samer.

537.　　　　　　　Me109E1 **3/JG52**
off Dover. Shot down by 610Sq in action
over the town. Fw A. Ziegler picked up by a
shore boat and made a POW. Based Coquelles.

538.　　　　　　　Spitfire I, P9496 **610**
over Hawkinge. Shot down in combat. Sgt
Else baled out badly wounded. Based Biggin
Hill.　　　　　　　　　　　　　　Cat 3

539.　　　　　　　Spitfire I, R6701 **616**
off Dover. P/O W.L. Walker baled out wounded in the foot after combat over the Channel and was picked up by the R.N. to be
admitted to hospital. Based Kenley.　Cat 3

540.　　　　　　　Spitfire I, R6632 **616**
Bekesbourne - Hoath. Force landed after an
attack by Me109's over Dungeness. F/O J.S.
Bell unhurt. Based Kenley.　　　　Cat 2

541.　　　　　　　Spitfire I, R7018 **616**
nr Canterbury. Crash landed after a hit in
the coolant system, taken during combat
over Dungeness, had stopped the engine.
F/O E.F. St Aubin hospitalised with burns.
Based Hornchurch.　　　　　　　Cat 2

542.　　　　　　　Defiant I, L7005 **264**
Chislet Park. Crash landed following action
with Me109's over Thanet. Sgts E.R. Thorn
and F.J. Barker slightly wounded. Based
Hornchurch.　　　　　　　　　　Cat 3

543.　　　　　　　Spitfire I, R6633 **616**
Dover area. Believed shot down by Hptm
Föcö of 4/JG51. Sgt M. Ridley killed. Based
Kenley.　　　　　　　　　　　　Cat 3

544.　　　　　　　Spitfire I, N3275 **616**
off Dover. Shot down in the Channel as
above. F/O G.E. Moberley killed.　　Cat 3

545.　　　　　　　Defiant I, L6985 **264**
Herne Bay. Shot down by Me109's following
the destruction of a Do17Z over Thanet, and
crashed in the sea. F/L A.J. Banham baled
out and was picked up. Sgt B. Baker missing
about 2 miles off shore. Based Hornchurch.
　　　　　　　　　　　　　　　　Cat 3

546.　　　　　　　Defiant I, L7025 **264**
Herne Bay. F/O I.R. Stephenson baled out
injured and was picked up by a fishing boat
but Sgt W. Maxwell missing. Based Hornchurch.　　　　　　　　　　　　Cat 3

547.　　　　　　　Me109E4, 5289 **4/JG3**
Reculver, Gray's Fm. Shot down over the N.
of Kent by 56Sq (F/O Marston). Uffz W.
Finke killed. Based Colombe or Conde-
Vaux.

548.　　　　　　　Me109E1, 3874 **6/JG3**
Chislet Marshes, Shuarts Fm. Possibly shot
down by 56Sq (Marston). Uffz F Buchner
killed.
　The site of this crash was excavated. In
September 1984 a body found was identified, at an inquest, as that of Buchner's.

Incident No. 568. The R.A.F. attacked this Do17Z of KG2 over Hornchurch resulting in it crashing on Sheppey.

549.   Hurricane I, V7340 **56**
Upstreet, Grove Ferry. Shot down into the River Stour by a Me109E. P/O Wicks baled out unhurt. Based North Weald.   Cat 3

550.   Spitfire I, R6595 **610**
Hawkinge. Severely damaged by enemy fighters over Folkestone and crashed in flames whilst attempting a force landing. P/O F.K. Webster killed. Based Biggin Hill.
                                          Cat 3
(The Unit's Form 541 gives this a/c as X4011, but that a/c was not written off until 5.11.40.)

551.   Do17Z2 **2/KG2**
Temple Ewell, nr Kearsney Rly Stn. Crashed and exploded.

552.   Spitfire I, R6970 or 6976 **610**
Hawkinge, Castle Hill. Shot down in combat with Me109's over Folkestone and force landed. F/O Lamb unhurt. Based Biggin Hill.
                                          Cat 2

554.   Do17Z3, 2646 **7/KG3**
off Foreness. Briefed to attack R.A.F. W. Malling but was shot down by a (?) Defiant of 264Sq. Lt Eggert was picked up by HSL 120 of 27 M.C.U. off the Goodwins. He was seriously wounded and died on the 28th. Uffz Ramm and Obgfr Knochenmuss missing, Uffz Haupt POW. Based St Trond.

557.   Spitfire I, K9827 **616**
Wye, Crundale House Fm. Shot down in a surprise attack by Me109's and had to force land. The a/c burned and Sgt Copeland was wounded. Based Kenley.   Cat 3

558.   Spitfire I, R6758 **616**
Adisham. Shot down by Me109's and had to force land. P/O R. Marples wounded in the leg by 20mm shell splinters and hospitalised. Based Kenley.   Cat 3

559.   Me109E1 **2/JG52**
Sandwich G.C., nr the Clubhouse. Shot down by the R.A.F. over Ramsgate. Based Coquelles. Fw A. Bacher made a POW.

560.   Hurricane I, R4121 **615**
off Sheerness. P/O J.A. McClintock baled out unhurt after being shot up by a Me109. Based Kenley.   Cat 3

561.   Do17Z, 3329, 5K + GR **7/KG3**
off Margate. Briefed to attack R.A.F. West Malling, but was shot down by fighters and crashed burning into the sea. Lt Sachse was killed but three other crew members were picked up by a fishing boat wounded. Based St Trond.

562.   Me109E1 **2/JG52**
Acol - Minster, Glebe Fm. Crashed and burned following combat over Margate. Obgfr W. Malecki made POW. Based Coquelles.

563.   Hurricane I, R4111 **615**
Herne Bay, W. of. F/L L.M. Gaunce baled out when his aircraft crashed in flames after an attack by a Me109E. He was picked up from the sea by a fishing boat and admitted to hospital. Based Kenley.   Cat 3

564.   Me109E1 **2/JG52**
Ramsgate area. Shot down by the R.A.F. and Uffz Hartlieb killed. Based Coquelles.

565.   Me109E1 **2/JG52**
Folkestone area. As above. Uffz Bokel made a POW.

567.   Do17Z2, 1160, 5K + AR **7/KG3**
Goodwins. Ditched after being shot up by the R.A.F. Uffz Reinhard and Ritzel missing; Fw Essmert POW; Gfr Huhn killed. Based Antwerp-Deurne.

568.   Do17Z, U5 + GK   **2/KG2**
Eastchurch. 2 miles S.W. Attacked by the R.A.F. over Hornchurch and was badly damaged. Later crashed on the Isle of Sheppey. Maj Gutzmann (Gruppe Kdr), Uffz Buhr, Schmolzer POW's; Oblt Hertel killed. Based Cambrai.

569.   **27.8.40**   Hurricane I, R4222   **501**
Hawkinge. Hit in the glycol tank by return fire from a Do215 over the Channel. S/L Hogan unhurt.   Cat 2

S/L H.A.V. Hogan
Was the Commanding Officer of a much weakened unit when it returned from France and was responsible for its re-birth.
   In July he had his first personal success when he shot down a Me109E and by October his score had risen to 6. Apart from a 'Damaged' on the 27th he did not increase his number of successes as that was his last combat.

570.   Lysander II, N1267   **26**
Maidstone, Rock Fm, Nettlestead. Stalled off a steep turn and crashed. P/O Smyth and Sgt Terry killed. Based W. Malling.   Cat 3

571.   **28.8.40**
            Do17Z3, 4251, 5K + LP   **6/KG3**
Foreness. Shot down by the R.A.F. over the Estuary. Lt Krug, Gfr Burghardt, Gailer and Brueckmann all wounded and POW's. Based Antwerp-Deurne.

572.   Defiant I, N1574   **264**
Wye, Kingswood. Shot down by Me109's over Thanet. P/O D. Whitley and Sgt R.C. Turner both killed. Based Hornchurch. Cat 3

573.   Defiant I, L7026   **264**
Ashford, Sillibourne Fm, Hinxhill. A Me109E of JG26 shot this aircraft down killing P/O's P.L. Kenner and C.E. Johnson. Based Hornchurch.   Cat 3

574.   Defiant I, N1569   **264**
Petham, Court Lodge Fm. Severely damaged by JG26 and force landed. P/O J.R. Bailey and Sgt O.A. Hardy unhurt.   Cat 2

575.   Hurricane I, P2718   **79**
Hythe area. Shot down in flames. Pilot baled out and swam ashore badly burnt. Based Biggin Hill.   Cat 3

576.   Me109E4, 5395   **Stab/JG51**
Denton. South Barham Fm. Shot down by the R.A.F. Oblt E. Kircheis (Geschwader Adj) baled out too late and broke his leg on landing. Based Wissant or Pihen.

577.   Hurricane I, P3938   **79**
Appledore Rly Stn. Landed with coolant system damaged in combat over Hythe. F/L G.D. Haysom unhurt. Based Biggin Hill.
                                              Cat 2

578.   Hurricane I, R4116   **615**
Throwley, Snoad Street Fm. Hit in engine by return fire from a Do17Z over Sandwich and had to force land. P/O J. Madle injured and admitted to hospital. Based Kenley.   Cat 3

579.   Defiant I, L7021   **264**
Faversham, Luddenham Marsh. Crashed in flames after combat with Maj Galland of JG26. S/L G.D. Garvin baled out slightly injured F/L R.C. Ash killed. Based Hornchurch.   Cat 3

580.   Me109E, 1353, 13 + 1   **7/JG26**
Goodnestone, House Fm. Shot up in combat over Canterbury, and force landed. Fw K. Straub was a POW. Based Caffiers.

581.   Me109E, 2743   **Stab/JG26**
Petham, South Chartham Down. As above Oblt G. Beyer (Geschwader Adj) baled out and made POW. Based Audembert.

582.   Hurricane I, L2005   **151**
Godmersham, Millthorpe. Set on fire during combat over the Estuary and crashed into a bungalow. P/O J.W. Alexander baled out badly burnt and was hospitalised. Based North Weald.   Cat 3

583.   Hurricane I, P3810   **79**
Biggin Hill (Base). The squadron returned from a rest period at R.A.F. Acklington on the 20th. On this day F/O O.V. Tracey made a head on attack against a Do17Z setting one engine alight. In the course of this his own engine was damaged causing it to lose oil. He arrived at Base during an air raid but had to land immediately so that his aircraft was further damaged by bomb splinters.
                                              Cat 2

584.   Me109E4, 2759   **II/JG54**
Channel. 85Sq were scrambled from Croydon to patrol Hawkinge. They sighted A.A. shell bursts over Dover and found 9 × Me109's at 15000ft. P/O Allard attacked one from 150yds astern and saw pieces of the wing break off. It then dived to crash on the high water mark near Folkestone. Uffz Kleeman missing. Based Hermalinghen.

585.   Me109E, 1436   **I/JG51**
off Folkestone Harbour. Thought to have been shot down by 85Sq (Allard). Pilot was unhurt. Based St Omer-Longuenesse.

586.   Me109E4, 5146   **III/JG3**
St Nicholas at Wade. Shot up over Canterbury later exploded in mid air. Obfw Trebing was killed. Based Desevres.

587.   Me109E
nr Tongue Lightship off Margate. Shot down by a 1Sq Hurricane. (Could have been one of two Me109's lost by JG26 and flown by Oblt G. Beyer or Fw Straub.).

588.   Spitfire I, R6832   **54**
Stockbury, Frid Wood. In the confusion of combat F/L A. Deere was shot down by another Spitfire whilst he himself was attacking a Me109E. Based Hornchurch.   Cat 3

589.   Hurricane I, R4117   **56**
Herne Bay, Westend. Crashed in flames after combat with enemy fighters over the Estuary. P/O M. Constable-Maxwell slightly injured. Based N. Weald.   Cat 3

590.   Hurricane I, V7382 **56**
Minster, Scocles Fm (Isle of Sheppey). Damaged by return fire from a Do17Z that it had engaged over the Estuary. F/O P.S. Weaver had to force land but was unhurt. Based North Weald.   Cat 2

591.   Spitfire I, P9511 **610**
Stelling Minnis. Shot up by Me109's over Dover and crashed on a house. P/O K.H. Cox was killed. Based Biggin Hill.   Cat 3

592.   Me109E4, 0941 **I/JG3**
Dover, Whitfield. Shot down by an unknown R.A.F. fighter. Lt Landry baled out badly wounded and died in hospital 23.9.40. Based Samer.

593.   Hurricane I, P3320 **151**
Eastchurch a/f. Crash landed after combat with the enemy over the Estuary. Sgt L. Davies was wounded. Based N. Weald. Cat 2

594.   Spitfire I, X4053 **54**
Westbere, Puckstone Fm Lake. Shot down by Me109's over Ramsgate. S/L D.O. Findlay baled out wounded. Based Hornchurch.
                                        Cat 3

595.   Spitfire I, L1046 **603**
off Dover. Failed to return from combat over the Channel. P/O D.K. McDonald's body was never recovered. Based Hornchurch.   Cat 3

596.   Spitfire I, R6751 **603**
Dover. As above. F/L J.L. Cunningham missing.   Cat 3

597.   Hurricane I, R4198 **56**
nr Hawkinge. Believed shot down by a Spitfire. P/O F.B. Sutton baled out badly burnt and was hospitalised. Based N. Weald. Cat 3

598.   Hurricane I, N2523 **56**
Acrise, Ladwood Fm. After a Me109 had been shot down this aircraft was itself attacked near Hawkinge. The fuel tank exploded and the aircraft burned. Sgt G. Smythe baled out unhurt. Based North Weald.   Cat 3

599.   Me109E, 1523, 14+ **7/JG51**
Alkam, Poulton Fm. Shot down by the R.A.F. Obfw A. Dau baled out to become a POW. Based St Omer or St Quentin.

600.   Me109E
Lympne. 12 miles NW. 10 × Hurricanes of 85Sq took off to patrol Tenterden at 18000ft and then vectored to intercept a raid of 20 × Me109's and a single ~Me110. S/L P. Townsend gave one of the opposition a short burst and it dived steeply to crash. The pilot was safe and made a POW. (No confirmation has been found of this report.)

601.   Me109E1, 3553 **7/JG3**
Channel. Shot down by the R.A.F. but the pilot was picked up by Seenotflkdo. Based Desevres.

Me109
Dymchurch. Shot down by F/O P.P. Wood-Scawen (85Sq) and confirmed by the R.O.C. He attacked from the stern quarter with 2 long bursts and followed the victim down for several thousands of feet.
(It is likely that these are one incident.)

602.   Spitfire I, N3105, XT-P **603**
Tenterden. French Hayes Fm, Leigh Green. Shot down by Me109's in flames. P/O N.J. Benson killed. Based Hornchurch.   Cat 3

603.   Me109E1, 6204, 4+ **I/JG54**
Capel le Ferne. Shot down by S/L G. Denholm (603Sq). It attempted to force land but hit H.T. cables and crashed. Fw Schoettle survived to become a POW. Based Guines or Yvrench.

604.   **29.8.40**
          3 × Me109E1, 4031, 6335 **III/JG3**
Channel. Shot down by the R.A.F. Based Desevres. 4031: Pilot picked up by Seenot-FkKdo. 6335: Pilot Uffz Pfieffer missing.
                              1181 **I/JG26**
Pilot missing. Obfw Graf von Treuberg killed. Based Audembert.

605.   Spitfire I, P9459, XT-N **603**
Upper Hardres, Bossingham. Had to force land following combat over Deal. F/L W. Rushmer wounded. Based Hornchurch.
                                        Cat 2

606.   Me109E
Dungeness. 11 aircraft of 85Sq were scrambled to patrol Maidstone and then vectored to Dungeness at 24000ft where they received a warning of 'bandits' to the north and intercepted. P/O Marshall attacked one of the hostiles as it went into a climbing turn with the result that it dived from 22000ft through cloud into the sea.

607.   Me109E3, 1166 **3/JG3**
off Folkestone. Failed to return to base. Possibly shot down by Sgt Lacey. Oblt Floerke killed. Based Samer.

608.   Spitfire I, R6753 **603**
Dymchurch, St Mary's Rd. Shot down by Me109's and crashed. P/O D. Pinkney slightly injured and to hospital. Based Hornchurch.   Cat 3

609.   Hurricane I, R4223 **501**
nr Hawkinge. Shot down in combat. Sgt W.J. Green is reported as landing by 'chute on a hill overlooking Elham, but another report has him rescued from the sea. Based Gravesend.   Cat 3

610.   Spitfire I, L1021 **603**
nr Lympne. P/O R.H. Hillary became separated from the rest of his formation and attached himself to 85Sq acting as 'weaver'. He subsequently crashed, so he may have been picked off as so often happened to pilots flying in this position. Based Hornchurch.   Cat 3

611.   Hurricane I, P3102 **501**
Acrise, Ladwood Fm. This aircraft was one
of a flight of three surprised by Me109's, and
shot up. It lost height and crashed into a
copse 500yds from the farmhouse, bursting
into flames, which in turn set the trees
alight. The resulting blaze could be seen as
far away as Dungeness. F/L J.A. Gibson
baled out landing at Mill Hill Cotts. Based
Gravesend.   Cat 3

612. **30.8.40**   Me109E4, 1623 **III/JG27**
off Dungeness. Shot down in combat with a
Hurricane of 253Sq (Gleave). Fw Lehrmann
killed. Based Guines or Plumetot.

613.   Me109E1, 1973 **2/JG52**
off Dover. Suffered engine failure and
ditched. Lt Geller missing. Based Peuplingues.

614.   Hurricane I, L1965 **253**
Wrotham, Percivals Fm. Shot down by a
Me109. P/O C.D. Francis killed. Based Ken-
ley.   Cat 3

615.   Spitfire, L1067, XT-D **603**
Snargate, Hope Fm. Shot down by Me110's
and had to force land. S/L G. Denholm
unhurt. Based Kenley.   Cat 3

The ever present fears that had to be faced
by young pilots involved not only the
thought of being killed but perhaps even
worse the thought of being crippled or dis-
figured.

G/Capt T.P. Gleave who was one of them
fighting through the Battle and towards the
end being shot down in flames said:

'I was about to pull up into an attack . . .
when I heard a click in my engine. A sudden
burst of heat struck my face, I looked down
into the cockpit. A long spout of flame was
issuing from the hollow wing root. The
flames increased until the cockpit was like
the centre of a blow-lamp nozzle.

The skin was already rising off my wrist
and hand and the other had started to
blister.'

After landing by parachute:

'My shoes looked like shoes and I found I
could walk . . my ankle and each side of my
right foot were burnt, my left scorched with
several small burns . . . my slacks had disappeared except for portions that had been
covered by my parachute harness.

The skin on my right leg from the top of
the thigh to just above the ankle had lifted
and draped my leg like an outsized 'plus
fours'. My left leg was in a similar condition.
My service gloves had almost burnt off
and the skin from my wrist and hands hung
down like paper bags. The underside of my
right arm and elbow was burnt and so was
my face and neck.'

There followed many painful weeks of
hospital treatment at East Grinstead under
Sir Archibald McIndoe, before he was able
to return to duty.

Many of the other surviving aircrew are
still, in 1987, requiring treatment to main-
tain mobility and reduce pain.

616.   Hurricane I, V6624 **85**
Smarden, Langley Fm. Shot down by gunners of a IV/KG1 Heinkel 111 or possibly of
a Me110. P/O Marshall baled out near Ashford. Based Croydon.   Cat 3

617.   Hurricane I, V7369 **151**
Rochester, Temple Street, Strood. This aircraft crashed during a routine patrol. Causes
not known. S/L E.B. King killed. Based
Stapleford Tawney.   Cat 3

618.   Spitfire I, X4248 **616**
West Malling. Shot down in a head on
attack by Me109's over base, crashing and
burning. F/O J.S. Bell killed. Based Kenley.
                                     Cat 3

619.   Me109E4, 6072 **II/JG54**
Chelsham, Layham Fm. Collided with Lt
Ziegler during an engagement with the
R.A.F. Oblt Rath baled out to become a
POW. Lt Ziegler crashed at Oxsted in
Surrey. Based Hermalinghen.

620.   He111H2, 5125 **11/KG1**
off Folkestone. Became separated from the
rest of the formation and was attacked by
Spitfires over the Coast. In the combat it
was forced to ditch, still harased by Sgt
Beardsley (610Sq). Uffz E. Burger, Gfr Feierabend, Hildebrand, Klappholz and Roggemann were picked up and landed at Dover.
Based Montdidier.

621.   Spitfire I, P9325 **222**
Eastchurch. Force landed with severe
damage after combat with Lw fighters over
Canterbury. Sgt S. Baxter unhurt. Based
Hornchurch.   Cat 2

622.   Spitfire I, R6720 **222**
Bekesbourne ALG as above. P/O Asheton
unhurt. Based Hornchurch.   Cat 2

623.   He111H2, 2782, A1 + JP **6/KG53**
Manston, north of Cheesemans Fm. Damaged by the R.A.F. during a raid on Radlett
and crashed. Fw Eckert killed, Gfr Koeler
severely wounded and died 2.9.40; Fw
Stockl, Gfr Glueck and Klapp all POW's.
Based Lille or Chartres.

624.   Heinkel111H2, 6818 **6/KG53**
off Sheppey. As above. Uffz Rascher, Roempert., Schall, Keuerleber and H. Wagner
picked up from the sea and made POW's.

625.   Me109E4, 2782 **8/JG2**
Dungeness area. Shot down in combat over
the Ness. Uffz Reith made a POW. Based
Bar le Duc.

626.   Me109E1, 3771 **3/JG27**
nr Faversham, Westwood Court, Sheldwich.
Damaged by 603Sq (F/O B. Carbury) over
London and had to force land. Fw E. Arnold
made POW. Based St Omer (?)

627.   Me109E, 6270   3/JG27
Westwell, Park House. Probably shot down
by 253Sq (Gleave). Pilot was Oblt Axthelm.

629.   Hurricane, P8816   501
Gravesend (Base). Force landed with a damaged radiator caused by return fire from a
He111 over the Estuary. Sgt J.M. Lacey
unhurt.   Cat 2

630.   Me109E4, 0804   II/JG26
Folkestone. Severely damaged in combat
over Folkestone and ditched. The pilot was
picked up by Seenotflkdo. Based Marquise.

631.   Me109E4, 5650   I/JG26
Channel. Ditched on the return flight after
combat with the R.A.F. Also picked up by
Seenotflkdo. Based Audembert.

632.   Hurricane I, P3802   253
W. Malling, Mereworth Wood. Force landed
after combat with Me109's. F/L G.A. Brown
wounded in the shoulder and later
hospitalised. Based Kenley.   Cat 3

633.   Spitfire I, R7021   603
W. Malling, Addington Park. This aircraft
had its tail shot off by a Me109E and
crashed. Sgt A. Sarre was fortunately able to
bale out unhurt. Based Hornchurch.   Cat 3

634.   Me109E4, 2765   4/JG2
Chatham. Walderslade. Shot down by 616Sq
(Gillam). Obfw K. Harbauer killed. Based St
Omer-Longuenesse (?).

635.   Hurricane I, P3213   253
nr Woodchurch, Plurenden Manor. Shot
down by II/JG26 (Fw Koch) over Dungeness.
Sgt J.H. Dickinson baled out dead. Based
Kenley.   Cat 3

636.   Hurricane I, P2631, SW-X   253
Biddenden. 1 mile south of. Shot down in
combat. Sgt S.F. Cooper unhurt. Based
Kenley.   Cat 3

637.   Hurricane I, V6548   43
Woodchurch. 1 mile south of. Shot down by
a Me109. S/L J.V. Badger very seriously
wounded and died in hospital 30.6.41. Based
Tangmere.   Cat 3

638.   Spitfire I, K9826   222
Barham, Marley. Shot up by Me109's so that
it crashed and burned. P/O H.P. Edridge
baled out burnt on the face. Based Hornchurch.   Cat 3
(This incident also reptd nr W. Malling.)

639.   Spitfire I, R6628   222
Bishopsbourne, Longham Pk. Shot down
and burned after crashing. Sgt J.I. Johnson
killed. Based Hornchurch.   Cat 3

640.   Spitfire I, P9443   222
nr Sittingbourne. Crash landed following
combat. F/L C.C. Matheson seriously injured. Based Hornchurch.   Cat 3

641.   Spitfire I, P9323   222
Minster, South Leas Fm. Suffered the same
fate as the other 222Sq aircraft. Sgt A.W.
Spears baled out unhurt.   Cat 3

642.   Me109E7, 6123   I/JG27
Minster (Isle of Sheppey). Shot down possibly by 222Sq over the Estuary. Oblt
Bertram baled out unhurt and was picked
up by Seenotflkdo. (This must have been a
courageous effort on the part of the pilot of
the seaplane, a slow and unmanoeuvrable
machine, well within R.A.F. radar cover and
not far from several fighter airfields.) Based
Guines, Plivot or Plumetot.

643.   **31.8.40**   Me109E4, 5393   6/JG26
Manston. Shot up by a Spitfire of 54Sq
(Gray) during a fighter operation over Canterbury. Uffz W. Heyer killed. Based Marquise.

644.   Me109E1, 3510   II/JG2
Channel. Ditched with severe damage
caused by R.A.F. fighters. Pilot rescued by
Seenotflkdo. Based St Omer (?).

645.   Me109E1, 5908   3/JG77
Channel. Ditched after combat with the
R.A.F. over S.E. England. Pilot picked up as
above. Based St Omer.

646.   Hurricane I, L1830   253
Eastry, nr Grove Ferry. Shot down by Lw
fighters whilst on an interception. S/L H.M.
Starr found dead at Hammil Brickworks.
Based Kenley.   Cat 3

647.   Me110, 3617   14/LG1
off Foreness. Shot down by the R.A.F. whilst
over the Estuary. Lt Eichorn was picked up
by a Margate fishing boat, but despite a
search for Uffz Growe and the finding of his
'chute, he remained missing. Based Caen.

648.   Me110, 3805   14/LG1
off Sheppey. Under much the same circumstances as above this aircraft ditched near
the Nore Lightship. The crew Fw Gottlob
and Obgfr Doepfer were picked up and
made POW's. Based Caen.

649.   Hurricane I, P2971   1RCAF
Staplehurst, Wanshurst Green. Abandoned
over Cranbrook. P/O G.C. Hyde baled out
burnt. Based Northolt.   Cat 3

650.   Hurricane I, P3858   1RCAF
Broomfield. Shot down by Me109's over
Cranbrook. F/O Sprenger baled out unhurt,
landing at Bray Court, Ulcombe. Based
Northolt.   Cat 3

651.   Hurricane I, P3869   1RCAF
Biddenden. Shot down over Cranbrook. F/L
V.B. Corbett baled out unhurt, to land at
Wittersham Rly level crossing. Based
Northolt.   Cat 3

652.   Me109E1, 4076   2/JG77
Elham, Elham Park Wood. Shot up by the
R.A.F. Oblt E. Priebe (Staffel Kapt) baled out
wounded and landed on the King George V
playing field. Made POW. Based St Omer.

654.   Hurricane I, P3166 **85**
Hawkhurst. After attacking two Me109's, part of the escort for Do17's attacking Croydon, this aircraft was hit by fire from a Me110 causing fuel to flood the cockpit. S/L P. Townsend was fortunate it did not ignite. He intended to force land but found himself in a densely wooded area at 1500ft and had to bale out landing in Bedgebury Park, Goudhurst, with his wrecked aircraft only half a mile away. He was hospitalised with a 20mm shell cap embedded in his ankle. Based Croydon.   Cat 3

655.   Me109E4, 5105 **1/JG77**
High Halden, Gate Fm. Shot down by F/L P.B. Robinson (601Sq) or Mentz (222Sq) and crashed. Oblt H.J. Ehrig (Staffel Kapt) made POW. Based St Omer.

I/JG77
This Geschwader was based at this time at Stavanger-Sola with detachments on other Norwegian airfields. I Gruppe was exchanged with I/JG51, presumably to rest the latter's pilots in a quiet theatre of war, and to give I/JG77 experience of more intensive activity. Eventually this Gruppe became IV/JG51.

656.   Hurricane I, P3115 **253**
Biggin Hill, Mace Fm, Cudham. Shot down in flames during an attack made on a Ju88. S/L T.P. Gleave baled out badly burnt and was hospitalised for a long period. Based Kenley.   Cat 3

657.   Me110D, 3381, S9+GK **EproGr210**
Wrotham Hill. Severely damaged when attacked by 85Sq aircraft over the outskirts of London, and had to force land. Uffz Glaeska made POW, Obgfr Schweda killed. Based Calais-Marck.

658.   Hurricane I, V6540 **501**
Gravesend (Base). Shot up by Me109's. Sgt Glowacki baled out slightly wounded. Cat 3

659.   Me109E1, 6092 **1/JG77**
Gravesend, Shornmead Fort. Shot down over the Estuary by 601Sq Spitfire (Sgt Taylor) and force landed. Fw Kramer made a POW. Based St Omer.

661.   Me109E, 4068, 8+ **I/JG77**
Walderslade - Boxley. Shot up over the Estuary. Uffz X. Keck baled out and was made a POW. (There are doubts as to the exact location, also reported as over the Channel and at Bluebell Hill.) Based St Omer.

662.   Me109E1, 3652 **I/JG77**
nr Marden, Court Fm, Hunton. Shot down by F/L Macdonald of 603Sq. Fw W. Evers seriously wounded and died later. Based St Omer;

663.   Do17Z3, 2669, 5K+LM **4/KG3**
Sandwich G.C. Had to force land after an attack on Hornchurch a/f and the following

engagement with the R.A.F. It had also sustained damage from A.A. fire. Obfw Lange, Fw Berndt and Wuensch and Uffz Krostopotsch all wounded and POW's. Based Antwerp-Deurne.

664.   Do17Z3, 3414, 5K+GN **5/KG3**
nr S. Goodwin. As above but shot down by a Hurricane of 310Sq. Fw Nickel drowned. Fw Gudat and Uffz Blasche and Sonntag all POW's.

665.   Hurricane I, N2530 **1RCAF**
Gravesend. Crashed and burned after an attack on Do17Z's. F/O J.P. Desloges baled out severely burnt. Based Northolt.   Cat 3

666.   Me109E1, 6309 **7/JG26**
West Kingsdown, Knatts Valley. Shot down by (?) 54Sq (Gribble and Norwell). Uffz H. Liebeck became a POW. Based Caffiers.

667.   Hurricane I, P3050 **79**
Hawkhurst, Conghurst Fm. Was set alight in combat with Me109's over New Romney and crashed. P/O W.H. Millington wounded in the leg and admitted to hospital. Based Biggin Hill.   Cat 3

668.   Spitfire I, P9337 **222**
Tenterden, 1 mile east of St Michaels. Shot up by enemy fighters over Ashford. P/O C.G. Davies burnt but alive. Based Hornchurch.
                                       Cat 3

669.   Spitfire I, N3233 **222**
Eastchurch a/f. Force landed with a damaged aircraft as a result of 20mm cannon fire from a Me109E. F/L A.I. Robinson slightly wounded. Based Hornchurch. Cat 2

670.   Hurricane I, R4091 **17**
Yalding. Damaged in combat with Me109's and had to force land. Sgt G.A. Steward unhurt. Based Tangmere.   Cat 2

671.   Me109E4, 1475 **6/JG3**
Lydd, R.A. Ranges. Shot down by P/O Millington (79Sq) during a sortie over the southeastern outskirts of London. Oblt K. Westerhoff burnt and made POW. Based Colombert (?).

672.   Me109E1, 3175 **4/JG3**
off Dover. Crashed after being damaged by the R.A.F. over London. Lt R. von Larisch killed. Based Colombert (?).

673.   Me109E1, 3464 **7/JG26**
Allington, Mill House Fm. Shot up by 85Sq Hurricane (Woods-Scawen) east of London. Fw M. Klar made a POW. Based Caffiers.

674.   Spitfire I, P9438 **72**
Biggin Hill. Shot up in combat over Dungeness. F/L F.M. Smith baled out badly burnt and wounded.   Cat 3

675.   Me109E4, 1184 **9/JG26**
Ulcombe, Jubilee Hill. Force landed after combat with (?) 54Sq P/O Gray. Oblt Fronhöfer made a POW. Based Caffiers.

676.   Hurricane I, P3877   79
Biggin Hill (Base). Attacked a Do17Z and
was damaged by its Me109 escort, over
base. P/O E.J. Morris wounded.   Cat 2

677.   Do17Z, 3316   2/KG76
Newchurch. Briefed to attack Hornchurch
and was itself attacked on the return journey by (?) 151Sq (Pattullo) over the Estuary.
Lt J. Kleppmeier, Obfw H. Lang, Fw H.
Pfachler and Uffz A. Bloss all wounded and
made POW. Based Beauvais.

678.   Spitfire I, P9457   72
Staplehurst, Munns Fm. Shot up by Lw
fighters over Dungeness. F/O E.J. Wilcox
killed. Based Biggin Hill.   Cat 3

679.   Do215, 0028   4/AufKlGr
Tunbridge Wells, south of. This was the last
aircraft in a formation when it was attacked
by Sgt Howes of 85Sq. It went down stream-
ing black and white smoke. Shortly afterwards 2 'chutes were seen to open and then
a tall column of smoke. Uffz Vogel killed;
Uffz Goebbels, Kamolz missing, Fw Mavrer
killed. Based in Belgium.
(A single unconfirmed report.)

680.   Spitfire I, X4054   54
Hildenborough, Gt. Hollanden Fm. Shot
down accidentally by a Hurricane shortly
after Sgt Gibbins had claimed a Me109E
shot down. The Spitfire crashed and burned,
but the pilot baled out, unhurt, except perhaps his feelings, and landed at Tinley
Lodge, Shipbourne. Based Hornchurch. Cat 3

681.   **1.9.40**   Me110   8/ZG26
Thames Estuary. Missing from a sortie over
S.E. England. Lw Q.M.'s records do not show
how it was lost or who crewed the aircraft.
Based Crecy.

682.   Me109E   II/JG27
Dover. Shot down in combat. Pilot's name
not recorded. Based Montreuil or Sempy.

683.   Me109E4, 1902   I/JG52
Orlestone. Shot down by the R.A.F. and
crashed. Obfw Gerber killed. Based Coquelles.

684.   Me109E, 1277   II/JG54
Ruckinge. Crashed after a collision which
occurred during a fighter sortie over Kent.
Oblt A. Stangl made a POW. Based Hermalinghen.

685.   Spitfire I, P9458   72
Pluckley, Elvey Fm. Crashed and burned
after being attacked by Me109's. F/L O.S.
Pigg was killed. Based Croydon.   Cat 3

686.   Spitfire I, X4109   72
Ham Street - Orlestone, Court Lodge Fm.
Shot down in a surprise attack by Me109's.
F/O D.F. Sheen baled out unhurt. Based
Croydon.   Cat 3

687.   Hurricane I, P3276   1
Ruckinge, Brisley Fm. Shot down by
Me109's. F/S F.G. Berry killed. Based North-
olt.   Cat 3

688.   Spitfire I, L1092   72
W. Malling a/f. Force landed with dead
engine due to severe damage caused by
enemy aircraft over Lympne. P/O B. Douthwaite unhurt. Based Croydon.   Cat 2
(There is doubt about this location.)

689.   Spitfire I, P9448   72
Leeds Castle. 12 Spitfires were despatched
to intercept a raid. In poor visibility they
were bounced by Me109's and this aircraft
was badly hit by cannon fire so that F/O R.A.
Thompson had to belly land.   Cat 2

691.   Spitfire I, L1056   72
W. Malling a/f. Severely damaged by
Me109's over Beachy Head and had to belly
land. Sgt M.H. Pocock was wounded in the
arm and leg. Later admitted to hospital.
Based Croydon.   Cat 2

692.   Hurricane I, N2477   85
Lympne a/f. Forced to land due to loss of oil
pressure and was caught on the ground in an
air raid. P/O G. Allard unhurt. Based Croydon.   Cat 2

693.   Hurricane I, P5185   253
Staplehurst, Clapper Lane. Shot down in
combat with Do215's (?) and Me110's over
Dungeness. P/O J.K. Clifton killed. Based
Kenley.   Cat 3

694.   Me110C, L1+OH   14/LG1
Bilsington, nr Ham Street, Tarpot Fm. Shot
down by the R.A.F. during a sortie over Kent
and force landed. Obfw Kobert and Fw
Meining unhurt and POW's. Based Tramecourt.

695.   Hurricane I, P3963   1RCAF
Shipbourne. Shot down in action by Do215's
and Me110's, crashing and burning. F/O
Kerwin baled out burnt. Based Northolt.
                                       Cat 3

696.   Hurricane I, L2062   79
Chelsfield. In combat over Biggin Hill was
shot down by Me109's. P/O E.R. Noble
wounded and baled out landing in Marley
Lake, Riverhead. Based Biggin Hill.   Cat 3

697.   Hurricane I, P2673, VY-E   85
Chelsfield, Court Road. Missing after combat over Kenley. Sgt J.H. Ellis missing,
believed killed. Based Croydon.   Cat 3

698.   Hurricane I, R4171   1RCAF
nr W. Malling. Shot down whilst attacking
Do215's and Me110's. F/O A. Yuile baled out
unhurt. Based Northolt.   Cat 3

699.   Do17Z, 3369, F1+AT   9/KG76
Dungeness Point. Was part of a raid of
150-200 Do17's with an escort of Me109's
and 110's. The target was Gravesend.
    The formation was sighted at 15000ft by
85Sq near Biggin Hill. P/O Allard carried out
an attack on a Do17 which had become
separated from the rest. It turned southward
and he climbed above it making three suc-
cessive attacks. Both of its engines began to

smoke and the port burst into flames. At this point the rear gunner baled out. Later the pilot force landed near the railway branch line. Obfw Illg, Fw Woehner and Uffz Maasen made POW's. Gfr Speiss killed. Based Cormeilles en Vexin.

700. Anson I, N9538 **500** **Detling** (Base). Destroyed on the ground in an air-raid. No aircrew involved. Cat 3

700A. Me110 **15/LG1** **Brasted,** Hosey Wood. Shot up over Eden bridge by P/O Mayhew (79Sq) and probably F/O Elsdon (72Sq). Fw M Jäckel and Flgr Rösler killed. Based Caen-Cariquet.

701. Hurricane I, P3217 **79** **Biggin Hill** (Base). Crashed on landing after combat with Me109's over base. Exact reason for crash and a/c No. not known. F/L G.D. Haysom injured. Cat 2

702. Hurricane I, W6670 **79** **Biggin Hill** (Base), Hawleys Corner. Severely damaged in the above combat and crashed. P/O Bryant-Fenn wounded landed by parachute at Dunton Green and was admitted to hospital. Cat 3

703. Me109E4, 4020 **III/JG53** **Chilham,** Hurst Fm. Shot up in combat over Thanet crashing and burning. Oblt Bauer killed. Based Sempy.

704. 2.9.40 Hurricane I, V7352 **249** **Bredgar.** Crash landed with battle damage after an encounter with Me109's over Rochester. F/L R.E. Wynn wounded. Based North Weald. Cat 2

705. Hurricane I, P2946 **253** **Ashford,** Longport, Crundale. Shot down by Lw fighters over Thanet. Sgt J. Metham wounded. Based Kenley. Cat 3

706. Me109E1, 4807 **1/JG51** **Womenswold,** Nethersole Park. During combat with P/O Gribble (54Sq) this aircraft flown by Lt G. Ruettowski shot down and the pilot killed. Based St Omer.

707. Me109E, 4850 **1/JG51** **Leeds Castle,** Abbey Fm. Crashed in flames after being shot up by S/L Leathart (54Sq). Lt H. Thoerl baled out unhurt and made POW.

708. Hurricane I, P3384 **249** **Meopham.** Hit by return fire from a Me110 of II/ZG26. P/O P.R. Burton unhurt. Based North Weald. Cat 2

709. Hurricane I, P2988 **249** **Aylesford,** Eccles Rec. Ground. Shot down in flames by a Me110 of 5/ZG26 after combat near Rochester. P/O H.J. Beazley unhurt and baled out. Cat 3

710. Hurricane I, P3803 **501** **Gravesend** (Base). Damaged in combat over base. Sgt W.B. Henn injured. Cat 3

711. Me110D1, 3309 **2/ZG26** **Birling,** White Horse Wood. Shot down by Sgt Rolls (72Sq) whilst it was on a bomber escort mission. Fw Schuetz killed, Gfr Stuewe wounded and POW. Based St Omer or Abbeville.

712. Me109E, 3584 **1/JG53** **Hythe,** on the ranges west of the town. Shot down by Sgt G.W. Jeffreys (46Sq). Uffz W. Karl unhurt made POW. Based Coquelles or Etaples.

713. Hurricane I, V7230 **501** **Sellindge,** Horton Priory. Force landed after combat over North Kent. P/O S. Skalski injured. Based Gravesend. Cat 2

714. Me110C4, 3536, 3U+GN **5/ZG26** **off Nore Light.** Shot down by the R.A.F. whilst on a bombing escort mission. Obfw Rochel and Uffz Schoefler unhurt. POW's. Based Crecy.

715. Me110D/O, 3269 **II/ZG2** **Eastry,** Venson Fm. Probably shot down by 249 Sq Hurricanes and exploded in the air. Fw L. Beil and Obgfr Oehl killed. Based Hermalinghen (?)

716. Me109E4, 1574 **III/JG54** **Chilham,** Hurst Fm, Mountain Street. Shot down in combat with (?) 303Sq. Oblt Schelcher's body was found when the site was excavated by Royal Engineers (T.A.) in the 1970's. Part of the aircraft is in the Kent Battle of Britain Museum at Hawkinge. Based Guines.

717. Me109E4, 6115 **4/JG2** **Charing,** Gale Hill Park, Little Chart. Whilst over Ashford was engaged by Sgt G.W. Jeffreys (46Sq). Uffz A. Glomb was seriously wounded. Based St Omer (?).

718. Me110, 3622, 3M+HK **I/ZG2** **Dover,** Hougham Without, St Radigans Abbey. Hurricanes of 249Sq attacked this aircraft causing it to crash and burn. Lt Schipper and Gfr Schockenhof were unhurt and made POW's. Based Amiens or Abbeville.

719. Me109E, 1167 **I/JG53** **Bilsington** (?). Shot down and lost in the sea. Oblt E. Kuehlmann missing. Based Couelles or Etaples.

720. Hurricane I, V6640 **253** **Appledore,** ½ mile south of Rly.Stn. F/O Bell-Salter baled out wounded and was further injured by a heavy landing as his 'chute was damaged. Based Kenley. Cat 3

721. Hurricane I, R4228 **111** **Detling a/f.** Force landed following an attack on a He111 over the Estuary. It was then caught in an air-raid on the R.A.F. Station. F/L H.S. Giddings unhurt. Based Debden. Cat 2

722. Spitfire I, K9938 **72** **Bekesbourne** ALG, nr Garrington Fm and 50yds from the railway line. Crashed and burned after a dogfight over Herne Bay. Sgt N.R. Norfolk safe. Based Croydon. Cat 3

46

723. Me109E4, 1452, 12+ **4/JG2**
W. Hythe, south of Lympne Castle. Force
landed due to damage sustained in combat
with F/L R.G. Reynell (43Sq). Uffz von Stein
became a POW. Based St Omer-Longuenesse (?).

724. Me109E, 6276 **I/JG53**
off Hythe. Failed to return from an escort
mission over the Channel. Shot down by (?)
F/L Reynell. Lt Riegel missing. Based Coquelles or Etaples.

725. Me109E4 **9/JG2**
Ulcombe, Streets Fm. Severely damaged by
A.A. over Tilbury and crashed. Lt Klüge
baled out severely wounded and died later.
Based Bar le Duc.

726. Hurricane I, V7420 **43**
Ivychurch - Fryland, ½ mile south of
Church. Set alight in combat with Me109's
over W. Kent and attempted a force landing. P/O Woods-Scawen baled out too late
and was killed. He is buried in Folkestone
Cemetery, Plot O Grave 25. Based Tangmere. Cat 3

727. Hurricane I, P3786 **43**
nr Ashford, Warehorne. In combat with
Me109's was shot down. F/L M.K. Carswell
baled out injured. Based Tangmere. Cat 3

728. Me109E4, 1569 **I/JG53**
Dover - Calais. After action with the R.A.F.
the pilot was picked up unhurt by Seenotflkdo. Based Coquelles or Etaples.

729. Anson I, MK-N **500**
Penshurst ALG. Force landed here as Detling
was u/s due to enemy bombing.

729A. Me109E4, 1632 **8/JG51**
Channel. Shot down returning from a sortie
over S.E. England. Lt Braun picked up by
Seenotflkdo. Based St Omer or St Quentin.

730. Anson I, MK-V **500**
Penshurst ALG. Had to force land as Detling
was u/s due to enemy bombing. P/O Leeson,
Sgts Marsden, Oughton and York safe.
Based Detling.

731. Hurricane I, P3903 **43**
Old Romney, Bell Corner. Shot down by
Me109's over E. Kent. P/O A. du Vivier ad-
mitted to hospital with wounds in the leg.
Based Tangmere. Cat 3

732. Spitfire I, X4241 (?) **72**
Monks Horton. Shot up over Lympne by Lw
fighters. F/L E. Graham unhurt. Cat 3

733. Me110D/O, 3197 **II/ZG2**
Channel. Shot down by (?) 249Sq during a
dogfight. Based Hermalinghen (?). Uffz
Deuker and Krapp missing.

734. Spitfire I, K9840 **72**
Hawkinge a/f. Severely damaged in combat
south of Dungeness and crashed on return
to base. W/C R.B. Lees wounded. Adv. Based
Hawkinge.,

735. Hurricane I, V7234 **501**
Lympne. Shot down by the Lw. Sgt H.C.
Adams reported unhurt. Based Gravesend.
Cat 2

736. Hurricane I, L1578 **501**
off Dungeness. Failed to return from ops.
over the Channel. May have been shot down
by Maj A. Galland. F/O A.T. Rose-Price missing. Cat 3

737. Spitfire I, X4181 **616**
Tonbridge, Brook Fm, Capel. Set on fire by a
Me110 over Maidstone area. F/L D.E. Gillam
baled out unhurt. Based Kenley. Cat 3

738. Me109E1, 3470 **8/JG54**
Ashford, Finns Fm, Kingsnorth. Crashed
attempting a force landing after being shot
up by a Hurricane of 46Sq (Ambrose) south-
east of Herne Bay. Uffz H. Elbers made
POW. Based Guines.

739. Spitfire I, N3056, XT-B **603**
Lenham, Warren Street. Shot down in com-
bat with Lw fighters over Maidstone. Sgt J.
Stokoe baled out wounded and hospitalised.
Based Hornchurch. Cat 3

740. Hurricane I, P3597 **46**
Sittingbourne, Borden. After combat over
the Estuary F/L A.C. Rabagliati force landed
unhurt. Based Stapleford Tawney. Cat 2

741. Me109E4, 1261 **1/JG52**
Sturry - Westbere, Tile Lodge Fm. Belly
landed after being shot up by P/O Ambrose
(46Sq). Had been engaged in a free lance
sortie off Eastchurch. Fw H. Verlings unhurt.
Based Coquelles.

742. Hurricane I, R4178 **303**
Elvington, ¾ mile NW. Damaged in combat
over the Channel and had to force land. P/O
M. Feric unhurt. Based Northolt. Cat 2

743. 3.9.40 Hurricane I, P3610 **253**
Woollage, Snowdown Mine. Cause not
known. P/O L.C. Murch unhurt. Based Kenley. Cat 3

744. Spitfire, X4277 **603**
off Margate. Shot down by Hptm Bode of
II/JG26. P/O R.H. Hillary picked up by Margate Lifeboat badly burnt. Based Hornchurch. Cat 3

745. Spitfire, X4262 **72**
Marden, north of the Rly. Stn. Crashed and
burned out. S/L Collins baled out wounded.
Based Croydon. Cat 3

746. Me109E1, 6290 **9/JG51**
Dover area. Shot down by the R.A.F. possibly by Sgt Frantisek (303Sq). The pilot was
wounded and made a POW. Based St Omer
or St Quentin.

Sgt Josef Frantisek
He was the son of a carpenter and panel beater in Moravia, Czechoslovakia. After qualifying as a car mechanic he enlisted in the Czech Air Force as a pupil pilot and on completion of his course was posted to No.5 Fighter Squadron.

He loved flying but was rather undisciplined and therefore frequently in minor trouble.

When his country was annexed by Germany he escaped to France and flew with the Armée de l'Air for a short time, but with the fall of France came to England with a group of other Czech airmen. After a conversion course he was posted to 303(Polish) Squadron.

He proved to be a skilful fighter pilot, but developed the habit of leaving the formation when the immediate action had finished to hunt for German stragglers, often over Dover.

His score of successes increased until, at the age of 27 years he was killed in an unexplained flying accident. At the time he was credited with 17 victories to which, according to the Polish Air Force, should be added 10 or 11 gained whilst flying in France.

747. Me110C4, 2146 **I/ZG2**
Herne Bay, N.E. of. An engine caught alight after combat with the R.A.F. during a freelance patrol and the crew Oblt Gottshalt and Uffz Hoffmann abandoned to be picked up by a shore boat which had gone out to search for them. Based Abbeville or Amiens.

748. Hurricane I, R2688 **303**
Tenterden - Woodchurch. Had engine damaged by a Me109 over the Channel whilst it was attacking another. The result of this was a forced landing. Sgt S.Wojtowicz was slightly injured. Based Northolt. Cat 2

749. Me109E4, 0823 **II/JG26**
off Margate. Failed to return from a sweep over the Estuary. Probably shot down by 603Sq (Pease). Oblt E. Roch missing. Based Marquise.

750. Hurricane I, P3782 **1**
Chart Sutton, Park House Fm. The exact circumstances of this incident are not known but P/O R.H. Shaw was reported missing. Based Northolt. Cat 3

750A. Whitley V, N1427, GE- **58**
Margate, 200yds W. of pier. This bomber ran out of fuel on return from ops. on Genoa. Crew S/L Bartlett, P/O Mitchell, and Sgts Coubrough, de Tilkin, Kerr and Caryll safe (?). Based Linton on Ouse. Cat 3

751. 4.9.40 Spitfire I, P9460 **72**
Tenterden, Shadoxhurst. Believed shot down by a Me110. P/O R.D. Elliott unhurt. Based Croydon. Cat 3

752. Spitfire I, X4263 **603**
Ashford, Elmsted. Force landed due to engine failure. Sgt A.S. Sarre unhurt. Based Hornchurch. Cat 2

753. Hurricane I, Z2309 **111**
W. Stourmouth, Dene Fm. Shot up by Me109E's. P/O J. Macinski baled out but was missing. Based Croydon. Cat 3

754. Hurricane I, R4172 **111**
5 miles east of **Folkestone.** Shot down in combat with Me109's. F/L D.C. Bruce missing. Based Croydon. Cat 3

755. Me109E4, 5026 **3/JG54**
off Dover. Shot down in combat with the R.A.F. (?) 111Sq (Giddings). Oblt Witt missing. Based Guines or Yvrench.

756. Me109E1, 4839 **3/JG54**
Folkestone, 6 miles off. Shot down by 111Sq (Wallace). Pilot not known as he was picked up by Seenotflkdo.

757. Spitfire I, N3048 **66**
Ashford, Mersham. Shot down by Lw fighters over the town. Sgt A.D. Smith baled out seriously wounded and died in hospital on the 6th. Based Kenley. Cat 3

758. Spitfire I, (?) P9378 **222**
Boughton Monchelsea. (?) Shot down by A.A. whilst attacking a Me109. P/O J.M. Carpenter was blown out of the cockpit when the aircraft was hit, to parachute safely landing at Renton, although slightly wounded. Based Hornchurch. Cat 3

759. Spitfire I, R6689 **66**
Bilsington, N. of Chequertree Fm. Shot down in action with Me109's over Ashford. P/O C.A. Cooke baled out slightly injured to land near Ham Street. Based Kenley. Cat 3

760. Me109E4, 5807 **I/JG77**
Channel. Shot down by the R.A.F. The pilot was wounded (?). Picked up by Seenotflkdo. Based at St Omer.

761. Me110C, 2089 **II/ZG76**
Penshurst, Smarts Hill. Crashed during combat with a Spitfire. Oblt Piduhn and Gfr Odene killed. Based Abbeville.

762. Spitfire I, X4278, ZD-D **222**
Chart Sutton, Amberfield Fm. Shot up by Me109's over Maidstone. F/O J.W. Cutts missing. Based Hornchurch. Cat 3

763. Spitfire I, K9962 **222**
Yalding, Collier Street. Sgt J.W. Ramshaw was seriously injured after combat, and later was found dead on arrival at hospital. Based Hornchurch. Cat 3

764. Spitfire I, X4052 **66**
nr Canterbury. Damaged in combat with enemy fighters over Thanet and had to force land. F/L G.P. Christie slightly wounded. Based Kenley. Cat 2

Incident No. 783. The Me109E of II/JG3 which crashed near Marden was credited to 234 Squadron (Hughes). The pilot Oblt von Werra was the only aircrew P.O.W. to escape back to Germany. (SE Press)

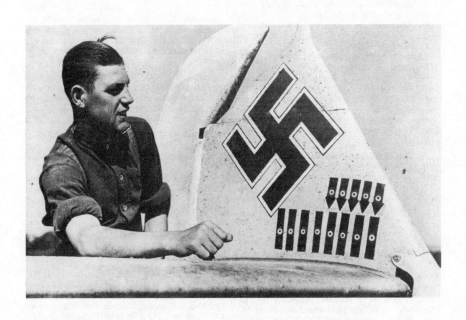

765. **5.9.40** Me109E1, 4017 **7/JG53**
Leysdown. Shot up in combat with the R.A.F. whilst on a sortie to London. Lt Deutsch missing. Based Sempy.

766. Hurricane I, P5181 **253**
Charing. Force landed for unknown reasons. Pilot probably P/O Murch. Based Kenley.
Cat 3

767. Spitfire I, X4264 **603**
Smarden. Shot up by Me109's over Biggin Hill. P/O W.P. Rafter wounded and to hospital. Based Hornchurch. Cat 3

768. Spitfire I, X4261 **603**
Over Kent. Failed to return following combat with Do17Z's and Me109's over Biggin Hill. F/L F.W. Rushmer missing. Based Hornchurch. Cat 3

769. Hurricane I, V6644 **501**
nr Herne Bay. Shot down in combat with Me109's over Canterbury. Exact location uncertain. P/O Skalski injured and to hospital. Based Gravesend. Cat 3

S/L S.F. Skalski
Flew with the Polish Air Force from 1936-39 and by the end of the Polish Campaign was credited with 4 successes. He then escaped to the U.K. by a tortuous route, joining the R.A.F. in January 1940.

His first operational posting was to 501Sq in August and by the end of the month had one further success.

In November a second posting took him to 46Sq and another to 249Sq.

By April 1941 he was a flight commander and six months later had been awarded the D.F.C. and was instructing.

Early in 1942 he returned to ops. with 316Sq, later becoming C.O. of 317Sq.

He formed and commanded a special unit, the Polish Fighting Team and with it took the first Spitfire IX's to N. Africa where they were attached to 146Sq.

On his return to the U.K. he became the first Pole to command an R.A.F. squadron, 601Sq.

As a Wing Commander he led No.2 Polish Wing where more successes took his final score to 18+, flying Mustangs.

When the War finished he was at the Advanced Gunnery School and had added a D.S.O. and bar to his decorations.

Post-war he returned to Poland where the Communist Regime imprisoned him, as happened to many senior Polish officers who had served with the Allies.

770. Me109E4, 1985 **I/JG3**
Aldington, Handen Fm, Clapp Hill. Damaged by fighters during a bomber escort mission and force landed (probably by Sgt Frantisek of 303Sq) over the Estuary. Lt H. Schnabel wounded and POW. Based Guines or Coulommiers.

771. Hurricane IIA, 312 or Z2312 **111**
Eynsford - Shoreham, nr Lullingstone Castle. Force landed after combat. Sgt F.H. Silk injured. Based Croydon. Cat 2
(This and the Hurricane 314 in incident 777 probably have the unusual numbers as they were part of a batch for the R.C.A.F. 1 RCAF Sq were also stationed at Croydon; 111Sq may have borrowed them temporarily.)

772. Spitfire I, P9422 **19**
Birling, White Horse Wood. Shot down by Me109's over the Estuary. S/L P.C. Pinkham killed. Based Duxford. Cat 3

773. Me109E, 1096 **I/JG54**
Maidstone, 6 Hardy Street. Shot down by F/O Haines (19Sq) in a low level chase across Kent (also reptd shot down by F/L Rabagliati). Uffz Hotzelmann baled out and broke both legs. Based Guines or Yvrench.

774. Me109E, 1949 **I/JG52**
Bethersden. Sgt Lacey (501Sq) shot this aircraft down. Uffz Kind killed. Based Coqelles.

775. Spitfire I, N3093 **72**
Elham, Park Wood. Shot down by Lw fighers and crashed. Sgt M. Gray killed. Based Croydon. Cat 3

776. Me109E, 1464 **5/JG3**
Dungeness. 10 miles SSW. Shot down from 15000ft by P/O Bowring. Pilot seen in the sea apparently unhurt. Based (?) Samer.

777. Me109E4, 3612 **I/JG3**
Channel. Had been in combat with the R.A.F. and ditched on the return flight. The pilot (probably Oblt Lammers) was picked up by Seenotflkdo. Based Samer or Colombert.

778. Me109E4, 1098 **II/JG54**
Thames Estuary. Shot down in combat with the R.A.F. This pilot was also picked up by Seenotflkdo. Based Guines or Yvrench.

779. Me109E **?**
off Reculver. Crashed into the sea and pilot killed.

781. Me109E, 0750 **I/JG3**
Faversham, Wichling. Shot down by 234Sq Spitfire (Doe), during a bomber escort mission and had to force land. Uffz H. Grabow unhurt and POW.

782. Hurricane I, P5207 **79**
Biggin Hill (Base). Damaged whilst attacking a Do17Z over base. F/L Haysom unhurt. Cat 2

783. Me109E4, 1480 **II/JG3**
Marden, Winchet Hill, Loves Fm. Shot down and had to force land. Oblt von Werra ('The one that got away') Gruppe Adj. His loss was credited to 234Sq (Hughes). Based Colombert.

Baron Lt F. von Werra
Had proved to be an effective pilot and an ardent Nazi. It was felt that he was destined for higher things in the Luftwaffe.

After becoming a POW he was included in a group of captured aircrew who were assessed as likely to attempt escapes, and shipped to Canada.

Even so he did escape and after a hard winter's walk crossed into the then neutral U.S.A. to be later repatriated to Germany.

After a personal meeting with Hitler and a great deal of propaganda appearances, he returned to operational flying only to be killed shortly afterwards.

784. Spitfire I, X4013 **72**
Elham, Covert Wood. F/O D.C. Winter was killed attempting to bale out after being shot up by a Me109E. Based Croydon. Cat 3

785. Spitfire I, X4034 **72**
Elham, Wildage Fm, Bladbean. After F/O D.F. Sheen baled out wounded a/c crashed.

786. Me109E, 2+ **8/JG2**
Detling. After being attacked by P/O J. Johnson, Oblt Metz collided with another flown by Fw Gotz. He then did a circuit and landed to become a POW. Based Bar de Duc.

787. He111H3, 6896, 1H+BC **II/KG26**
nr Chatham, Strood Rural. Shot down by 17Sq (Chew and Czernin). Obfw Vetter, Fw Wilde, Uffz Stenzel, Obgfr Wart all missing. Based Dinard.

788. Spitfire I, X4057 **222**
E. Langden, nr Pineham. Hit by A.A. during an attack on a Me109E over Dover and crashed burning. Sgt Chipping baled out wounded. Based Hornchurch. Cat 3

789. He111H, 2632, A1+GR **7/KG53**
off Herne Bay. Failed to return from a bombing mission. May have been shot down by 17Sq Hurricanes near Gravesend. Fw Bohn killed; Uffz Bickl, Bolz, Rosenburger and Gfr K. Haak missing. Fighters chased this aircraft into the sea 200yds from Margate Hook. Shore boats went to the location but found only floating debris. Based Lille.

790. Spitfire I, N3162 **41**
Manston (Base). Was attacked by Me109E's whilst it was shooting down a He111 over the Estuary. P/O E.S. Lock slightly injured. Based Hornchurch. Cat 2

791. Me109E1, 5375 **Stab/JG53**
St Nicholas at Wade - Monckton. Force landed after being shot up by the R.A.F. Hptm W. Mayerweissflog unhurt and POW. Based Sempy (?).

792. Spitfire I, K9944 **66**
N. Kent. Was in combat over the Medway when it was shot down by Me109's. F/L G.P. Christie was wounded and hospitalised. Based Kenley. Cat 2

793. Spitfire I, N3029 **66**
As above P/O J.R. Mather unhurt. Cat 2

794. He111H3, 3338, A1+CR **III/KG53**
off the Nore. Hit by A.A. fire after a raid on Thameshaven and ditched. Fw Agner, Uffz Armbruster and Lenger and + Gfr Nowotny were picked up by the R.N., Fw Waier killed. (It appears likely that 17Sq were involved.) Based Lille-Vendeville.

795. Me109E1, 3627 **5/JG27**
nr Appledore Rly Stn, Bussbarn Fm. Was damaged in combat with the R.A.F. near Elham (? 46Sq Sgt Hurry) and crashed. Lt H. Strobel was killed. His remains were exhumed when the site was dug 5.9.86 and the engine is in the Kent Battle of Britain Museum at Hawkinge. Based Fiennes.

797. 6.9.40 Hurricane I, 314 **111**
nr Dartford. P/O Bowring reported that he had been shot down by a He113(!) after force landing with an arm wound. Based Croydon.

798. Me109E4, 1216 **3/JG53**
Thames Estuary. Shot down by the R.A.F. whilst it was on a bomber escort mission to Tilbury Docks. Thought to have crashed off the Kent Coast. Oblt Riegel missing. Based Sempy.

799. Me110D/O, 3405, 3U+HR **7/ZG26**
Thames Estuary. As for above. Fw Kaufmann and Gfr Schumann missing. Based Arques.

800. Me109E4, 5347 **I/JG53**
Thames Estuary. Shot down by a Spitfire of 602Sq. Oblt Geghardt killed. (Also reptd as crashing north of Hastings, but does not appear in the Sussex Police records.) Based Sempy.

801. Me109E, 3877 **7/JG26**
Channel. Shot down whilst on a sortie to Kenley. Gfr P. Holzapfel missing. Based Caffiers. This or No.831 may be the e/a that crashed at Lydd, Swamp Fm with the body of its unidentifiable pilot.

802. Hurricane I, R4229 **249**
Maidstone, nr Sutton Road. Whilst attacking a formation of Ju88's escorted by Me109's and Me110's, S/L J. Grandy was shot up and his aircraft caught fire. He baled out slightly wounded and was hospitalised. Based N. Weald. Cat 3

803. Hurricane I, V6612 **501**
Elham, Clavertye Wood. Shot up in combat with the Lw over Ashford. P/O H.C. Adams was killed when his 'chute failed to open and he fell in Park Wood. Based Gravesend. He was promoted the day he was killed. Cat 3

804. Hurricane I, V6646 **501**
Charing, Long Beech Wood. As above. Sgt O.V. Houghton killed. Cat 3

805. Hurricane I, P3516 **501**
Westwell, Cowleas Fm, Kempton Manor. As above. Sgt G.W. Pearson killed. Cat 3

806.   Hurricane I, V7290 **303**
Pembury, Fletchers Fm. Shot down by return fire from a He111. Sgt Karubin slightly injured. Based Northolt.   Cat 2

807.   Hurricane I, P3032 **253**
Ruckinge, Golden Wood. Crashed during a routine patrol, cause not known. S/L W.P. Cambridge killed after baling out. Based Kenley.   Cat 3

808.   Me110C4, 2145 **Stab/ZG26**
off Dover. Shot down over the Channel when on an escort mission. An engine caught fire due to an electrical fault. Oblt Viertel baled out to be a POW but Uffz Roth was killed. The bombers' target was Hawker's factory. Based Lille-Vendeville.

809.   Hurricane I, P3974 **303**
Hexstable - Wilmington, nr H.T. cables. S/L Krasnodebski was badly burnt when he was shot down in the middle of a dogfight of about 100 aircraft. He baled out, went into free fall because his flying suit was burning, and to avoid the other aircraft. After falling about 10000ft his 'chute opened and he landed barely conscious. His injuries were such that he did not fly again for twelve months. Based Northolt.   Cat 3

S/L Z. Krasnodebski
Was born in Poland in 1904 and was a pilot in the pre-War Polish Air Force. He flew from Zulenka airfield against the Lw units bombing Warsaw.

After the very short campaign he escaped via Rumania, Italy, Yugoslavia and France to the U.K.

By August 1940 he was joint C.O. of 303Sq with S/L Kellett (R.A.F.), and as eager as all the other Poles to become operational. This was delayed until they could all understand enough English and understood R.A.F. radio procedure. Post-War he settled in Canada.

810. **6.9.40**   Hurricane I, V7284 **303**
Biggin Hill. Force landed badly damaged by return fire from a Do215 (?) including a missing starboard aileron. S/L Kellett slightly wounded. Based Northolt.   Cat 3
(So 303Sq had both its Polish and R.A.F. C.O.s incapacitated.)

811.   Hurricane I, L1892 **111**
nr Kenley (? in Kent). Shot down by return fire from a Ju88 and crashed. Sgt L.J. Tweed baled out wounded. Based Croydon.   Cat 3

812.   Hurricane I, P2686 **1**
Chiddingstone, Brownings Fm. After being shot up by the rear gunner of a Me110, south of Penshurst, P/O G.E. Goodman baled out with a sprained shoulder. Based Northolt.
          Cat 3

813.   Hurricane I, V6647 **601**
Pembury, Kippings Cross. Was over Mayfield when it was shot up by a Me109E. P/O H.T. Gilbert baled out wounded.   Cat 3

S/L R.G. Kellett
Was a pre-War member of 600(Aux)Sq, (County of Yorkshire), having been commissioned in 1934, and was mobilised with this unit in August 1939.

In May 1940 he was promoted to command 249Sq, but was then posted to fill the difficult post of Commanding Officer of 303(Polish)Sq with S/L Krasnodebski as Polish Commander.

He had his first operational success in August and by the end of September had increased his score to 5 + 2 probables, and had been awarded the D.F.C.

When 303Sq became fully operational he moved to 96Sq in command and stayed with them until March 1941 when, as a W/C he went to R.A.F. North Weald as Wing Leader.

Coming off ops. at the end of 1942 with a score of 8 kills he received the D.S.O. and a posting to Air Ministry.

Post-War he returned to the Auxiliary Air Force as Commanding Officer of 615Sq.

814.   Hurricane I, P3382 **601**
East Sutton, Boynton Court. Shot down over Mayfield. F/O L. Topolnicki baled out wounded and was hospitalised. Based Tangmere.   Cat 3

815.   Hurricane I, P8818 **601**
Tunbridge Wells, High Brooms Viaduct, Southborough. Was attacked by enemy fighters over the town. F/Lt W.H. Rhodes-Moorhouse killed. Based Tangmere.   Cat 3
(The Merlin engine and other relics are at the Kent Battle of Britain Museum, Hawkinge.)

816.   Ju88A, 3176, F1+LP **6/KG76**
off Littlestone. Shot down by A.A. and the R.A.F. Oblt Wagner and Uffz Geyer missing Uffz Haenel and Obgfr Kohn killed. Based Creil.

817.   Hurricane I, V7243 **303**
Beckenham, Langley Pk. G.C. Shot down and burst into flames. Sgt Rogowski baled out. Based Northolt.   Cat 3

818.   Hurricane I, R4179 **303**
Sundridge. F/L Forbes force landed and the aircraft crashed hitting an embankment.
          Cat 2

819.   Hurricane I, P3363 **601**
Brenchley, Matfield. Shot down by Me109's. F/L C.R. Davis killed. Based Tangmere; Cat 3

820.   Me109E4, 1138 **3/JG52**
Seal, Stone Street. Shot down by the R.A.F. over Kent. Oblt Waller baled out to be a POW. Based Coquelles.

821.   Spitfire I, N3070 **72**
Goudhurst, Finchcocks Fm. Shot down in a head on attack on a Me110 over Maidstone. P/O R.D. Elliott baled out landing unhurt at Wanshurst Green. Based Croydon.   Cat 3

822.   Me109E, 1129   8/JG53
Stoke Marshes, on the mudflats. Shot down
by P/O Bennions (41Sq) in combat over the
Estuary and exploded over the mouth of the
Medway. Uffz Hempel killed. Based Sempy.

823.   Hurricane I, V7386   **111**
Sutton at Hone. After being attacked by
Me109's over the Estuary had to force land.
F/O B.H. Bowring slightly injured. Based
Croydon.   Cat 2
(This was his second force landing of the
day.)

824.   Me109E7, 5567   **II/LG2**
Hawkinge a/f. Hit by A.A. whilst on a
bomber escort mission over Chatham. Force
landed as a result of small arms fire from
the ground. (The complete aircraft was salvaged for evaluation by R.A.E. Farnborough.)
(Most of the E7's seem to have been allo-
cated to the Lehr Geschwader.) This aircraft was flown by Fw W. Gottschalk. Based
Cambrai-Epinoy.

825.   Me109E1, 3225   **3/JG27**
off Nore boom. Reported as being shot
down by 303Sq (Feric). Oblt W. Schueller
baled out to be a POW. Based Guines or
Plumetot.

826.   Me109E7, 3736   **II/LG2**
off the Nore. Shot down by A.A. during a
bomber escort mission. Lt H. Gueltgen made
POW. Based St Omer or Cambrai.

827.   Hurricane I, P3089   **303**
nr Lenham. Shot down by a Me109E whilst
making a solo attack on a Me110 during a
patrol with 1Sq. F/O W. Janussewicz was
unhurt. Based Northolt.   Cat 2

828.   Me109E, 6318   **7/JG27**
Whitstable - Canterbury, Blean. Shot down
by F/O McKenzie (41Sq). Uffz E. Nittmann
unhurt and made a POW. Target reported as
Tilbury Docks. Based Guines (?).

829.   Me109E4, 1506   **7/JG53**
Manston, Vincents Fm. Shot down by the
R.A.F. during a free lance sortie over the
Estuary, and had to force land. Pilot was
Uffz G. Schulte. Based Sempy.

830.   He111H3, 6902   **2/KG26**
Kent. Failed to return after an attack on
London. Exact location not known. Lt
Schactebeck killed, Fw Jessen, Uffz Has-
lache, Fasz and Jahme missing. Based Moor-
becke.

831.   Me109E1, 3578   **7/JG26**
Channel. Believed shot down when a sortie
over Kenley was intercepted. Gfr Bieker
missing. Based Caffiers. (See No.801)

832.   Me109E4, 5044   **Stab/JG2**
Headcorn, Plumtree Fm. During an ad-
vanced fighter sweep was shot down by the
R.A.F. Lt Himmelheber was made a POW.
Based Bar le Duc.

833.   Me109E4, 2762   **5/JG27**
Tonbridge, Bank Fm, Tudeley. Severely
damaged by fighters whilst escorting
bombers. Fw E. Braun baled out, POW.
Based Fiennes or Montreuil.

834.   Me109E4, 2781   **7/JG26**
Hothfield. Crashed after combat over Ken-
ley. Oblt H.M. Christinnecke made POW.
Based Caffiers.

835.   Ju88A, 8104, F1 + HP   **6/KG76**
Tonbridge, Tanyards Fm. Hit by A.A. and
then by fighters during a raid on London and
had to force land. Lt Kernnbach, Uffz Agel,
Obfw Schumacher and Gfr Riesel all POW's
unhurt. Based Cormeilles en Vexin.

836.   **7.9.40**   Me109E, 5385   **II/JG26**
Pluckley, Sheerland Fm. Cause of crash not
known. Oblt Krug (Staffel Kapt) missing.
Based Marquise.

837.   Me109E, 0735   **II/JG26**
Dover, Shakespear Cliff. Shot down. Uffz E.
Braun missing. Based Marquise.

Of this period Gunther Rail of JG52 said:
  'We really wasted our fighters. We did not
have enough to begin with, and then we
used them in the wrong way, for direct close
escort. We were tied to the bombers flying
slowly — sometimes with our flaps down,
over England. We could not use our height
advantage, nor our superiority in the dive.'

838.   Me110C5, 2208   **4(F)14**
Channel. Failed to return from a recce.
mission. Lt Goedsche and Oblt Russel killed.
Based ?

839.   Me109E1, 6271   **8/JG3**
Channel. Shot down by the R.A.F. Pilot
picked up unhurt by Seenotflkdo. Based
Desevres.

840.   Me109E1, 4840, 7 +   **3/JG51**
Bethersden. Shot up by the R.A.F. whilst
escorting bombers to London. Uffz R.
Zurlage baled out to be a POW. Based
Wissant or St Omer.

841.   Spitfire I, P9466   **234**
nr Biggin Hill. Crashed after combat with
enemy fighters. S/L J. O'Brien killed. (Also
reported as over St Mary Cray.) Based
Middle Wallop.   Cat 3

842.   Spitfire I, X4009   **234**
Sevenoaks, Bessels Green. as above. F/L P.
Hughes killed by blast when a Do17Z was
shot down. Exactly how is uncertain.   Cat 3

843.   Spitfire I, N3228   **602**
Maidstone. Scrambled to 15000ft over Hawkinge and then damaged by return fire from
a Do17Z over south London. P/O O. Hanbury unhurt. Based Westhampnett.   Cat 2?

844.   Spitfire I, R7022   **72**
Eynsford. Crash landed following action
with He111's and Me109's over the Estuary.
Sgt White slightly injured in the leg and
head. Based Croydon.   Cat 2

845.   Me109E4, 6342 2/JG51
Channel. Failed to return from a bomber
escort mission to London. Obfw Stroehlein
missing. Based Wissant or St Omer.

846.   Me109E4, 5249 III/JG3
Thames Estuary. Shot down into the sea.
Oblt Goettmann killed. Based Desevres.

847.   Hurricane I, V7309 43
Sutton Valence, Babylon Fm. Crashed and
burned out after combat over Ashford. Sgt
A. Deller baled out burnt and injured. Based
Tangmere.   Cat 3

848.   Spitfire I, X4321 66
Hawkinge a/f. Force landed after combat.
P/O C. Bodie unhurt. Based Kenley.   Cat 2
(Also reported as at Sellindge.)

849.   Spitfire I, N3225 66
Hawkinge area (?). Damaged in combat with
enemy aircraft and had to force land. P/O I.
Cruikshanks unhurt(?). Based Kenley. Cat 2

850.   Hurricane I, R4114 249
Hollingbourne. Shot down by Me109's over
Maidstone. P/O R. Fleming killed. Based
North Weald.   Cat 3

851.   Hurricane I, V6574 249
Eastchurch. Crash landed following combat
over Maidstone. Sgt R. Smithson wounded.
                                    Cat 2

852.   Hurricane I, P3890 303
Elham, Selstead. Shot down by a Me109E
whilst attacking a Do17Z over the Estuary.
P/O Daszewski baled out severely wounded
in the thigh. Based Northolt.   Cat 3

853.   Hurricane I, L1615 504
Faversham, Sandbanks Fm. On a section
patrol south of the Estuary at 20000ft. F/O
K. Wendel was badly burnt after being shot
down by Me109's later dying of his injuries
to be buried at Faversham. Based Hendon.
                                    Cat 3

854.   Hurricane I, R4230 249
Eastling. After combat with Me109's over
Maidstone, Sgt F. Killingback baled out
wounded. Based North Weald.   Cat 3

855.   Hurricane I, P3021 504
Eastchurch. Force landed with a cannon
shell through the canopy and the fuel tank
after an engagement over the Estuary. Sgt
B.M. Bush unhurt(!). Based Hendon.   Cat 2

856.   Hurricane I, P3594, GN-O 249
Faversham. Caught fire after an attack on a
He111. F/O P. Wells baled out wounded and
was hospitalised. Based North Weald. Cat 3

857.   Me110C4, 2216 I/ZG2
Hoath, Old Tree Fm. Crashed in flames after
being shot up by the R.A.F. during an escort
mission for bombers. Lt Kislinger killed and
Uffz Dahnke baled out unhurt made a
POW. Based Abbeville or Amiens.

858.   Hurricane I, P3049 257
Sheppey, Spitend Point, Elmley. Shot down
in combat over the Estuary. F/L Beresford
killed. Probably shot down by Oblt Föcö.
Beresford's body was found when the site
was dug in September 1979. Based Debden.
                                    Cat 3

859.   Hurricane I, V7254 257
Thames Estuary. As above F/O L. Mitchell
missing.   Cat 3

Major A. Galland claimed two Hurricanes
shot down early in September over the
Thames Estuary with both pilots baling out.
They seem most likely to have been those in
incidents 858, 859 or 876.

860.   Spitfire, X4256 602
Failed to return from combat over Biggin
Hill. P/O H.W. Moody missing. (It has not
been possible to pinpoint the site of this
crash.) Based Westhampnett.   Cat 3

861.   Spitfire I, N3198 602
Bidborough, Fosters Fm, Haysden Lane.
Crashed in flames after being shot up by
enemy aircraft over Biggin Hill. F/O W.H.
Coverley baled out badly injured and died.
His body was not found, in an orchard, until
the 15th. Based Westhampnett.   Cat 3

862.   Spitfire I, K9839 602
Wrotham, West of. Crash landed after the
glycol tank was damaged by return fire from
a Do17Z over Biggin Hill. P/O E. Aries
unhurt. Based Westhampnett.   Cat 2

863.   Spitfire I, P9467 603
Thames Estuary. Shot down. Sgt A. Sarre
baled out slightly injured. Based Hornchurch.   Cat 3

864.   He111H, 2777, A1 + DN II/Kg53
Isle of Grain. Shot down by the R.A.F. during
an attack on Thameshaven. The crew set
fire to the crash after a forced landing. Oblt
Breuer, Uffz Bergmann, Ofw Pitzkar and
Gfr Ulrich all POW's. Ogfr Neumann killed.
Based Lille-Vendeville.

865.   Spitfire I, N3196 603
Sutton Valence. Force landed after combat
over London. P/O B. Stapleton unhurt.
Based Hornchurch.   Cat 2

866.   Hurricane I. V7317 257
nr Sittingbourne, Bredgar. Force landed
severely damaged after combat with the Lw
over the Estuary. Sgt D. Hulbert unhurt.
Based Debden.   Cat 2

867.   Me109E, 5798 I/LG2
Wickhambreux, Little Stour. Shot down by a
310Sq Hurricane (Sgt Furst) during combat
over Canterbury. Uffz Guetting baled out,
POW. Based Calais-Marck.

868.   Hurricane I 79
West Malling. Landing with damage sustained over base. P/O Stones slightly
wounded. Based Biggin Hill.   Cat 2

869.   Spitfire I, X4254   **72**
Biggin Hill. Crashed after being badly damaged by Me109's over the Estuary. F/O T. Elsdon severely injured. Based Croydon.
                                                    Cat 2

870.   Me109E3, 5091   **3/JG51**
Borden, Old Street. Shot down by ground fire whilst on a mission escorting bombers over Kent. Gfr H. Werner baled out and was a POW. Based St Omer or Pihen.

871.   Me109E4, 5811   **1/JG77**
Rolvenden. Shot down during a Jabo operation by S/L Johnson (602Sq). Oblt Goltzsche made a POW. Based St Omer.

872.   Me110C4, 3117   **I/ZG2**
Deal, Eythorne. Crashed following a fighter attack whilst on bomber escort duty. Fw J. Ottersbach dead, Hptm Oligschlager missing. Based Abbeville or Amiens.

873.   Do17Z, 2596   **Stab/KG76**
Sevenoaks, Sundridge. Attacked by the R.A.F. during a photo. recce. mission over London Docks. Obfw Schneider, Uffz Rupprecht and Obgfr Schneider killed; Fw Rosche baled out unhurt and POW. Based Cormeilles en Vexin.

874.   Me110C4, 3570   **II/ZG2**
Birchington. 5 miles off. Ditched following combat with the R.A.F. Uffz Galla killed; Oblt Brede unhurt and POW. Based St Omer or Hermalinghen.

875.   Me109E1, 3320   **5/JG2**
off Folkestone. Shot down by 41Sq (F/O W. Scott) during an escort mission. Uffz W. Melchert made a POW. Based Oye Plage or Mardyck.

876.   Hurricane I, V7437   **310**
Sheppey, Capel Fleet, Harty Marsh. This Czech aircraft crashed following combat with Me109's over the Estuary. Sgt J. Koukal had lost contact with the rest of the flight and joined up with a formation of fighters heading for the Gravesend area. He shot down a Me109 from 20000ft but was himself hit in the fuel tank. His cockpit filled with flames and he was drenched in petrol. As he dived to 7000ft the second tank exploded blowing him clear of the wreck. He landed by 'chute very badly burnt and had to crawl 50yds to a farmhouse for help.

He was admitted to hospital at E. Grinstead, but it was 2½yrs before he returned to operational flying.

Before joining the R.A.F. he had flown with the Armée de l'Air in France and had been credited with 6 Me109's destroyed.

The site of the crash was dug in 1966, and in 1972 Koukal visited the Battle of Britain Museum and was presented with a piece of his aircraft.

877.   Hurricane I, P3025   **111**
Newchurch, nr boundary with Burmarsh. In combat over the Channel was severely damaged. Sgt T. Wallace was slightly wounded but managed to bale out south of Ashford. Based Croydon.   Cat 3

878.   Me109E4, 3909, White 8   **1/JG2**
Dover, St Radigans Abbey, Hougham. Had an engine failure during an escort mission to London. Oblt A. Gotz unhurt but POW. Based Beaumont le Roger or Bar le Duc.

879.   Spitfire I, N3169   **222**
Sutton Valence, nr Boundary with Headcorn. Force landed following action south of Maidstone. Sgt J. Burgess unhurt.   Cat 2

880. 8.9.40   Me109E7, 1171   **8/JG53**
Channel. Collided with a Me109 flown by Oblt Witmeier. Oblt Kuhnert (Staffel Kapt) killed. Based Sempy.

881.   Me109E1, 3478   **I/JG53**
Channel. Involved in the above incident. Pilot, Oblt Witmeier. May have crashed on the French Coast. Based Etaples or Coquelles.

882.   Spitfire I, R6756   **41**
off Dover. Crashed in flames during a squadron patrol, presumably shot down by the Luftwaffe. F/O W. Scott killed. Based Hornchurch.   Cat 3

883.   Hurricane I, P3201   **46**
Bearsted, Green Pastures, Thurnham Lane. Shot down whilst attacking Lw aircraft over Sheppey. Sublt J.C. Carpenter baled out but was killed. Based Stapleford Tawney. Cat 3

884.   Hurricane I, L2061   **605**
Wrotham, Trottscliffe. Shot down by Me109's in flames over Tunbridge Wells, crashing and burning out. F/O J. Fleming baled out at 20000ft and delayed opening his 'chute. Because of severe burns and injuries was admitted to hospital. Based Croydon.   Cat 3

885.   Hurricane I, V6631   **46**
Hollingbourne. Crashed after combat over Sheppey. F/L N. Burnett wounded and to hospital. Based Stapleford Tawney.   Cat 3

886.   Hurricane I, P3053   **46**
Meopham Green. Shot down by Me109's whilst attacking another. P/O P. McGregor unhurt.   Cat 3

887.   Me109E4, 0867   **I/JG53**
Seal. Shot down in fighter combat with the R.A.F. Uffz B. Adelwart killed. Based Coquelles.

888.   Do17Z, 3415   **5/KG2**
Leeds, Broomfield. Was attacked by 46Sq (Sgt S. Andrews) and exploded in the air. Oblt Ziems, Uffz Flisk, Trost, Selter all killed. Based St Leger.

889.   Do17Z, 2668   **5/KG2**
Farningham. Crashed following combat but probably shot down by A.A. whilst on ops. to London. Oblt Schneider, Obgfr Hoffmann, Uffz Schumacher and Flgr Kohl all wounded and POW's.

Incident No. 901. This crater with small pieces of wreckage was formed when a ME110C of III/ZG26 was shot down by A.A. at Borden. (Kent Messenger)

890.   Do17Z, 1130 **5/KG2**
As above. Lt Landenburger, Obgfr Lotter, Flgr Schuetz all killed; Obfw Stroebel POW. This aircraft exploded over the Rly. Stn.

891. **9.9.40**   Hurricane I, P3667 **249**
Rochester, Cooling. Force landed during a routine patrol. Cause unknown. Sgt H. Davidson unhurt. Based N. Weald.   Cat 2

892.   Hurricane I, P2680 **607**
E. Peckham, Stilstead Fm. Crashed after combat with a Do17Z and Me109 escort. Sgt R. Spyer slightly wounded. Based Tangmere.
                                            Cat 3

893.   Spitfire I, L1077 **92**
Lydd, Midley. Crashed after being shot up by a Me109E over Biggin Hill. P/O C. Saunders had leg wounds and was hospitalised. Based Biggin Hill.   Cat 3

894.   Hurricane I, P2912 **607**
nr Knockholt. Force landed with seized engine after combat with Lw fighters in the Mayfield area. Sgt P. Purnell-Phillips slightly wounded in the ankle. Based Tangmere.
                                            Cat 2

895.   Hurricane I, P2728 **607**
Goudhurst, Bockingfold Fm. Crashed after combat with enemy aircraft over Mayfield. P/O G. Drake killed. Based Tangmere. Cat 3

896.   Hurricane I, P3574 **607**
Goudhurst, Lime Tree Fm. As above. P/O S. Parnall killed.   Cat 3

897.   Hurricane I, P3117 **607**
Cranbrook, Mt Ephraim. As above. P/O J. Lenahan killed.   Cat 3

A rough introduction to fighting in the Southeast, for 607 Squadron.

898.   Spitfire I, X4058 **222**
Southfleet. Shot down by Me109's and crashed on landing. P/O T. Vigors unhurt. Based Hornchurch.   Cat 2

899.   Hurricane I, V6639 **253**
Cobham, Park Fm. Force landed after an attack on Ju88's. F/O R.F. Watts unhurt. Based Kenley.   Cat 2

900.   Spitfire I, N3049 **66**
Edenbridge - Cowden. Shot down by Me109's over E. Grinstead. P/O G. Corbett baled out slightly wounded. Based Kenley.
                                            Cat 3

901.   Me110C, 2137, 2N + FM **III/ZG76**
Sittingbourne, Borden. Shot down by A.A. Both Uffz Bierling and Kurella killed. Based Laval or Yvrench.

902.   He111H3, 5713, V4 + BL **3/KG1**
Sevenoaks, Sundridge. Shot down by (?) 19Sq (Blake) after a raid on London. Oblt Kiunka, Uffz Marck and Stumbaum, Obfw Heidrich and Gfr Reinecke all POW's. Based Rosieres en Santerre.

903.   Me109E1, 6316 **7/JG3**
Flimwell, Coopers Field (also reptd Lamberhurst Pillary Fm). Force landed due to combat damaged engine. Uffz Massmann
unhurt and POW. Based Desevres.

904.   Me109E4, 1508 **I/JG53**
Biggin Hill, Old Jail Lane. Crashed in flames
as a result of an attack by R.A.F. fighters. Fw
H. Honisch baled out, POW. Based Etaples
or Coquelles.

905.   Me109E1, 6280 **6/JG27**
Benenden, Mounts Fm. Shot down during a
bomber escort mission probably by 222Sq
(Whitbread). Uffz A.Rauwolf baled out to be
a POW. Based Fiennes or Montreuil.

906.   Spitfire I, R6596 **92**
Biggin Hill (Base). Force landed with aircraft
badly damaged as a result of combat with
bombers and escort attacking the airfield.
P/O A.R. Wright unhurt.   Cat 2

907.   Spitfire I, P9372 **92**
As above. P/O Watling baled out badly
burnt on hands and face.   Cat 3

908.   Me109E1, 3906 **3/JG54**
Channel. Shot down by the R.A.F. and
ditched. Pilot and his condition not known.
Based Guines or Yvrench.

909.   Me109E1, 6103 **1/JG54**
Channel. As above. Fw Biber missing.

910.   Me109E4, 0963 **4/JG53**
Channel. As above. Oblt Schulze-Blank
Staffel Kapt missing. Based Denain-Prouvy.

911.   Me109E4, 5351 **7/JG3**
Channel. As above but ditched. Fw Bauer
missing. Based Desevres.

912. **11.9.40**   2 × Albacores **826**
(a) **in the Straits of Dover.**
(b) **Staple,** L7098
Six of these F.A.A. aircraft were bounced by
Me109's over the Channel, the above crashing as a result, another two crashed at R.A.F.
Bircham Newton (base) on return.   Cat ?

913.   Me110C4, 3376 **2/ZG2**
Failed to return from a sortie over Kent,
exact location of crash not yet found. Based
Abbeville or Amiens. Gfr Kling and Sossner
missing.

914.   Hurricane I, V6549 **46**
Sandhurst, School Fields. Shot down over
north Kent. Sgt de Cannart d'Hamale baled
out landing near Bodiam with head injuries.
Based Stapleford Tawney.   Cat 3

915.   Hurricane I, P5200 **501**
nr Maidstone (?Ightham). Shot down by
Me109's over the town. Sgt T. Pickering
unhurt. Based Kenley.   Cat 3

916.   Hurricane I, V6682 **249**
nr Benenden. Crashed after attacking
He111's over the Estuary and N. Kent. Sgt
W.L. Davis baled out wounded. Based N.
Weald.   Cat 3

917.   Hurricane I, P3038 **229**
Hastingleigh, Combe Grove Fm. Shot down.
P/O M. Ravenhill baled out and was admit-
ted to hospital. (Also reptd as at Combe
Corner.) Based Northolt.   Cat 3

918.   He111H3, 5680 **I/KG26**
Burmarsh, 1 mile W. Damaged by A.A. and
the R.A.F. over London. Crashed and burned
out. Fw Friedrich and George, Uffz Dreyer,
Hoffmann and Stirnemann all POW's.
Based Moerbeke.

919.   He111, 3157 **3/KG26**
Edenbridge, Marsh Green. Briefed to bomb
London Docks and was shot down by the
R.A.F. Fw Westfalen, Gfr Zaehle and Uffz
Herms killed. Oblt Abendhausen and Uffz
Hauswald baled out made POW's. The dead
were firstly buried at Dormansland
Cemetery and then transferred to Cannock
Chase.

920.   He111H3, 3215 **2/KG26**
Channel. Crashed in the sea after the above
raid. Fw Horn killed but three other N.C.O.'s
picked up by Seenotflkdo.

921.   Hurricane I, P3770 **504**
Newchurch, S. of Brookland. Shot up over
the Kent coast and burned after the crash.
P/O A. Clarke missing. A subsequent dig on
the site showed no sign of the body, but a
handkerchief marked 'Clarke' was found.
Based Hendon.   Cat 3

922.   Hurricane I, V7242 **303**
Westerham - Brasted, Hog Trough Hill. Shot
up by Me109's over the southern outskirts of
London and then crashed and burned, in a
chalk pit where the fire brigade could not
reach the wreckage. Sgt Wojtowicz killed.
Based Northolt.   Cat 3

923.   Hurricane I, N2466 **229**
Horsmonden, Goudhurst Rd, Spelmonden.
Caught fire during combat with He111's
over Maidstone and crashed. P/O K. Carver
baled out burnt and was hospitalised. Based
Northolt.   Cat 3

924.   Hurricane I, P2796 **73**
Detling, Coldblow Lane. Crashed following
combat with Me110's over Sheppey. Sgt H.
Webster unhurt. Based Debden.   Cat 3

925.   Me110D2, 3392, 3U + DM **4/ZG26**
Margate. 3 miles off. Failed to return from
an escort mission, believed shot down by
the R.A.F. The lifeboat was launched to
search for a crashed aircraft reported by the
Coastguards, but only a patch of fluorescent
dye was found. Based Amiens or Hermalinghen. Oblt Birkner and Uffz Kleiber missing. This aircraft may have been shot down
by 73Sq. Based Crecy.

926.   Me110D2, 3400, 3U + HP **6/ZG26**
As above but believed to have been a victim
of 17Sq (Baynes) over Margate Sands. Lt
Volk missing and Obgfr Hoffmann killed.

927.　　　Me110D4, 3625, 3U + HM　**6/ZG26**
As above also claimed by 17Sq (Czernin).
Oblt Henken and Fw Radelmeier killed.

928.　　　　　　Hurricane I, V6665　**303**
Pembury, Hitchins Fm. Shot up south of
London and crashed. F/O A. Cebrzynski
severely injured and died a week later.
Based Northolt.　　　　　　　　　　Cat 3

929.　　　　　　　Spitfire I, K9793　**92**
off Dungeness. With P/O Edwards in P9464
intercepted a large formation of enemy
bombers at 20-25000ft on course for
London. P/O F. Hargreaves missing presumed lost at sea. Based Biggin Hill.　Cat 3

930.　　　　　　Me109E7, 2029　**I/LG2**
Wrotham Hill, Pilgrims Way. Shot down by
the R.A.F. south of London. Uffz Heckmaier
killed. Based Calais Marck.

931.　　　　　　Hurricane I, R2682　**238**
Lydd, Little Scotney Fm. Failed to return
from chasing a Ju88 over Romney Marsh.
Sgt Duszynski missing. Based Middle
Wallop.　　　　　　　　　　　　　Cat 3

932.　　　　　　Hurricane I, V6670　**1RCAF**
Old Romney. Crashed and burned out after
an engagement with He111's over Tunbridge
Wells. F/O P. Lochnan unhurt. Based
Northolt.　　　　　　　　　　　　Cat 3

933.　　　　　　He111H3, 3233, V4 + KL　**3/KG1**
Hildenborough, Stocks Green Road.
Attacked and damaged by the R.A.F. during
a sortie to bomb London Docks. Force
landed. Uffz Hirsch Pfeifer, Puempel,
Kramer and Steinecke all POW's. (Also
claimed by the A.A.) Based Montdidier.
Possibly shot down by F/O J.N. McKenzie
(41Sq).

934.　　　　　　Spitfire I, X4325　**41**
Dunton Green, Pole Hill. Shot down during
an attack on a Ju88 and abandoned over
Sevenoaks. P/O G.A. Langley baled out
unhurt. Based Hornchurch.　　　　Cat 3

935.　　　　　　Spitfire I, P9513　**92**
Hawkinge. Force landed after combat with
Me109's. P/O Wade safe. Based Biggin Hill.
　　　　　　　　　　　　　　　　Cat 2

936.　　　Me110C4, 3231, 3U + LT　**9/ZG26**
Meopham, Barnes Cote, Harvel. Failed to
return from combat over the Estuary, may
have been shot down by 73Sq Hurricane
(Robinson). Oblt Junghans and Gfr Eckert
missing. Based St Omer or Barley.

937.　　　Me110C4, 1372, U8 + HL　**2/ZG26**
Charing, Cobham Fm. Developed engine
trouble during a bomber escort mission and
was attacked by the R.A.F. and force
landed. Fw Brinkmann and Uffz Kreusphow
POW's.

938.　　　　　　Me109E4, 5276　**1/JG3**
off Dover. Collided with another flown by
Obfw Hessel and ditched. Oblt Keller

picked up by (?) Seenotflkdo. Hessel crashed
at base. Based Guines or Coulommiers.

939.　　　　　　Spitfire I, R6613　**92**
Wye. Crashed following combat with
Me109's over Folkestone. F/L J. Paterson
slightly injured. Based Biggin Hill.　Cat 3

940.　　　　　　Spitfire I, P9386(?)　**19**
Shoreham (nr Eynsford). Force landed after
being damaged by fire from a Lw bomber.
F/S G.C. Unwin unhurt. Based Fowlmere.
　　　　　　　　　　　　　　　　Cat 2

941.　　　　　　Spitfire I, P9464　**92**
Smeeth, Manor Fm, Evegate. Shot down by
Me109's. P/O H.D. Edwards killed. The
wreck was not found until 7.10.40. Based
Biggin Hill.　　　　　　　　　　　Cat 3

942.　　　　　　Spitfire I, P9513　**92**
Biggin Hill. Shot down by Me109's for the
second time on this day. P/O T.S. Wade
unhurt. Based Biggin Hill.　　　　Cat 2

943.　　　　　　Spitfire I, X4339　**66**
Wye, Wye Court Fm. Force landed with
combat damage. P/O I.J. Cruikshank slightly
injured. Based Gravesend.　　　　Cat 2

944.　**13.9.40**　　　Hurricane I, P2793　**501**
Boughton Monchelsea. Had radiator shot off
during combat over Maidstone. Sgt Lacey
baled out unhurt. Based Kenley.　Cat 3

945.　**14.9.40**　　　Me109E1, 5813　**I/JG26**
Stone, Beacon Hill (nr Faversham). Shot
down by 253Sq (Sgt Dredge) and exploded
over the site. Oblt K. Dähn killed. (Also
reptd shot down by Rabagliati (46Sq) nr
Maidstone.) Based Audembert.

946.　　　　　　Hurricane I, L2039(?)　**73**
Newenden. Shot up over Tonbridge. S/L M.
Robinson baled out wounded and admitted
to hospital. Based Debden.　　　Cat 3(?)
(Although this is recorded as Cat 3 it is listed
as being transferred to Admiralty November
1942.)

947.　　　　　　Spitfire II, X4265　**222**
Detling. Force landed as a result of combat
damage received during a fight with
Me109's. Sgt I. Hutchinson unhurt. Based
Hornchurch.　　　　　　　　　　Cat 2

948.　　　　　　Hurricane I, L1981, TP-E　**73**
Dover, Ringwould. Damaged my Me109's
over the Estuary and force landed. Sgt A.E.
Marshall unhurt. Based Debden.　Cat 2

949.　　　　　　Hurricane I, V7446　**73**
Gravesend a/f. Landed damaged as a result
of an engagement over the Estuary. Sgt M.
Leng unhurt. Based Debden.　　　Cat 2

950.　　　　　　Hurricane I, TP-L　**73**
Staplehurst, Overbridge. Enemy aircraft
damaged this fighter over Maidstone and
Sgt Griffin baled out but had to be admitted
to hospital with a dislocated shoulder and
leg wounds. Based Debden.　　　Cat 3

951.   Hurricane I, P2542 **73**
Chart Sutton, Parkhouse Fm (also reptd
Sutton Valence). Crashed. Sgt J. Brimble
killed. Based Debden.   Cat 3
(In later years the site was excavated and
Brimble's body found.)

Not the best of days for 73 Squadron.

952.   Me109E1, 3854, 4+ **1/JG77**
Boxley, Long Barn Fm. Force landed and
burned following combat with the R.A.F.
whilst on a free-lance patrol. Fw H. Ettler
made POW. Based St Omer.

953.   Hurricane I, P5184 **253**
Sittingbourne, Bredgar, Swanton Fm.
Crashed in flames shot down by Me109's.
Sgt W. Higgins killed. Based Kenley. Cat 3

954.   Hurricane I, P3804 **253**
Stone (nr Faversham). As above, Sgt J.
Anderson baled out and was hospitalised
with severe burns.   Cat 3

955.   Spitfire I, K9960 **72**
Orlestone. Abandoned after combat over
Ashford. Sgt H. Bell-Walker baled out
unhurt. Based Biggin Hill.   Cat 3

956.   Spitfire I, R6605 **41**
Staplehurst, Chapel Lane. Shot down during
a squadron patrol. Exact circumstances not
known. S/L R. Lister baled out wounded.
Based Hornchurch.   Cat 3
S/L Lister has said himself that he crashed
near Canterbury.

957.   Me109E, 2014, 1+ **6/LG2**
Gt Chart, Thanet Wood, New Street Fm.
Shot down by a Spitfire of 72Sq. Uffz V.
Blazejewski baled out unhurt and was made
POW. Based Calais-Marck.

958.   Hurricane I, V7209 **73**
W. Malling. Force landed with bullets in its
radiator. F/L Beytagh unhurt. Based Debden.
                                      Cat 2

959.   Spitfire I, R6624 **92**
Faversham, Sole Street Hse, Norton. Shot up
by Me109's and crashed. P/O H. McGowan
baled out wounded and was admitted to
hospital. Based Biggin Hill.   Cat 3

960.   Spitfire I, X4327 **66**
Hollingbourne. This aircaft was shot down
by enemy fighters over Maidstone. P/O R.
Robbins seriously injured and admitted to
hospital. Based Gravesend.   Cat 3

961.   Spitfire I, X4051 **92**
Biggin Hill (Base). Returned with damage
sustained on patrol over Canterbury and
force landed. Sgt Mann injured.   Cat 2

962.   Spitfire I, N3029 **66**
Gravesend (Base), 1 mile S.E. Force landed
due to engine failure. Sgt P. Willcocks
unhurt.   Cat 2

15.9.40
On this day R.O.C. Dungeness reported 8 Lw
aircraft, 6 × Me109's, 1 × Do17Z and 1 ×

He111 shot down in their area. 605Sq
claimed 6 × Do17Z's shot down.
   The following facts give some idea of the
difficulty of correlating claims and losses.
   In the whole of Kent on the 15th, 13 ×
Do17's none in the Dungeness area, one was
finally credited to 605Sq. Two were shot
down by unidentified fighters. Two 605Sq
Hurricanes shot down by Do17's gunners
whilst attacking.

963.   Hurricane I **213**
Maidstone, nr Kent Police H.Q. Sgt M.E.
Crosskell baled out after being attacked by
Me109's. (The pilot confirmed this when he
appeared on BBC/TV in 1986.) Based Tang-
mere.   Cat 3

964.   Me110C3 **14/LG1**
Thames Estuary. Failed to return from an
escort mission. Thought to have been shot
by the R.A.F. Margate L.B. searched for an
aircraft 3 miles N.E. of Whitstable, which
may have been this aircraft. Lt Adametz and
Obgfr Stief both missing. Based Caen-Carpiquet.

965.   Me109E4, 6160 **I/JG53**
over Kent Coast. Shot down by the R.A.F.
Uffz Schersand killed. Based Coquelles or
Etaples.

966.   Me109E4, 1345 **I/JG53**
Isle of Sheppey. Another victim of the R.A.F.
Obfw Muller wounded and POW. Claimed
by 603Sq (Denholm). Based as above.

967.   Do17Z, 1176 **5/KG3**
Thames Estuary. Shot down en route to Lon-
don. Hptm Puettmann (Staff Kapt) and Fw
Franke killed. Oblt Langenheim missing; Fw
Falke POW. Based Antwerpe-Deurne.

968.   Me109E4, 4802 **3/JG77**
off Dungeness. Failed to return to base. Uffz
Meixner missing. Based St Omer.

969.   Hurricane I, L2122 **605**
Tonbridge, Drux Fm, Plaxtol. Shot down in
an engagement with Do17Z's and Me109's
over Croydon. P/O R.E. Jones slightly injured
and baled out. Based Croydon.   Cat 3

970.   Hurricane I, N2537 **229**
Staplehurst Rly. Stn. Was over Sevenoaks
when it was shot down by enemy fighters.
P/O G. Doutrepont killed. Based Northolt.
                                      Cat 3

971.   Do17Z, 2578 **8/KG76**
off Herne Bay. Shot down after a bombing
op. over London. Fw Keck and Uffz Osenow
killed; Uffz Heitmann and Zahn missing.
The lifeboat searched in vain for this aircraft. Based Cormeilles en Vexin.

972.   Hurricane I, V6616 **229**
Staplehurst, Duckhurst Fm, Clapper Lane.
Shot down in action with Do215's and
Me110's over Sevenoaks. P/O R. Smith baled
out with leg wounds. Based Northolt. Cat 3

973.   Me109E4, 1590   **3/JG53**
Biggin Hill, Mullard Wood, Norheads Fm.
Whilst on the southern outskirts of the City
was shot down by the R.A.F. Oblt J. Haase
(Staffel Kapt) baled out but his 'chute failed
and he was killed. Claimed by 603Sq
(McPhail). Based Coquelles or Etaples.

974.   Me109E4, 5197   **1/JG53**
Bekesbourne, Adisham Court. Shot down by
a Spitfire of 41Sq (F/O A.D. Lovell) over
Canterbury and crashed. Fw H. Tschoppe
baled out badly burnt. Based as above.

975.   Do17Z, 2555, F1 + FS   **8/KG76**
Shoreham, Castle Fm. 609Sq Spitfires (F/O J.
Dundas and P/O Tobin) shot down this air-
craft. Fw Heitsch, Pfeiffer and Sauter all
POW's; Fw Schmid killed. Based Cormeilles
en Vexin.

976.   Hurricane I, P3080   **1RCAF**
Tunbridge Wells. Attacked by Me109's and
shot down. F/O Nesbitt baled out wounded
to be admitted to hospital. Based Northolt.
                                                Cat 3
977.   Hurricane I, P3876   **1RCAF**
As above, F/O R. Smither killed.   Cat 3

978.   Me109E4, 5205   **Stab/JG3**
Bilsington, Hanns (or Hornes) Fm. Shot
down during a free-lance sortie. Oberst Lt
von Wedel unhurt and POW. May have
been shot down by Dover A.A. Based Samer.
This senior officer was the official Lw
historian. It is reported that his engine was
riddled by fire from a Hurricane so that it
seized. He then crashed into a farmhouse,
killing the farmer's wife, Mrs A. Daws and
her 4 year old daughter.

979.   Hurricane I, P3865, TP-K   **73**
Sittingbourne, Nouds Fm, Teynham. Shot
down by Me109's over Maidstone. P/O R.
Marchand killed. Based Debden.   Cat 3

980.   Do17Z, 3322, F1 + DT   **9/KG76**
Seal, Underriver. Force landed and burned
out after being shot up by 46Sq (Sgt Tyrer)
and 257Sq (F/L Brothers and P/O Mortimer).
Uffz Malter killed; Obfw Streit, Fw Raab
and Teuffert all POW's. Based Cormeilles
en Vexin.

981.   Spitfire I, P9324   **41**
Gravesend. Shot down by Me109's. P/O G.A.
Langley killed. (Also reptd shot down at
Thurrock, Essex.) Based Hornchurch.   Cat 3

982.   He111H3, 6843, A1 + GM   **II/KG53**
Frittenden, Burgess Fm. Damaged by the
R.A.F. and A.A. over Kent, and had to force
land. Fw Grassl killed; Maj Grube, Oblt
Schirning, Obfw Schmittborn, Fw Nagel and
Uffz Schilling all baled out and POW's.
Based Lille.

983.   Hurricane I, V7433   **501**
Sevenoaks. Force landed with radiator
trouble after combat with Me109's over Ashford. S/L Hogan unhurt. Based Kenley. Cat 2

984.   Do17Z, 2651, F1 + FL   **3/KG76**
Sturry north. Shot down by 66Sq (F/L Gillies)
and 46Sq (Sgts Jeffreys and Hurry), also involved F/L Leather and P/O Pollard (611Sq)
and P/O Bodie (66Sq). Obfw Niebler, Fw
Wissmann and Uffz Schatz killed; Oblt
Wilke and Uffz Zremer POW's. (Was this a
special with 5 crew or was one of the above
from another aircraft?) Based Beauvais.

985.   Spitfire I, R6606(?)   **92**
nr Goudhurst. Whilst on patrol P/O R.H.
Holland baled out, reason not recorded, and
was slightly injured. (Also reptd Leeds
Castle.) Based Biggin Hill.   Cat 3

986.   Me109E1, 3619   **3/JG53**
Dymchurch Redoubt. Severely damaged by
the R.A.F. whilst acting as escort to a bomb-
ing mission, and had to force land. Uffz K.
Feldmann unhurt POW. Based Coquelles or
Etaples.

987.   Me109E   **2/JG53**
Bearsted, Gore Wood, Aldington Court Fm.
Crashed and burned after combat with
fighters. Oblt R. Schmidt killed. Based as
above.

988.   Hurricane I, P2760   **501**
Chilham, E. Stour Fm. Severely damaged by
a Me109E whilst carrying out an attack on a
Do17Z over Ashford. P/O A. van den H.
d'Ertsenrijck killed. The a/c wreckage fell
into the river. Based Kenley.   Cat 3

989.   Hurricane I, N2481   **504**
Dartford, Hartley. Shot up over the southern
outskirts of London and dived full throttle
into a house. P/O J. Gurteen killed. Based
Hendon.   Cat 3

990.   Me109E4, 1606   **3/JG3**
Charing, Thorn Fm, Pluckley Brickworks.
Shot down by the R.A.F. Oblt H. Reum-
schuessel (Staffel Kapt) baled out unhurt
and POW. Based Coulommiers.

991.   Me109E4, 2803   **9/JG51**
Paddock Wood, Skinners Corner, Mascalls.
Shot down by the R.A.F. crashing and ex-
ploding. Fw F. Klotz killed. Based St Omer.

992.   Hurricane I, L2012   **605**
Yalding, the Leas. Hit by return fire from a
Do17Z whilst he was attacking, causing P/O
T. Cooper-Slipper to lose control and collide
with the mid-fuselage of the bomber. He
baled out slightly injured landing at Church
Fm, Marden. Based Croydon.   Cat 3

993.   Hurricane I, R4087   **310**
Isle of Grain, Stoke. Shot up by enemy
fighters over the Estuary. Sgt J. Hubacek
baled out slightly injured in the foot. Based
Duxford.   Cat 3
(Possibly a victim of Maj A. Galland.)

994.   Do17Z, 4200, 5K + JN   **5/KG3**
Marden, Widehurst Wood. Attacked by
605Sq Hurricanes whilst on a bombing
mission to London. Crashed after a collision
with L2012 (Plot 992). Obfw Rilling killed;

Obfw Hoebel and Howind, Fw Zimmermann, all baled out, POW's. Based Antwerp-Deurne.

995.   Hurricane I, V6566 **249**
W. Malling a/f. Crash landed after being severely damaged by Me109's whilst itself attacking a He111 S.E. of London. P/O K. Lofts unhurt. Based North Weald.   Cat 2

P/O K.T. Lofts
A Kentish man from Canterbury who flew Gladiators with 615Sq in France and converted to Hurricanes in May 1940. By September of that year he was credited with six victories and several shared.

In October he was posted to 249Sq as a flight commander and awarded a D.F.C. for his continuing successes. After a spell of instructing at 52 OTU he formed and commanded 340Sq, the first Free French squadron, in 1942, but did not fly with them operationally, being posted as C.O. of 154Sq. and sailing with them to the Middle East.

On returning to the U.K. he was, as W/Cdr, the C.O. of 66Sq.

He survived the War only to be killed in a flying accident.

996.   Do17Z3, 2881 **4/KG3**
Isle of Grain, Stoke. Shot down by (?) 501Sq during a bombing raid over the Estuary. Uffz Wien, Fw Goertz, Gfr Schild and Weymar all POW's. Based Antwerp-Deurne.

997.   Do17Z3, 3457, 5K + JM **4/KG3**
Dartford, Barnhurst G.C., Perry Street. Probably shot down by 504Sq Hurricanes (S/L Sample). Uffz Burballa and Hansburg, Flgr E. Bormann killed. Lt Michaelis POW. Based Antwerp-Deurne.

998.   Hurricane I, N2705 **504**
nr Dartford. Crashed following combat over S.E. ̄ngland. F/O M. Jebb died in hospital 19.9.40. Based Hendon.   Cat 3

999.   Me109E4, 3266 **7/JG51**
Dover, St Margarets at Cliffe. Had a fire during an escort mission and following combat with 605Sq Hurricane (Currant). Lt K. Bildau baled out unhurt and made POW. Based St Omer or St Quentin.

1000.   Me109E4, 3182 **I/JG52**
Smarden, N.E. of. Lost control following a collision with another Me109 during a free-lance patrol over Kent. Lt H. Birthol baled out landing at Boundsend Fm, Staplehurst to be POW. Based Coquelles or Laon.

1001.   Me109E7, 2058 **3/LG2**
Isle of Sheppey, Shellness Point. Force landed following an attack by the R.A.F. whilst on bomber escort. Uffz A. Klick unhurt, POW. Based Calais-Marck.

1002.   He111H2, 5718, A1 + LN **II/KG53**
Benenden, Trafford Fm. Shot down by the R.A.F. Fw Mayer and Gfr Hoffmann killed; Lt Baensch, Uffz Bauer and Buttler POW's. Based Lille-Vendeville (?).

1003.   Me109E1, 2685 **1/JG3**
Tenterden, St Michaels. Fighters shot this aircraft down whilst it was on a free-lance sortie over Kent. Obfw F. Hessel baled out to be a POW. Based Guines or Coulommiers.

1004.   Me109E7, 2061 **1/LG2**
Sittingbourne, Hartlip. Shot down by Sgt Wojciechowski (303Sq) over the Estuary. Uffz H. Streibing baled out unhurt and POW. Based Calais-Marck.

1005.   Do17Z, 2304, U5 + HN **5/KG2**
Shot down by F/L Oxspring (?) (66Sq) and the A.A. during an operation over London, causing it to crash into houses. Uffz Boehmel (or Bochmel), Huber killed; Uffz Möbious and Gfr Birg missing. Based St Leger or Arras.

1006.   Hurricane I, P3113, AK-F **213**
Hawkhurst. Shot down in combat with an Me109. Sgt R. Llewellyn but severely wounded in the arm. Based Tangmere. Cat 3

1007.   Hurricane I, P3939 **303**
Lower Stoke, Isle of Grain. Shot down in combat with Me109's over the Dartford area. Sgt T. Andruszkow baled out unhurt. Based Northolt.   Cat 3

1008.   He111H1, 2771, A1 + AN **II/KG53**
W. Malling a/f. Force landed after an attack by R.A.F. fighters whilst it was bombing London Docks. Uffz Lange and Sailer killed; Fw Behrend, Lichtenhagen and Uffz Zilling all POW's. Based Lille-Vendeville or Chartres.
F/O Simpson (229Sq) credited with a half share.

1009.   Hurricane I, P2836 **238**
Pembury, Kent College. Aircraft hit an oak tree. Sgt L.M. Pidd had baled out but landed dead. Based Middle Wallop.   Cat 3

1010.   Hurricane I, P3920 **238**
W. Malling. Force landed with severe damage sustained during an attack on a He111H. F/L M. Blake unhurt. Based Middle Wallop.   Cat 2

1011.   Hurricane I, P3577 **303**
Thames Estuary. Failed to return from combat with Me109's off Gravesend. Sgt Brzezowski missing. Based Northolt.   Cat 3

1012.   Spitfire I, X4324 **603**
Leeds Catle, Kingswood. Shot down by the Lw P/O A. Pease killed. Based Hornchurch.
                                             Cat 3

1013.   Do17Z, 3440, U5 + PS **8/KG2**
Chatham, The Chase. Shot down by 253Sq Hurricane (Sgt Innes) whilst it was on an op. to bomb London Docks. Oblt Kittmann, Uffz Langer and Stamfer + Kriegsberichter (War Correspondent) Koehler all baled out to be POW's. Based Cambrai or Arras.

1014.   Do17Z, 3458, 5K + GN **5/KG3**
Bedgebury, Combwell Wood. Collided with

a Hurricane (P/O P.J. Stephenson) and crashed. Oblt Becker-Ross, Obfw Bruckner and Fw Hensen killed; Fw Brinkmann missing. A Homeguard Private J. Waters also killed. Based Arras or St Leger.

1015. Hurricane I, V6688 **607**
Cranbrook (?). Set alight in the above incident over Appledore. P/O Stephenson slightly wounded abandoned by parachute. Based Tangmere. Cat 3
(This crash was at Swiss Park, Cranbrook.)

1016. Me109E1, 3759 **Stab I/JG77**
Lympne, Stuttfall Castle. Shot down by the R.A.F. Oblt H. Kunze (Gruppe Adj) killed. Based St Omer.

1017. Hurricane I, V6698 **253**
Lympne. Force landed after being damaged during a head on attack against a formation of Do215's over the Channel. P/O A. Barton unhurt. Based Kenley. Cat 2

1018. Do17Z, 3405, U5+FT **9/KG2**
off Herne Bay. Shot down by P/O Pattullo (46Sq) whilst it was on an attack against London. Obfw Staib and Uffz Hoppe killed; Gfr Hoffmann and Zierer POW's. Hoppe's body was later washed up at Shellness, Isle of Sheppey. Based Cambrai-Niergnies.

1019. He111H2, 5481, A1+GL **3/KG2**
Sandhurst, Bourne Fm. Shot up by Spitfires (92Sq) whilst on the way to London. Uffz Lehner and Ruetig killed; Oblt Buechler, Gfr Richter and Stamminger baled out and were POW's. Based Lille-Vendeville.

1020. Me110C3 **13/LG1**
N. Kent. Intercepted by the R.A.F. en route for London as bomber escort. Shot down by S/L Kellett (C.O. 303Sq). Lt Gorisch and Uffz Gericke missing. Based Tramecourt.

1021. Me110C3, 3802 **13/LG1**
Ashford, Hothfield Fm. As above. Shot down by 303Sq (Feric) whilst over the Estuary. Oblt Muller and Fw Hoffmann killed.

1022. Do17Z, 3230 **9/KG2**
nr Cranbrook. This aircraft was on a London raid when it was shot down by the R.A.F. Fw Glaser and Krummheuer with Uffz Lenz killed. Uffz Sehert made a POW. Based Arras or Cambrai.

1023 Blenheim, R2067(?) **25**
nr Biggin Hill. Reported as a night accident but does not appear in the F541 so may have been on practice interceptions, F/O's Miley and H. Lambert and LAC J. Wyatt killed, P/O B. Hooper unhurt. (Also reported as a Beaufighter but not likely as the unit did not have this type until October; it could not have carried a crew of 4.) Based Hornchurch. Cat 3

1024. **16.9.40** Hurricane I, N2589 **605**
Detling a/f. Force landed with severe damage after being attacked by a Me109 flown by Maj Mölders of JG51, over Kent. P/O E. Watson wounded. Based Croydon. Cat 2

1025. Spitfire I, R6616 **92**
Biggin Hill (Base). Undercarriage was damaged due to a side-slip on landing. P/O H. Hill unhurt. Cat 2

1026. **17.9.40** Spitfire I, X4409 **41**
Stelling Minnis. After combat with Me109's over Manston, P/O Baker had to force land, but was unhurt. Based Hornchurch. Cat 2

1027. Hurricane I, V6669 **1RCAF**
Strood, High Halstow. Crash landed with a damaged oil system after combat. F/O E. Briese unhurt. Based Northolt. Cat 2

1028. Hurricane I, P3929 **607**
Bethersden, Tuesnoad Fm. Had to force land after being shot up by Hptm Neumann I/JG27. P/O G.H. Welford injured. Based Tangmere. Cat 2

1029. Hurricane I, P3933 **607**
E. Peckham, The Bell, Beltring. Also thought to have been shot up by Hptm Neumann and crashed. Sgt J. Lansdell killed. Based Tangmere. Cat 3

1030. Hurricane I, V7357 **501**
nr Harrietsham, Wrinsted Court, Frinsted. Whilst carrying out a solo attack on a formation of Me109's over Ashford Sgt Lacey was shot down but managed to bale out safely. Based Kenley. Cat 3
(This site was dug by the Shoreham Aircraft Preservation Society in September 1986 and the Merlin engine and other items recovered.)

Sgt J.H. Lacey
A Yorkshireman from Wetherby, he joined the R.A.F.V.R. in 1932 and later became a flying instructor with the Yorkshire Flying Club.
At the outbreak of War he was posted to 501Sq going with that unit to France.
When he returned to the U.K. he had a score of five victories. After another in July he was awarded the D.F.M. and by October when he had reached a total of 23, a Bar to the D.F.M. and commissioned.
He continued to fly operationally until July 1941 when he was posted as an instructor to 57 O.T.U., but in the following March was once more on ops. and claiming three Fw190's as damaged before once more coming off operational flying by a spell as Chief Flying Instructor at R.A.F. Milfield.
Later he was Senior Instructor on a team sent to India to convert Hurricane squadrons to Thunderbolts, and as C.O. of 17Sq, when he scored his final and 28th victory against a Japanese Oscar over Burma.
Post war he remained in the R.A.F.

1031. Hurricane I, P3820 **501**
Bethersden, Tuesnoad Fm, Daniels Wood. Shot down in flames over Ashford. Sgt E.J. Egan killed. Based Kenley. Cat 3

Incident No. 1036. Crashing in Maidstone this Ju88 wrecked a house and killed its crew. (One photograph shows part of the wing and the dive brake.)   (Kent Messenger)

1032.   Me109E4, 5141 **9/JG53**
Thames Estuary. Shot down by 19Sq (Sublt Blake). Oblt Stoll (Staffel Kapt) missing. Based Sempy.

1033.   Me109E4, 1228 **9/JG53**
Thames Estuary. As above. Oblt Seliger missing.

1034.   Hurricane I, V7529 (?) **504**
Faversham, Shepherds Hill, Selling. Sgt Helcke lost control during a simulated attack by another fighter, crashed and was killed after baling out. Based Hendon. Cat 3

1035.   Me109E4, 3177 **9/JG53**
Dunkirk, Bishopden Wood. Shot down by 303Sq Hurricane (Sgt Wojciechowski) over N. Kent. Uffz M. Langer killed. Based Sempy.

1036.   Ju88A1, 2152 **I/KG54**
Maidstone, St Andrews Close. Shot down by a Defiant night fighter of 141Sq (Sgts Chard and Laurence). Lt Ganzlmayr, Obfw Faschinger, Uffz Bauer and Schloessler killed during a night raid. Based Evreux.

1037. **18.9.40**   Me109E4, 5388 **1/JG27**
Sittingbourne, Squirrel Wood, Stockbury. Shot down over the Estuary by the R.A.F. Oblt Kraftschick missing. Based Guines or Plumetot.

1038.   Me109E4, 2669 **1/JG77**
Ramsgate - Deal. As above, Gfr Still killed.

1039.   Hurricane I, V6600 **501**
Staplehurst, Overbridge Fm. Shot up by Me109's over Tonbridge. Sgt C. Saward baled out unhurt. Based Kenley.   Cat 3

1040.   Spitfire I, X4323 **603**
Ashford, Kennington. As above. P/O P. Howes killed. Based Hornchurch.   Cat 3

1041.   Spitfire I, N3193 **92**
Hollingbourne. Crashed and burned following combat with Me109's. P/O R. Mottram burnt and hospitalised. Based Biggin Hill.
                                    Cat 3

1042.   Spitfire I, N3283 **92**
Appledore. Whilst patrolling Gravesend was severely damaged in combat with Me109's resulting in engine failure and a crash landing. F/O A. Bartley uninjured. Based Biggin Hill.   Cat 2

1043.   Do215, 0038 **4/AufKlaerung**
Yalding, Collier Street. Shot down by the R.A.F. whilst on a photo. recce. mission over Kent. Fw Schuetz killed; Uffz Linsner and Wiesen baled out to be POW's. Based Berlin-Staaken, but individual aircraft operated from any occupied airfield in Europe.

1044.   Spitfire I, X4337 **72**
Hawkinge a/f. Force landed after an attack by M109's. Sgt Norfolk unhurt. Based Biggin Hill.   Cat 2

1045.   Spitfire I, R6704 **72**
Gravesend a/f. As above but attacked over the town. Sgt H.J. Bell-Walker seriously wounded. (Also reptd at Whitfield.) Based Biggin Hill.   Cat 2

1046.   Hurricane I, P3859 **1RCAF**
Thames Estuary. P/O E. Beardmore baled out slightly wounded. (Also reptd off Dungeness.) Based Northolt.   Cat 3

63

1047.   Spitfire I, P9368 **72**
Dover, Martin Mill. Force landed after being seriously damaged in combat. P/O J. Lloyd seriously wounded. Based Biggin Hill. Cat 2

1048.   Spitfire I, R6603 **66**
Petham, Denge Wood. Shot up in combat over Canterbury. Sgt D. Corfe injured and admitted to hospital. Based Gravesend.
                                    Cat 3

1049.   Hurricane I, V6620 **501**
nr Charing. Crashed following combat with He111's and Me109's over W. Malling. S/L H. Hogan baled out. Based Kenley.   Cat 3

1050.   Hurricane I, V7442 **46**
Chatham, Boxley. Shot up over the town. Sgt G.W. Jeffreys baled out but was killed due to parachute failure. Based Stapleford Tawney.   Cat 3

1051.   Hurricane I, V6554 **46**
Chatham, Chestnut Avenue, Walderslade. Shot down in combat over the town. P/O P. LeFevre baled out with minor injuries. Cat 3

1052.   Hurricane I, P3816 **46**
Walderslade. The site of this crash was dug and some items are in the Battle of Britain Museum. Sgt C. Hurry baled out after being shot up, burnt and wounded. Based Stapleford Tawney.   Cat 3

1053.   Me109E1, 2674 **9/JG27**
Sandwich, Royal St Georges G.C., Willow Fm. Probably shot down by 41Sq Spitfires. Gfr Glöckner force landed and set his aircraft on fire. Based Guines or Senon.

1054.   Me109E, 6327 **9/JG27**
Sellindge, Harringe Court. Force landed due to damage sustained in combat with 41Sq near Maidstone, whilst on a bomber escort. Fw E. Schulz severely wounded and died 12.12.40 as a POW. Based Guines or Senon.

1055.   Spitfire I, X4170 **19**
Eastchurch a/f. Force landed with a glycol leak the tank having been damaged by enemy action over the Estuary. P/O W. Lawson unhurt. Based Duxford.   Cat 2

1056.   Spitfire I, R6772 **222**
Challock, Clock House Fm. Crashed and burned after being shot up by Me109's over Canterbury. Sgt I. Hutchinson landed at Molash by parachute, slightly injured. Based Hornchurch.   Cat 3

1057.   Ju88A1, 3142, 3Z + BS **8/KG77**
Sheppey, Minster. Shot down by the R.A.F. during a bombing operation over the Estuary. Fate of crew uncertain but four N.C.O.'s thought to have been missing. Based Laon.

1058.   Ju88A1, 5097, 3Z + ES **8/KG77**
Sheppey, Mocketts Fm, Harty. Shot down before reaching the Target, Tilbury Docks. Obfw Semerau, Fw Damschen (who fell from the aircraft), Uffz Eggert and Treutmann all killed. (A Jumo engine from it is at the Kent Battle of Britain Museum.)

1059.   Spitfire I, R6925 **66**
Dover, Coldred. Shot up in combat over the Estuary. P/O J. Mather baled out unhurt. Based Gravesend.   Cat 3

1060.   Ju88A1, 5104, 3Z + DT **9/KG77**
Cooling, Cooling Court. Also on Tilbury Dock. Uffz Kurtz and Koehn killed; Uffz Burkart missing; Uffz Glaeseker made POW. Based Laon-Couvron.

1061.   Me109E1, 4842, 10+ **II/JG53**
Ash, Guilton. Shot down by F/L Oxspring (66Sq) during a free-lance sortie over Kent. Lt E. Bodendick baled out severely wounded a POW. Based Coquelles.

1062.   Ju88A1, 3162 **8/KG77**
off the Nore Light. Probably shot down by 303Sq. Oblt Fuchs killed; Gfr Foelinger missing; Fw Stier and Obgfr Baumann POW's. Based Laon-Couvron.

1063.   Ju88A1, 5100, 3Z + HS **8/KG77**
off Sheerness. As above but likely to have been shot down by 92Sq after the raid. Oblt Weber and Fw Kripmann killed; Gfr Neuweg missing; Fw Goern POW. Weber's body was washed up on the beach at Minster. Based Laon Couvron.

1064.   Ju88A1, 3173, 3Z + ED **III/KG77**
Eastry, The Mill. Shot down after the raid. Maj Kless (Gruppe Kdr) and Oblt Lauth killed; Fw Himsel and Uffz Proebst baled out POW's.

In addition to the above six losses, another KG77 aircraft was lost at an uncertain location and appears in the 'Imprecise' list. A black day for this unit, the III Gruppe.

1065. **19.9.40**   Ju88A1, 7058 **I/KG51**
Channel. On an operational sortie over the south coast reported missing. Cause unknown. Obfw Luckard and Uffz Henker killed; Fw Walter and Gfr Roeder missing. Based Paris-Orly.

1066.   Ju88A1 **I/KG51(?)**
Deal, 3 miles off. Shot down by the R.A.F. Exact fate of crew not known. Based Etampes.

1067. **20.9.40**   Spitfire I, X4410 **72**
Sittingbourne, Stiff Street. Shot up over Canterbury. P/O D. Holland baled out severely wounded and died in hospital. Based Biggin Hill.   Cat 3

1068.   Spitfire I, N3203 **222**
Higham, Hermitage Fm. Shot down by Me109's. P/O H. Whitbread killed. Based Hornchurch.   Cat 3

1069.   Hurricane I, R2686 **253**
Lyminge, Postling. Crashed and burned after an attack by Me109's. P/O A. Barton slightly injured but admitted to hospital. (Also reptd at Hythe.) Based Kenley.   Cat 3

1070. Hurricane I, R6736 **253**
Hildenborough. Crashed following combat over Maidstone. Sgt R.A. Innes unhurt (?). Based Kenley. Cat 3

1071. Spitfire I, X4417 **92**
Dover, W. Hougham. Crashed after combat with Maj Molders of JG51. (There does not seem to be such an incident on his claims list.)
also reported
Biggin Hill, Keston. Crashed into the tops of trees after being in combat over Calais. It had been hit by a 20mm cannon shell, which is thought to have entered through the canopy killing P/O H. Hill. The aircraft seems to have flown itself back and was seen to fly almost directly across the air-field. For a month it was missing until the crew of an Anson sighted the wreckage in the trees with the pilot in the cockpit.

There is a P/O H.E. Hill buried at Hawk-inge which would tend to support the former explanation. It has not been possible to clarify this further. F541 states that it was patrolling Gravesend at 5000ft when it crashed and burned out.

1072. Spitfire I, N3248 **92**
Dover - Dungeness. Shot down by Maj Molders the aircraft falling into the sea. Sgt P. Eyles missing. Based Biggin Hill. Cat 3

1073. Me109E4, 2789 **9/JG27**
Faversham, Ospringe. Shot down by (?) 92Sq (Saunders). Uffz Clauser killed. Based Guines or Senon.

1074. Spitfire I, X4101 **41**
Lympne a/f. Force landed after being dam-aged in combat. P/O G. Bennions unhurt. Based Hornchurch. Cat 2

1075. **21.9.40** Me109E4, 3716 **5/LG2**
off Dover. Shot down by A.A. during a sortie over Dover. Pilot rescued unhurt by Seenot-flkdo. Based Calais-Marck.

1076. Spitfire I, N3032 **92**
Manston. Crashed after attacking escorted bombers. Sgt T. Sherrington unhurt. Based Biggin Hill. Cat 2

1077. **23.9.40** Anson I, N4914 **1CACU**
East Langdon. A flight of Spitfires of 41Sq (P/O J.N. McKenzie, Sgt Bamberger and two others had flown from Hornchurch to Hawk-inge to escort an Anson over the Channel to a position near the French coast where it was to act as front gun spotter.) One Spitfire aborted with engine trouble and the Anson and escort were intercepted by 20+ Me109's.

The Anson dived to sea level and headed for home. On arrival it belly landed and two of the crew were killed. Fate of the fighters not known other than that McKenzie sur-vived. Based Hawkinge. Cat 3(?)

1078. Hurricane I, P8812 **73**
Rodmersham, Ludgate, Lynsted. A victim of Me109's over Sheppey. Sgt M. Leng baled out and was injured in a heavy landing. Based Castle Camps. Cat 3

1079. Me109E4, 3735 **8/JG26**
Isle of Grain, Grain Port. Was hit in the radiator by P/O J. Drummond (92Sq) over North Kent and had to force land. Obfw A. Kuepper unhurt and POW. Based Caffiers.

1080. Spitfire I, P9371 **92**
nr W. Malling a/f. Crashed after attempting a force landing which resulted from damage sustained in combat over Gravesend. P/O J.G. Pattison severely wounded in the leg and admitted to hospital. He was incapacitated for 8 months. Based Biggin. Cat 2

1081. Me109E4, 1969 **4/JG2**
nr Folkestone Rly. pier. Shot down by F/L Cosby and Sgt Glew (72Sq) whilst it was on escort duty. Army personnel, Lt M. Jacobs and L/Cpl Ebbington swam out to assist the pilot, Uffz Dilthey who was injured, until they were picked up by a boat. Based St Omer-Longuenesse..

1082. Me109E4, 5817 **8/JG26**
Biddenden. Shot down by F/L Kingcome (92Sq). Obfw G. Grzymalla baled out unhurt and was made a POW. Based Caffiers.

1083. Hurricane I, L2036 **73**
Thames Estuary, nr Lightship 93. Shot down by Me109's. P/O N. Langham-Hobart picked up with severe burns. Based Castle Camps. Cat 3

1084. Hurricane I, P2960 **257**
Eastchurch, Groves Fm. Shot up by Me109's over Thames Estuary whilst on patrol. Sgt D. Aslin baled out badly burnt and was hospitalised. Sgt Aslin not listed in Form 541. Also reported at Godmersham. Based Debden. Cat 3

1085. Hurricane I, P3226 **73**
As for No.1083. P/O D.S. Kinder picked up. Cat 3

1086. Spitfire I, X4063 **72**
nr Sittingbourne, Bapchild. Was in combat over Gravesend when it was shot down by a Me109E crashing and burning, but P/O B. Brown escaped wounded. (Also reptd at Eastchurch.) Based Biggin Hill. Cat 3

1087. Me109E1, 6343 **Stab/JG3**
Dover Straits. Shot down by a Hurricane of 303Sq. Oblt Hopp killed. Based Colombert or Samer.

1088. Me109E1, 1516 **3/JG54**
Barham, Broom Park. Shot down by Spitfires of (?) 92Sq. Obfw Knippscheer baled out and was killed. Based Coquelles or Etaples.

65

1089. Me109E4, 6304 **7/JG3**
off Kingsdown. Shot down by (?) 603Sq (Boulter) during a free-lance sortie. Uffz K. Elbing baled out to be POW. Based Desevres.

1090. Hurricane I, P2879 **229**
St Mary Hoo, in marshes. Shot down whilst acting as squadron weaver. P/O D. Allcock baled out wounded, at Westcliff and was hospitalised. Based Northolt. Cat 3

1091. Hurricane I, V7445 **73**
Elmley, in the River Swale. Shot down by enemy fighters over Sheppey. Sgt F. Perkin baled out landing at Harty Ferry. Based Castle Camps. Cat 3

1092. 24.9.40
A force of Blenheims, five from 139Sq + 6 from 114Sq were despatched on an anti-shipping strike in the Channel, to include E-boats.

Blen IV, T1794 **139**
Dover, 9 miles east. Missing without trace after an attack on E-boats. S/L M.F. Hendry, Sgts Arrowsmith and Davidson all missing. Based Horsham St Faith. Cat 3

1093. Blen IV, R3885 **139**
Manston. Badly damaged and had to force land. F/O Turnbull + Sgts Jones and Ward safe. Cat 3(?)

1094. Me109E **?**
S.E. Dover. Was acting as top cover for the above shipping and attacking Blenheim R3698, P/O Hunt 139Sq, when it was shot down by the gunner.

1095. Spitfire I, X4340 **72**
Biggin Hill (Base). Damaged in combat over Swanley, but believed to have just reached base. F/S J. Steere unhurt. (This pilot had flown 1315-1420 and 1525-1615 hours.) Cat 2

1096. Spitfire I, X4356 **92**
Strood, Higham Marshes. Crashed with damage to starboard wing and coolant system as a result of fire from a Me109 over Maidstone. Sgt W. Ellis unhurt. Based Biggin Hill. Cat 2

1097. Hurricane I, P3878, YB-W **17**
off Chatham. Shot down by a Me109. P/O H. Bird-Wilson baled out burnt and was picked up from the sea. Based Debden. Cat 3

1098. Spitfire I, X4427 **92**
Biggin Hill (Base). Returned severely damaged in the wing as a result of combat over Maidstone. S/L R. Lister wounded in the leg and arm and hospitalised. Cat 2

1099. Spitfire I, N3118 **41**
off Dover. Shot down during a squadron patrol off Dover. Sgt J. McAdam baled out and was picked up. Based Hornchurch. Cat 3

1100. Spitfire I, R6604 **41**
nr Dover. After forced landing. Sgt E. Darling unhurt. Cat 2

1101. He111H4, 6964, 1T + GH **1/Kgr126**
off Gravesend. Failed to return from ops. over the Estuary. Believed shot down by 66Sq (Oxspring and Reilly). Lt Z.S. Drews, Uffz Mellin, Gfr Blau and Flgr Saal all missing. (Also reptd as having been attacked north of Hastings when hits were seen on both engines.) The presence of a naval officer suggests a shipping recce. Based (?) Rennes.

On this day, 24th September, Major A. Galland, then Commanding Officer of JG26, claimed an unspecified victory over an R.A.F. fighter over the Thames Estuary. This could have been incidents 1096 or 1097.

He also states that he reported to Goering on the subject of inflated claims;

'At the great altitudes where aerial battles take place, it was impossible except on rare cases to follow the victim down to its final crash in order to verify the kill.

'Even if the German figures of enemy aircraft destroyed were perhaps over-estimated, the fact that their (R.A.F.) fighter strength did not diminish could only be accounted for in this way.'

1102. 26.9.40 Me109E4, 5369 **3/JG51**
off Dungeness. Shot down by the R.A.F. whilst on a sortie over the Channel. Fw Meudner missing. Based Wissant or Pihen.

1103. Hurricane I, V7470 **253**
Dungeness. Shot down by Me109's. P/O W.M. Samolinski missing. Based Kenley. Cat 3

1104. Hurricane I, P2958 **253**
off Folkestone. Ditched with combat damage. F/L G.R. Edge baled out and was picked up by a trawler, injured. Based Kenley. Cat 3

1105. Hurricane I, V6673 **303**
Biggin Hill. Force landed with combat damage sustained over Southampton. Sgt M. Belc safe. Based Northolt. Cat 2

1106. 27.9.40 Blenheim, T2221, PZ-J **53**
Detling (Base). Crashed on take off. P/O Richie and Sgt Gotham unhurt; Sgt Trafford injured. Cat 3

1107. Me109E7, 2062 **I/LG2**
Thames Estuary. Shot down by 46Sq(?) (Pattullo and Tyrer). Oblt Bühl (Staffel Kapt) missing. Based Calais-Marck.

1108. Hurricane I, P3647 **1RCAF**
Edenbridge, Hever. Shot down as a result of combat with Ju88's and Me109's over north Kent. F/O O. Peterson killed. Based Northolt. Cat 3

1109. Hurricane I, L1696 **303**
Borough Green, Crowhurst Fm. Was attacked by Me109's and crashed. P/O L. Paskiewicz killed. Based Northolt. Cat 3

1110.   Hurricane I, N2401, AK-Q **213**
Seal, Wilderness G.C. Shot up by Lw fighters near Gatwick. F/L L. Schwind killed. Based Tangmere.   Cat 3

1111.   Spitfire I, X4480 **92**
Biggin Hill (Base). Damaged by a Me109E over Sevenoaks and returned to base with a large section of tailplane missing. P/O J. Mansell-Lewis unhurt.   Cat 2

1112.   Spitfire I, N3068 **72**
W. Wickham, 70 Queensway. Shot down by Me109's over Sevenoaks. F/O P. Davis-Cooke baled out but was dead on landing at 66 Bourne Way. Based Biggin Hill.   Cat 3

1113.   Spitfire I, X4422 **92**
Farningham, Sparepenny Lane. Patrolling Maidstone at 20000ft when involved in combat and crashed. P/O J.A. Paterson was killed. Only his second day on the unit. Based Biggin Hill.   Cat 3

1114.   Spitfire I, K9940 **72**
Force landed with damage to header tank after combat, over Sevenoaks. Sgt J. White unhurt. Based Biggin Hill.   Cat 2

1115.   Ju88A1, 2164, 3Z + IK **2/KG77**
off Lydd. Shot down by the R.A.F. Fw Krebs and Uffz Hertlein killed; Uffz Schmidt and Sergocki unhurt and POW's. Based Laon.

1116.   Ju88A1, 8090, 3Z + DH **1/KG77**
Cudham, Angas Home. Hit by A.A. on the flight to London. Gfr Zabel baled out but was killed due to 'chute failure. Obfw H. Müller and R. Müller with Uffz Kollmannsmager landed safely and made POW's.

1117.   Me109E, 1538 **8/JG54**
Boughton, Brenley House. Damaged by the R.A.F. and attempted to force land but hit a fence and somersaulted over the road to crash in flames. Oblt Schon killed. Based Guines or Yvrench.

1118.   Spitfire I, K9846 **41**
nr E. Malling. Shot down over the airfield by Me109's. Sgt E.V. Darling baled out wounded in the shoulder and was admitted to hospital. Based Hornchurch Adv. Rochford.
                                              Cat 3

1119.   Spitfire, R6884, EB-S **41**
Mereworth, Swanton Lane. As above, Sgt F. Usmar baled out with leg wounds and was hospitalised.   Cat 3

1120.   Spitfire I, X4237 **19**
Wye, Court Fm. Shot up over Canterbury by Lw fighters. Sgt D.G. Cox wounded. Based Duxford.   Cat 3

1121.   Spitfire I, X4328 **616**
Throwley, Workhouse Cottages. Attacked by Me109's whilst acting as a weaver. F/O D.S. Smith seriously wounded and died 28.9.40. (Also reptd Faversham.) Based Duxford.   Cat 3

1122.   Hurricane I, V6608 **310**
Godmersham, Woodsdale Fm. F/O G. Sinclair baled out after being shot up over Thanet. He landed safely at Chilham. Based Duxford.   Cat 3

1123.   Hurricane I, V6645 **501**
Sittingbourne, Teynham Court. Reason for crash not known but F/O E. Gunter baled out to die as a result of parachute failure. Based Kenley.   Cat 3

1124.   Hurricane I, P2967 **242**
Milstead, Mintching Wood, Bluetown. Shot down by Me109's crashing in flames. F/O M. Homer killed. Based Coltishall.   Cat 3

1125.   Spitfire I, X4352 **19**
Coldred (nr Dover). Shot down by Me109's over Canterbury. P/O E. Burgoyne killed. Based Duxford.   Cat 3

1126.   Hurricane I, V6576 **242**
nr Sandwich. Force landed with engine trouble and finally on fire after combat over Dover. F/L G. Ball unhurt. Based Coltishall.
                                              Cat 2

1127.   Spitfire I, N3244 **603**
Folkestone, ¼ mile off. Pilot believed wounded in combat with Me109's over the Channel. He attempted to regain the Kent coast but had to abandon over the sea and his 'chute failed to open. He was picked up later. P/O Cardell killed. Based Hornchurch.
                                              Cat 3

1128.   Spitfire I, X4250 **603**
Folkestone beach. Force landed in an attempt to rescue P/O Cardell. P/O Dexter unhurt, commandeered a boat but only succeeded in picking up the dead body. Based Hornchurch.   Cat 3

1129.   Me109E4, 1447 **6/JG27**
Maidstone, Hales Fm, Eccles. Exploded in mid-air over Aylesford after combat with 19Sq (Blake). Uffz Schiedt killed. Based Sempy (?).

Sublt A.G. Blake, RN
Joined 19Sq on 1st July 1940 to fly Spitfires from Duxford. On the 9th he shot down a He111H3 of 3/KG1 over N.E. London at 1750hrs followed by a Me109E on the 15th. In the latter attack his own aircraft was damaged but he force landed uninjured. He also shared a He111 on that day. The 17th saw him add another Me109E1 W.N. 1228 and a second W.N. 5141 both from 9/JG53 to the East of London. At 1231hrs the Me109 in the above incident and yet another unidentified Me109.

He was killed in action on the 29th at 1650hrs flying over Chelmsford having, in four short weeks, more than made his mark.

1130.   Me109E1, 3431, 3 + **5/JG52**
High Halden, Brick House Fm. Shot down during a forward sweep over the Estuary and crashed. Fw H. Hoffmann baled out POW. Based Peuplingues.

1131.   Spitfire I, R6755 **41**
nr W. Malling. Shot down during a squadron patrol and burned out. F/L E. Ryder baled out unhurt. Based Hornchurch.   Cat 3

1132.   Me109E1, 3907, 8 + **II/JG52**
Hollingbourne, Broad Street. Crash landed after being damaged by (?) 66Sq (Allen). Oblt C. Treiber wounded and POW. Based Peuplingues.

1133.   Hurricane I, P3756 **46**
Rochester a/f. Force landed with engine trouble after combat with the Lw over North Kent. P/O Mrazek unhurt. Based Stapleford Tawney.   Cat 2

1134.   Me109E1, 6245 **4/JG52**
Petham. Shot down by the R.A.F. during a free-lance sweep. Lt H. Geist POW. Based Peuplingues.

1135.   Ju88A1, 5103, 3Z + CL **3/KG77**
Horsmonden, Hononton Park. Shot down whilst en route for London, crashing and burning. Uffz Damerius, Hastrich and Merschen killed; Uffz Ludwig wounded and POW, Sgts Cameron and Parson of 66Sq both claimed this a/c at the same time. Based Laon-Couvron.

1136.   Me109E4, 5181 **4/JG52**
St Nicholas-at-Wade, Morrison House Fm. Shot down by the R.A.F. whilst it was on a free-lance sweep over Kent. Fw F. Bogasch made a POW. Based Peuplingues.

1137.   Spitfire I, P9519 **66**
nr Orpington. Hit by own A.A. during an attack on a Ju88 (which crashed) and had to force land. P/O G. Corbett unhurt.   Cat 3

1138.   Ju88A1, 4118, 3Z + DP **6/KG77**
Sevenoaks, Seal. Shot down as above. Oblt Seif, Fw Eichinger and Uffz Gebhardt killed. Fw Zinsmeister wounded POW. Based Asche.

1139.   Ju88A1, 0293, 3Z + DC **II/KG77**
(?) Penshurst, Vexour Fm. Shot down by A.A. and R.A.F. Oblt Lutze, Fw Adler and Zeller killed; Uffz Brodbeck made POW. Based Asche.

1140.   Ju88A1, 8099, 3Z + EL **3/KG77**
Faversham, Graveney Marsh. Force landed after being attacked by the R.A.F. Uffz Ruhlandt, E. Richter, G. Richter and Gefr Reiner all POW's. Based Laon-Couvron.

1141.   Me109E1, 3442, 12 + **4/JG52**
Sandwich, Northbourne Park. Severely damaged by the R.A.F. with the result that it hit H.T. cables. Gfr E. Bosch wounded and made POW. Based Peuplingues.

1142.   Spitfire I, R6622 **92**
Dartford, Hesketh Park. Shot down by Me109's and crashed exploding on impact. Sgt T.G. Oldfield killed. Based Biggin Hill.
                                        Cat 3

1143.   Spitfire I, R6760 **92**
Biggin Hill (Base). Crashed on landing with combat damage. Sgt H. Bowen-Morris unhurt.   Cat 2

1144.   Hurricane I, V6622 **249**
W. Malling. On patrol over the Estuary with 46Sq when they intercepted 12 × Ju88's. This a/c was shot down by their defensive fire when south of London. P/O Barclay unhurt. Based North Weald.   Cat 2

1145.   Spitfire I, P9364 **222**
Hollingbourne, Greenway Court. Cause not known, but it failed to return from a sortie. Sgt E. Scott missing. Based Hornchurch.
                                        Cat 3

1146.   Me109E1, 3217 **9/JG3**
Selling, Owen Court Fm. Shot down by the R.A.F. Uffz Struwe believed baled out to be a POW. Based Desevres.

1147. **28.9.40**   Hurricane I, V7497 **501**
E. Sutton, Parsonage Fm. Attacked by Me109's over Deal and shot down, crashing and burning out. P/O E. Rogers baled out wounded. Based Kenley.   Cat 3

1148.   Hurricane I, P3417 **501**
Ulcombe, Strawberry Plantation, College House. Shot down by Me109's. P/O Harrold killed. Based Kenley.   Cat 3

1149.   Spitfire I, X4409 **41**
Chilham, East Stour Fm. Whilst over Charing was shot down by Me109's, exploding over the farm. The engine was 300yds north of the buildings. P/O H. Chalder baled out seriously wounded to die in hospital on 10.11.40. Based Hornchurch.   Cat 3

1150.   Spitfire I, L1076 **603**
Gillingham, Brompton Barracks. F/L H.K. Macdonald was killed when Me109's shot down this aircraft. Based Hornchurch. Cat 3

1151.   Spitfire I, X4426 **41**
Lynsted, Erriotts Fm, Dadmans. Shot up over Charing and F/O J. Boyle killed. Based Hornchurch.   Cat 3

1152.   Spitfire I, X4345 **41**
Pluckley. Crash landed after being shot up in the above incident. P/O E. Aldous slightly injured.   Cat 3

1153.   Hurricane I, P3828 **605**
Lamberhurst, Bewl Bridge. Attacked by Me109's, aircraft crashed. P/O R. Hope baled out landing at Ticehurst. Based Croydon.   Cat 3

1154.   Hurricane I, V6617 **249**
Sittingbourne, Blacketts Fm. Shot down over Faversham. P/O A.G. Lewis baled out badly burnt and hospitalised. Based Hornchurch.
                                        Cat 3

1155. **29.9.40**   Spitfire, N3035 **66(?)**
Gravesend (Base). Force landed following combat with enemy fighters. Sgt P. Willcocks wounded.   Cat 2

1156.   **30.9.40**   Me109E4, 3447   **II/JG2**
Channel. Failed to return from action with the R.A.F. Gfr Schumacher missing. Based Mardyck or Oye Plage.

1157.   Me109E4, 0847   **2/JG2**
Channel. As above. Pilot Fw Hermes missing. Based Mardyck or Audembert.

1158.   Do17Z3, 4227, 5K + HR   **8/KG3**
Was shot down whilst on a bombing attack over the S.E. Presumably by the R.A.F. Fw Bauer, Salomo and Schierling + Uffz Schonn and Schroff all missing. Based St Trond.

1159.   Ju88A1, 3067, 4D + BZ   **IV/KG30**
As above. Oblt Richter, Fw Laege, and Uffz Fuchs missing (4th member of crew?). Based Gilze-Rijen.

1160.   Me109E1, 4820   **9/JG26**
Thames Estuary. Shot down by (?) 66Sq. Gfr H. Hornatschek killed. Based Caffiers.

1161.   Hurricane I, L1657   **501**
Hawkenbury, Little Bayhall Farm. Force landed following combat with Me109's over Maidstone. F/O N. Barry unhurt. Based Kenley.   Cat 2

1162.   Hurricane I, N2652   **229**
Ightham Place. After combat over Edenbridge P/O N. Stansfield had to bale out slightly wounded. Based Northolt.   Cat 3

1163.   Hurricane I, P2815   **229**
Ightham, Church Road. As above F/O M. Ravenhill killed.   Cat 3

1164.   Hurricane I, P3227, RE-R   **229**
Hartley, Ash. Damaged in the above combat. P/O F. Robshaw slightly wounded. Cat 2

1165.   Me109E1, 3391   **7/JG51**
Leigh, Kennards Fm. Shot down by the R.A.F. Flgr K. Hubel killed. Based St Omer or St Quentin.

1166.   Me109E1, 5116   **9/JG54**
Tonbridge, east of Golden Grn. Shot down and claimed by 66Sq (Oxspring) crashing and burning. Uffz Braatz killed. Based Sempy.

1167.   Me109E, 3417   **4/JG52**
Detling a/f. Whilst on bomber escort duty was shot up over the Estuary by the R.A.F. Gfr E. Mummert unhurt and POW. Based Peuplingues.

1168.   Me109E, 5175   **7/JG52**
nr Strood. Severely damaged by the R.A.F. during an escort sortie and had to crash land. Uffz Poschenrieder seriously injured and made POW. Based Sempy.

1169.   Hurricane I, P3663   **303**
Lydd on beach. Whilst on a combat patrol over mid Channel was damaged by Me109's and had to force land as soon as he crossed the coast. P/O J. Radomski uninjured. Based Northolt.   Cat 2

1170.   Me109
Canterbury. Tyler Hill, Honey Wood. This a/c blew up, some of the wreckage fell on the Artillery Barracks and Old Park Fm. (May have been the Me109 in Incident 1160.)

1171.   Hurricane I, R4112   **229**
nr Lydd. Force landed after being hit by return fire from a Do215(?) formation whilst making a solo attack. P/O V. Ortmans unhurt. Based Northolt.   Cat 2

P/O V.M. Ortmans
Served with the Royal Belgian Air Force, flying Fairey Foxes before the War.
    After his country's fall he made his way through France and Spain to Gibraltar. On arrival in the U.K. he was posted to 229Sq and had his first success in 17.9.40.
    In October 1941 he was shot down, becoming a POW but not before he was credited with 7 victories and 2 probables. Included in these successes was Hptm Balthaser of JG2, one of the top scoring Lw aces.
    He survived the war, but like so many was killed in a flying accident.

1172.   Spitfire I, P9394   **41**
Hawkinge. Force landed after combat with engine trouble over Dungeness. Sgt R. Beardsley unhurt. Based Hornchurch. Cat 2

1173.   Hurricane I, P3037   **229**
'Over Kent'. Abandoned during a squadron patrol, believed shot down. P/O L. Way unhurt after baling out. Based Northolt.
    Cat 3
(It is hard to understand this vagueness when the pilot was unhurt.)

1174.   Hurricane I, (?)V7411   **229**
As above, Sgt C. Hodson force landed slightly injured.   Cat 2

1175.   **1.10.40** Me109E4, 5814, 9 +   **1/JG51**
Shadoxhurst, Chequers. Shot down by 41Sq (P/O Lovell) over Ashford. Uffz Garnith baled out to be a POW. Based St Omer-Longuenesse.

1176.   **2.10.40**
    Me109E4, 5901, 7 + 1   **8/JG53**
E. Peckham, Addlested Fm. Crash landed after an attack by 603Sq (Hartas). Oblt Fiel unhurt, POW. Based Sempy.

1177.   Me109E4,5374   **8/JG53**
Biggin Hill, Sutherland Avenue. Shot down by the RAF over the southern outskirts of London. Oblt Stronk killed. Based Sempy.

1178.   Me109E4, 6370   **8/JG53**
Goudhurst, Forge Fm. Shot down by (?)603Sq (Dexter) whilst on a bombing raid escort and had to force land. Gfr Zag made a POW.

1179.   **4.10.40**   Ju88A1, 6116   **II/LG1**
off Dungeness. Shot down by 605Sq (Currant and Milne) over the Channel. Gfr Jahn and Schoeffmann killed; Uffz Kirchbauer and Kross missing. Based Cambrai-Epinoy.

1180.   **5.10.40**   Blenheim IV, R2771 **53**
Manston. Crashed in circuit and burned, whilst attempting a force landing. P/O K.A. Faulkner and Sgt Fielder seriously injured; Sgt Hall killed. Based Detling.

1181.   Hurricane I, P3873 **1RCAF**
Smarden, Dering Fm. Shot down by the Lw over Canterbury. F/O P.O.H. de Molson baled out wounded and was admitted to hospital. Based Northolt.   Cat 3

1182.   Me110, 3382, S9+FH **1/EproGr210**
Lympne. Shot down by (?) 303Sq over S.E. England. Oblt Weimann (Gruppe Kdr) and Uffz Hübner missing. Based Calais-Marck.

1183.   Me110(?)   **EproGr210**
nr Lympne. Shot down by Sgt Belc (303Sq).

1184.   Spitfire I, X4544 **72**
Biggin Hill (Base). Was in mid-air collision with K9989 soon after take off. Sgt R. Staples unhurt.   Cat 2

1185.   Spitfire I, K9989 **72**
Farnborough, Kent. Crashed and burned. P/O N. Sutton killed.   Cat 3

1186.   Spitfire I, K9935 **72**
Biggin Hill (Base). Damaged by Me109's in action over the Channel and returned to base. F/S J. Steere unhurt.   Cat 2

1187.   Spitfire I, N3285 **66**
Gravesend (Base). Force landed at base after being damaged by enemy fighters over Tenterden. P/O C. Bodie unhurt.   Cat 2

1188.   Spitfire I, X4543 **66**
As above, Sgt B. Wright unhurt.   Cat 2

1189.
Me110D3, 3383, S9+GH **1/EproGr210**
Ashford, Millbank Place, Kingsnorth. Shot down by (?) 303Sq. Fw Duesnig and Keppitsch killed. Based Calais-Marck.

1190.   Me109E4, 1564, 3+ **1/JG53**
Pluckley, Sheerlands Fm. Crashed and burned after combat with 501Sq Hurricanes. Lt Zeis baled out unhurt (also reptd shot down by 41Sq Bamberger). Based Coquelles or Etaples.

1191.   Me109E4, 1804, 10+ **1/JG53**
Aldington, W. of Frith Fm. Shot down by 41Sq (Mileham). It belly landed with Uffz Gehsla slightly wounded to be a POW.

1192.   Spitfire I, X4473 **66**
Detling a/f. Force landed after being shot up over Tenterden. P/O J. Kendal slightly injured but needed hospitalisation. Based Gravesend.   Cat 2

1193.   Spitfire I, K9807 **603**
Chilham. Was abandoned over Dover after being attacked by Me109's. P/O J. Morton baled out burnt. Based Hornchurch.   Cat 3

1194.   Hurricane I, P3892 **303**
Lyminge, Stowting. Crashed in flames after combat with Me109's. F/O W. Januszewicz killed. Based Northolt.   Cat 3

1195.   Me109E1, 4865, 2+ **1/JG3**
Bethersden, Runsell Fm. Shot down by (?) 41Sq (Lock), crashing and burning out. Fw von Herwarth-Bittenfeld baled out wounded, and badly burnt to be a POW. Based Guines or Coulommiers.

1196.   **6.10.40**   Spitfire I, K9940 **72**
Biggin Hill (Base). Severely damaged during a bombing raid on the airfield.   Cat 2

1197.   **7.10.40**   Hurricane I, P2993 **1RCAF**
Biggin Hill. Force landed after being badly damaged by a Me109E. F/O Nesbitt unhurt. Based Northolt.   Cat 2

1198.   Hurricane I, V6800 **501**
Darenth. Shot up by Me109's over Wrotham. F/O N. Barry fell to earth dead at Wilmington. Based Kenley.   Cat 3

1199.   Spitfire I, N3109 **603**
Godmersham, Hurst Fm. Shot down by II/JG26. F/O H.K. Matthews killed. Based Hornchurch.   Cat 3

1200.   Spitfire I, N3267 **41**
Folkestone, Postling. Shot up by Me109's. P/O D.A. Adams baled out unhurt. Based Hornchurch.   Cat 3

1201.   Me109E
Eastry, Thornton Fm. Aircraft written off. Cause unknown. Pilot made POW. See 1221 9.10.40.

1202.   Hurricane I, P3089 **303**
Rochester, Borstal. On a decoy a/f, crashed and burned out whilst attempting a forced landing. P/O B. Mierzwa unhurt. Based Northolt.   Cat 3

1203.   Hurricane I, P3620 **257**
Horton Kirby. Force landed for unknown reasons. P/O S.E. Andrews unhurt. Based Martlesham Heath.   Cat ?

1204.   Hurricane I, P3677 **605**
Sevenoaks, Park Fm, Brasted. Shot up by Me109's over Westerham. P/O C. English killed. Based Croydon.   Cat 3

1205.   Me109E1, 3665, 10+ **5/JG27**
Goudhurst, Bedgebury Wood. Shot down by 605Sq Hurricanes whilst it was on an escort mission for 4/LG2 Jabos, and had to force land. Uffz Lederer wounded POW. Based Sempy.

1206.   Hurricane I, V7305 **605**
Bexley. Crashed and burned after combat over London. P/O I.J. Muirhead baled out unhurt. Based Croydon.   Cat 3

1207.   Spitfire I, X4326 **66**
Gravesend (Base). Damaged in combat and force landed. P/O H.M. Heron unhurt. Cat 2

1208.   Me109E4, 0751 **9/JG27**
Headcorn, Oak Fm. Shot down by fighters over London. Uffz Bartsch made POW. Based Guines or Senon.

70

1209.   Me109E4, 5566   **4/LG2**
Tunbridge Wells, Spa G.C. Shot down by (?)
603Sq (Carbury). Uffz Moerschel wounded
and POW. This was a fighter bomber. Based
St Omer-Fort Rouge.

1210.   Me109E4, 4853   **2/JG51**
Sandgate, 2 miles off. Shot down by S/L
Hogan and P/O McKenzie (501Sq) whilst it
was acting as escort to the above Jabo raid.
Lt E. Meyer was picked from the sea and
made a POW. (Remains of the wing, fuselage and engine are on display at the Kent B.
of B. Museum, Hawkinge. Based Pihen or
Wissant.

1211.   Me109E4, 5391, +A   **4/LG2**
Greatstone, 2 miles off. Another Jabo victim
for the R.A.F. The wreck was located and
marked for a possible recovery effort in the
future. The pilot Uffz Bley was saved by the
Dungeness L.B. to be a POW. Based St
Omer-Fort Rouge.

1212.   Hurricane I, V6799   **501**
Folkestone - Capel le Ferne. The pilot had to
force land after ramming a Me109 which
also crashed. P/O K.W. McKenzie was
picked up. (This may have been Me109E
Werke Nr 4853 in Incident 1210.)   Cat 2

1213.   **8.10.40**   Spitfire I, R6779   **66**
Upchurch, Bayford Marsh. Bounced by
Me109's at 20000ft over the Medway falling
in flames. P/O G. Corbett killed. Based
Gravesend.   Cat 3

1214.   Spitfire I, K9847   **72**
Sevenoaks, Halstead, Force landed as a
result of engine failure. Sgt N. Glew unhurt.
Based Biggin Hill.   Cat 2

1215.   Spitfire   **72**
Biggin Hill (Base). Damaged in combat with
enemy fighters. Pilot unhurt.   Cat 2

1216.   Spitfire   **72**
Biggin Hill. As above.

(The details missing were not included in the
unit's F.541. If a check is made through the
details in this work referring to units stationed at Biggin Hill, the reader may feel
that relevant facts are too often missing
from the records. If so the responsibility for
this must rest with the Intelligence staff of
the station and squadrons.)

1217.   Spitfire I, N3043   **66**
Rochester, Valley View Road, Borstal. In
combat over the Medway was shot down by
a Me109E. Sgt R. Ward baled out but was
killed. Based Gravesend.   Cat 3

1218.   Me109E4, 1656   **4/JG3**
Channel, 1½ miles SW Abbot's Cliff, nr
Folkestone. Shot down by the R.A.F. during
a sortie to London, and ditched severely
damaged. Oblt Voigt made POW. Based
Colombert or Samer.

1219.   **9.10.40**
                 Ju88A5, 0311, 4D + EP   **6/KG30**
Thames Estuary. Failed to return from ops.
over S.E. England. Shot down by (?) 1Sq
(Davies and Pilkington (?)). The crew of 4
NCO's missing. Based Gilze-Rijen.

1220.   Me109E4, 1573   **9/JG54**
off Dover, 10m. Shot down by 41Sq (?)
(Walker) over the town. Lt Eberle killed.
Based Guines.

1221.   Me109E4, 0966   **1/JG77**
Eastry, Vensons Fm. The pilot's dinghy accidentally inflated in the cockpit in a way
which caused him to lose control and it
crashed. Lt Escherhaus uninjured and made
a POW. Based St Omer.

1222.   Spitfire I, X4597   **92**
Ashford, Smeeth, The Ridgeway. Shot down
by Me109's. Sgt E. Frith baled out badly
burnt, dying in hospital on the 17th. Based
Biggin Hill.   Cat 3

1223.   Me109E4, 5327, 6+   **7/JG54**
Hawkinge, west of. Meridan Hunt Fm. Damaged in combat with 222Sq (F/O E. Thomas)
whilst it was itself attacking a 41Sq aircraft
over Chatham. Forced to land. Fw Schweser
set the wreckage of his aircraft alight before
becoming a POW. Based Guines.
(There are reports of this crash at other sites.
Parts of aircraft are at the Kent B. of B.
Museum, Hawkinge.)

1224.   **10.10.40**
                 Spitfire IIA, P7446   **421Flt**
Gravesend (Base). Sustained damage from
20mm cannon fire and had to force land.
The controls had also been damaged by
excessive evasive action. Sgt M.A. Lee
unhurt.   Cat 2
(Some of the unit's aircraft on 'Jim Crow'
sorties were unarmed. This might account
for the excessive evasive action.)

1225.   Me109E1, 4143   **4/JG53**
off Ramsgate. Failed to return from ops. Probably shot down by 603Sq (Carbury). Oblt
Vogel (Staffel Kapt) missing. Based Denain-
Prouvy.

1226.   Hurricane I, V7537   **249**
Cooling Marshes, Shades House. Crashed
during a routine patrol, hitting two cottages
and killing three civilians. Possibly due to
anoxia. Sgt Bayley killed. Based North
Weald.   Cat 3

1227.   Hurricane I, L1928   **253**
Maidstone, Albion Place. Crashed into a
house. Cause unknown. Sgt H.H. Allgood
killed. Based Kenley.   Cat 3

1228.   **11.10.40**   Spitfire I, K9870   **72**
Sittingbourne, Milton Regis. Shot up by
Me109 and fell in flames whilst on a convoy
escort off Deal. P/O P. Poole baled out
wounded. Based Biggin Hill.   Cat 3

1229.   Spitfire I, N3121 **66**
Eastchurch, Newhook. Crashed in poor visibility. Sgt P. Willcocks unhurt. Based Gravesend.   Cat 2

1230.   Spitfire I, R6777 **72**
Biggin Hill (Base). Involved in a taxying accident prior to take off. Sgt N. Glew unhurt.
                                   Cat 2

1231.   Hurricane I, V6676 **73**
Strood, Dillywood, Frindsbury. Shot down whilst acting as a weaver. Sgt R. Plenderleith baled out slightly burnt and was admitted to hospital. Based Debden.   Cat 3

1232.   Spitfire I, X4562 **66**
Elham, Covert Wood. Shot down by Me109E possibly Maj Mölders (Geschwader Kmde) JG51 in combat over Canterbury. P/O J. Pickering injured and in hospital. Based Gravesend.   Cat 3

1233.   Spitfire I, X4255 **66**
Hawkinge. Crash landed after its oil tank exploded over the Channel, whilst in the process of chasing a Me109E was itself attacked by Maj Mölders. P/O H. Allen severely concussed. Based Kenley.   Cat 3

1234.   Hurricane I, V6570 **253**
nr Tunbridge Wells. Shot down in combat for the third time in the Battle, P/O L.C. Murch baled out and was hospitalised with a broken arm. Based Kenley.   Cat 3

1235.   Spitfire IIA, P7303 **421Flt**
nr Newchurch. Shot down by Lw fighters and crashed. Sgt C. Ayling killed. (The unit's F.541 has this crash at Hawkinge.) Based Gravesend.   Cat ?

1236.   Me109E, 6267 **5/JG27**
off Deal. Shot down by (?) 41Sq. Uffz Wiemann wounded and picked up by Seenotflkdo. Based Sempy.

1237.   Hurricane I, L1666 **253**
Staplehurst, Pagehurst (a pre-War A.L.G.). Made a forced landing after an interception patrol. Cause not known. Sgt R. Innes (?) unhurt. Based Kenley.   Cat 2

1238.   Spitfire I, P9447 **41**
Eastchurch, Gt Bells Fm. Shot down by Me109's. P/O J. Lecky baled out but was killed. This site was dug and a helmet marked 'Lecky' found. Based Hornchurch.
                                   Cat 3
(Also reptd at Preston Hall, nr Maidstone.)

1239.   Spitfire I, X4554 **41**
West Kingsdown, South Ash Manor. Collided with X4052 during a climb to intercept an enemy. Sgt L.R. Carter baled out unhurt. Based Hornchurch.   Cat 3

1240.   Spitfire I, X4052 **41**
Wrotham, Crooked Billet, Ash. As above. F/O O'Neil baled out but his 'chute failed to open and he was killed.   Cat 3

1242. **12.10.40**   Me109E4, 5256 **4/JG52**
Sheerness. Shot down by fighters over the Estuary. Uffz Reichenbach killed. Based Peuplingues.

1243.   Me109E7, 5793 **2/LG2**
off Kent Coast. Failed to return from a sortie over the Channel. Probably shot down by 92Sq (Tuck). Pilot killed. Based Calais.

1244.   Spitfire I, P9338 **72**
Capel le Ferne. Lost formation and crashed for unknown causes. P/O H. Case killed. Based Biggin Hill.   Cat 3

1245.   Hurricane I, P3755 (?) **257**
Detling a/f. Force landed with aircraft damaged during combat with Me109's over Deal. P/O K. Gundry slightly injured by 20mm shell splinters. (Also reported as hit by own A.A. over Dungeness.) Based N. Weald.
                                   Cat 2

1246.   Hurricane I, P6555 **257**
Sellling, Saffrey's Fm. Force landed after combat over Deal. P/O J. Redman unhurt.
                                   Cat 2

1247.   Hurricane I, V7313 **249**
Wickhambreux. Shot down. Adj G. Perrin (FFAF) baled out slightly injured and admitted to hospital. Based N. Weald.
                                   Cat 3

1248.   Me109E4, 4869 **StabII/JG54**
Tenterden, Small Hythe Chapel Holding. Shot down by F/L S. Tuck (92Sq) during action over Kent and had to force land. Lt Malischewski made a POW. Based Hermalinghen.

1249.   Hurricane I, V7426 **145**
Cranbrook, Coursehorn Fm, Chittenden. Shot up by Me109's over Hastings. Sgt J. Wadham killed. Based Tangmere.   Cat 3

1250.   Hurricane I, P3022 **605**
New Romney, Littlestone G.C. Shot up by the Lw over Dungeness. Sgt P. McIntosh killed. Based Croydon.   Cat 3

1251.   Spitfire IIA, P7441 **421Flt**
Boughton Malherbe. Whilst on patrol from Gravesend at 30000ft shadowing enemy aircraft was attacked by a Me109E and the pilot wounded in the neck and arm, whilst the controls were shot away. He struggled to open the canopy whilst falling to 1000ft. He eventually escaped to open his 'chute at only 700ft. F/L C.P. Green landed at Pembles Cross where he was found by Army personnel. Based Gravesend.   Cat 3

421 Flight
When new tactics were thought up it was often the practice to form a small flight to investigate them operationally, later forming it into a squadron if successful.
    This flight was set up for reconnaissance over the French Channel ports; to shadow enemy air formations as a back up for the radar chain; and to watch for enemy shipping movements. It also had a secondary

function of search and protection for A.S.R. units. As such it was known in the Service as a 'Jim Crow' unit. When first formed it had four Hurricanes and borrowed Spitfires from 66Sq which was its parent unit. Later it received its own Spitfires which were coloured P.R.U. blue (almost Navy blue).

To enhance performance their finish was highly polished. In some cases armament was stripped out.

In January 1941 they were brought up to full strength and re-numbered 91 Squadron.

It is of interest to note that a similar flight No.422 was formed at R.A.F. Shoreham in an endeavour to develop single engined night fighters.

1252. Me109E3, 1966 **1/JG52**
Harrietsham, Deans Hill. Shot down by (?) the R.A.F. whilst it was on a sortie over Kent. Oblt Buesgen (Staffel Kapt) baled out uninjured to be a POW. Based Laon.

1253. Me109E, 4132 **2/JG52**
Hollingbourne, Chantry Fm. Shot down whilst escorting Jabos to London. Oblt Sauer baled out slightly wounded. Based Laon-Couvron.

1254. Me109E, 5283, 3 + **3/JG52**
Brabourne Down, Weekes Lane. Abandoned after being attacked by the R.A.F. Also on escort duties. Fw Voss baled out uninjured.

1255. Spitfire I, X4591 **92**
Folkestone, Bartholomews Wood, Postling. Shot down by Lw fighters whilst over Hawkinge. F/O A.J.S. Pattinson killed. He had been briefed to patrol Maidstone and the A20. Based Biggin Hill. Cat 3

1256. Hurricane I, V7298 **257**
Wittersham, High House Fm, Stone. Shot up by Me109's over Dungeness. P/O C. Capon baled out slightly wounded. (Confirmed by an eye witness.) Based N. Weald. Cat 3

1257. 13.10.40 Hurricane I, P3536 **17**
Rochester, river Bank. Shot down by own A.A. during a squadron patrol over Chatham. P/O J. Rose baled out wounded and was hospitalised. Based Debden. Cat 3

1258. Me109E4, 0860, 7 + 1 **7/JG3**
Hastingleigh, Cuckold Coombe. Force landed after being attacked by 66Sq (Oxspring) during a chase across Kent. It had been part of a Jabo escort, and was sighted at 31000ft over Maidstone.

F/L Oxspring made a diving attack with only half his guns working and with severe icing on the canopy. Fw Rungen was made a POW (also claimed by F/L Kingcome of 92Sq). Based Desevres.

1259. Spitfire I, N3285 **66**
Gravesend (Base). Damaged during an attack on Me109's over Maidstone and forced to return to base. P/O C. Bodie unhurt. Cat 2

1260. Spitfire I, X4479 **66**
Rochester, nr Halling Ferry. Force landed damaged after the Maidstone combat. S/L R. Leigh unhurt. Based Gravesend. Cat 2

1261. Hurricane I **46**
Biggin Hill. Force landed after an attack on Me109's over Dungeness. Sgt L.H. Pearce wounded. Based Stapleford Tawney. Cat 2

1262. 14.10.40 Me109E
Sandwich Bay. This aircraft fell into the sea and not located. The pilot was picked up and became a POW.

1263. 15.10.40 Hurricane I, R2684 **302**
Wrotham. Force landed due to engine trouble. P/O J. Malinski unhurt. Based Northolt. Cat 2

1264. Hurricane I, V6756 **253**
Dunton Green. Severely damaged in combat. Sgt E.H. Kee unhurt. Based Kenley. Cat 2

1265. Spitfire I, X4418 **92**
High Halstow, Wybornes Fm. Was shot up in combat over the Estuary by Me109's. F/L C.B. Kingcome baled out wounded and was admitted to hospital. Based Biggin Hill. Cat ?

1266. Spitfire I, X4178 **41**
Thames Estuary. Shot down by Hptm Föcö of 4/JG51. Sgt P. Lloyd killed, his body being washed up near Herne Bay 27.10.40. Based Hornchurch. Cat 3

1267. Me109E1, 3535 **4/JG51**
Lamberhurst, Owl Castle Fm. Shot down by 92Sq (Fokes) over Kent. Uffz Hoehn baled out and became a POW. Based Desevres or Marquise.

1268. Me109E4, 1294, 7 + 1 **8/JG3**
Sandwich, Princes G.C. Damaged by 229Sq (Brown) whilst on a free-lance fighter sortie and had to force land. Obfw Bauer unhurt. POW. Based Desevres.

1269. Me109E7, 3734 **StabI/LG2**
Elham, Spruce Lawns. The aircraft exploded during a Jabo mission, probably shot down by 92Sq (Sgt Kingaby). Lt L. Lenz dead. Based Calais-Marck.

1270. Hurricane I, (?)P3124 **229**
Stockbury, South Street Fm. Shot down in flames by Me109's and crashed into the farm buildings. S/L A. Banham baled out burnt. Based Northolt. Cat 3

1271. Spitfire I, R6838 **92**
off Hoo Marina. Shot up by Me109's over the Estuary. Sgt K. Parker killed. Based Biggin Hill. Cat 3

1272. Spitfire IIA, P7444 **421Flt**
Broadoak, Blaxland Fm. Damaged in combat with enemy fighters and crashed attempting a force landing. Sgt M.A. Lee wounded and hospitalised. Based Gravesend. Cat 2

1273.   Hurricane I, N2546 **605**
Gillingham, Darland, Spekes Bottom. Shot
down by Me109's over the town. F/L I. Muirhead killed. Based Croydon.   Cat 3

1274.   Hurricane I, P2752 **302**
High Halstow, Stoke. Shot up and burned
as a result of fighter action over Chatham
Sgt Wedzik baled out and was hospitalised.
Based Northolt.   Cat 3

1275.   Spitfire I, R6642 **92**
off Kent Reach, Bee Ness Jetty. Shot down
by enemy fighters. P/O J. Lund baled out
and was picked up by HMS Nysan. Based
Biggin Hill.   Cat 3

1276.   Hurricane I, V7351 **257**
Hawkinge a/f. Force landed after an engage-
ment with Me109's. P/O G. North unhurt.
Based North Weald.   Cat 2

1277.   Me109E4, 2790 **8/JG27**
Ashford, Trimworth Manor, Olantigh. Shot
down by the R.A.F. Oblt Deicke (Staffel
Kapt) baled out and was POW. Based
Guines or Senon.
(This site was dug post-war and the wreck
found at 18ft deep.)

1278.   Hurricane I, V6787 **501**
Rochester a/f. Force landed with a glycol
leak as a result of combat over Sheppey.
F/O R. Dafforn unhurt. Based Kenley. Cat 2

1279.   Spitfire I, L1089 **222**
Hougham. Force landed out of fuel and
damaged by a Me109E. Sgt J.T. Dunmore
unhurt. Based Hornchurch.   Cat ?

1280.   Hurricane I, V6550 **46**
Gravesend, Albion Parade. Shot up over the
Estuary by Me109's. F/S E. Williams missing.
Based Stapleford Tawney.   Cat 3

1281. Spitfire I(?), (?) P7446 or X6412 **421Flt**
Gravesend (Base)(?). Force landed with a
seized engine due to big end failure. P/O
Lawrence unhurt.   Cat 2

1282.   Hurricane I, V6789 **46**
Gravesend G.C. Abandoned over the Estu-
ary following combat with Me109's. Sgt A.
Gooderham baled out slightly burnt. Based
Stapleford Tawney.   Cat 3

1283. **16.10.40**   Hurricane I, V6878 **249**
Rolvenden. Force landed after being hit by
return fire from Do17's or 215's. P/O K. Lofts
unhurt. Based North Weald.   Cat 2

1284. **17.10.40**   Hampden I, L4195 **49**
Hollingbourne - Lenham. Crashed in poor
visibility on return from operations in the
Bordeaux area. (Probably sea mine laying.)
Sgt R. Potter W/Opr killed; P/O Evans, Sgt
Molyneux and LAC Glover all injured. Based
Scampton.   Cat 3

1285.   Hurricane I, P3537 **253**
Yalding, Gains Hill. Crashed due to engine
failure. P/O T. Nowak unhurt. Based Kenley.
                                       Cat 3

1286.   Hurricane I, LZ-V **421Flt**
Detling a/f. Force landed with a seized
engine following violent evasive action to
escape from attacks by Me109's. Sgt A.W.
Spears unhurt. Based Gravesend.   Cat 2

1287.   Hurricane I, Z2312, LZ-O **421Flt**
Gravesend (Base). Crashed on landing after
combat with Me109's which caused severe
damage. F/S J. Gillies injured.   Cat 2

1288.   Spitfire I, R6800, LZ-N **66**
Sevenoaks, Crockham Hill. Shot up by Maj
Mölders (Kmde of JG51), P/O H. Reilley
killed. Based Gravesend.   Cat 3
(At this time 66Squadron and 421 Flight
were both using 'LZ' as squadron a/c codes.)

P/O H.W. Reilley
A citizen of the U.S.A. flying with the R.A.F.
and one of the two Americans killed in the
Battle of Britain, the other being William
Fiske.

1289.   Me109E7, 4138 **I/JG53**
Channel. Shot down by the R.A.F. maybe
222Sq (McMullan). Hptm Mayer (Gruppe
Kdr) killed. Based Coquelles or Etaples.

1290.   Spitfire II, P7360 **74**
nr Hollingbourne. Shot down by Lw from
20000ft after scrambling from Biggin Hill.
F/O A. Ricalton killed. Based Biggin Hill.
                                       Cat 3

1291.   Me109E4, 1106 **3/JG53**
Manston. After being attacked over the
Estuary by P/O Draper (74Sq) Oblt Rupp
belly landed unhurt with a severely damaged aircraft. Based Coquelles.

1292.   Hurricane I, P3174 **213**
Pluckley, Weeks Fm, Egerton. Shot down by
enemy fighters and P/O Atkinson killed.
Based Tangmere.   Cat 3

1293.   Hurricane I, V6866 **213**
Tenterden. Shot up by enemy aircraft at
20000ft and had to force land. Sgt Stevens
unhurt. Based Tangmere.   Cat 2

1294.   Hurricane I, V6735 **302**
nr Sittingbourne. Force landed, causes not
known. P/O Kleczkowski unhurt. Based Northolt.   Cat 2

1295. **18.10.40**
             Ju88A1, 8050, L1+NT **III/LG1**
over Kent. Failed to return after a mission to
bomb London. Shot down by (?) 229Sq (Ortmans and Bright). The crew of 4 N.C.O.'s
missing. Uffz G. Battre, Obgfr H. Pfeiffer,
Gfr K. Donner and F. Rohmer. Based
Chateaudun.

1296.   Ju88A1, 7160, 9K+EC **II/KG51**
As above. Shot down by the R.A.F. Hptm H.
von Claer, Lt J. Sonntag, Obfw A. Stegmuller
and Fw H. Marte all missing. Based Paris-
Orly.

74

Incident No. 1307. Obfw W. Friedmann crashed at Welling whilst on a fighter-bomber sortie to London.
(Bexley Libraries)

1297. Hurricane I, V6571, WX-Q **302** **Detling,** Harp Fm, Boxley. Ran out of fuel having lost his bearings in deteriorating weather, whilst on a routine patrol, and crashed. P/O A. Zukowski killed. Based Northolt. Cat 3

1298. Hurricane I, P2918, WX-Y **302** **nr Maidstone**(?) As above, P/O B. Bernas unhurt. Cat 2

1299. **19.10.40** Spitfire I, R6922 **92** **Bethersden,** Tuesnoad Fm. Crashed reason not known. Sgt L. Allton killed. Based Biggin Hill.

1300. Hurricane II, Z2352 **421Flt** **Old Swanley,** Clements Street. Force landed. P/O D. Parrott slightly injured. Based Gravesend. Cat 2

1301. **20.10.40** Spitfire IIa, P7445 **421Flt** **Gravesend** (Base). Returned to base after a spotting flight extensively damaged in tail rudder and radiator by cannon fire, but Sgt A. Spears was unhurt. Cat 2

1302. Me109E4, 1525 **9/JG54** **New Romney,** North Fording House. Shot down by F/L McKellar (605Sq) whilst it was on a free-lance sweep over Kent. Fw A. Iburg (or Jowig?) slightly wounded and made a POW. Based Guines.

1303. Spitfire I, X4599 **66** **Gravesend** (Base). Force landed at base after combat damage. Sgt H. Cook unhurt. Cat 2

1304. Me110C5, 2228, L2+MR **7/LG2** **Goudhurst,** Bockingfold Fm. Shot down by 92Sq whilst it was on a photo. recce. mission of the Estuary, crashing and burning. Oblt Lemmerich made POW; Uffz Ebeling killed Based Calais-Marck.

1305. Spitfire I, X4412 **92** **Biggin Hill** (Base). Was in combat with the above Me110 whose gunner damaged it. On return to base had to force land. Pilot (unknown) unhurt. Cat 2

1306. Spitfire I, N3113 **92** **Tonbridge,** Waterfield. Also damaged by Me110 No.2228 and had to force land. F/O J. Villa unhurt. Based Biggin Hill. Cat 2

1307. Me109E4, 2780, 1+ **6/JG52** **Welling,** Wickham Street. Attacked by the R.A.F. during a bombing mission to London and exploded over Woolwich. Obfw Friedmann fell clear of the wreckage but his 'chute failed to open. Based Peuplingues.

1308. Me109E7, 2059 **3/LG2** **Lenham** Heath, Chapel Fm. Shot down by F/O Mungo-Park (74Sq) whilst it was on a Jabo raid to London. Uffz Mairl baled out but his 'chute caught fire and he was killed. (This was also claimed by McKellar of 605Sq.) Based Calais-Marck.

1309.   Me109E, 5930 **5/JG52**
Mereworth. Shot down by Spitfires near R.A.F. W. Malling whilst on the above raid. Fw Bielmaier baled out unhurt. (Also reptd shot down by 41Sq nr Biggin Hill.). Based Peuplingues.

1310.   Spitfire IIA, P7370 **74**
Maidstone, Cox Heath. Shot down by Lw over the town. Sgt T.B. Kirk baled out wounded and died in hospital 22.7.41. Based Biggin Hill.   Cat 3

1311.   Spitfire IIA, P7426 **74**
Cowden. Shot up by Me109's over south London. Sgt C. Hilken baled out wounded and was hospitalised. Based Biggin Hill. Cat 3

1312.   Spitfire IIA, P7355 **74**
Brasted. Sustained severely damaged oil cooler in combat with enemy fighters and crash landed with a seized engine. P/O B. Draper unhurt.   Cat 2

1313. **21.10.40**   Blenheim IV, R3699 **53**
Tonbridge, Dernier Road. Became uncontrollable and had to be abandoned. Two houses were damaged and one civilian killed in the crash. P/O Meakin injured, Sgts Hutson and Hadnam unhurt. Based Detling.
                                                       Cat 3

1314. **22.10.40**   Wellington I, R3158 **75**
Manston. Crashed on landing after returning from ops. over Germany. There were no other losses amongst the bomber force. F/O Elliott, Sgts Musselwhite, Johnson-Barrett, McClaughlin and Day safe (?). Based Mildenhall.   Cat 3

1315.   Spitfire IIA, P7364 **74**
Tonbridge, Hadlow Place. Shot down in combat with Me109's. P/O R. Spurdle baled out unhurt. Based Biggin Hill.   Cat 3

1316.   Hurricane I, R4074 **46**
Newchurch Church, Shot up over Dungeness by Lw fighters. Sgt J. Morrison killed. Based Stapleford Tawney.   Cat 3

1317.   Me109E4, 1124, 10+ **2/JG26**
Littlestone G.C. Shot down by 257Sq (F/O Coke) breaking up in the air. The bulk of the wreckage fell in the sea. Uffz H. Arp killed. Based Audembert or Marquise.

1318.   Hurricane I, R4195 **257**
Lydd, ¼ mile south of church. Came under A.A. fire during combat with Me109's and crashed. P/O N. Heywood killed. Based N. Weald.   Cat 3

1319.   Hurricane I, V6851 **257**
Shadoxhurst, Moat Fm, ½ mile south of village. Whilst over Folkestone was shot up by Me109's, crashed and burned out. Sgt R. Fraser killed. Based North Weald.   Cat 3

1320. **24.10.40**   Defiant I, N1688 **141**
Biggin Hill. Ran into an unlit vehicle which was stationary on the airfield, after landing from night opts. Crew unhurt (?). Detached Gatwick.   Cat 2

1321. **25.10.40**
                       Me109E4, 1080, 2+ **6/JG53**
off Lydd. Failed to return from a sortie may have been shot down by 66Sq over Tunbridge Wells. Uffz Schulz missing. Based Dinan-Prouvy (?).

1322.   Me109E4, 4100 **9/JG51**
off Dover. Shot down during action with the R.A.F. Pilot rescued from the sea unhurt. Probably a victim of 41Sq (McAdam). Based St Omer-Longuenesse.

1323.   Spitfire I, X4170 **66**
Tunbridge Wells, Capel. Shot down by Me109's over the town. F/O Oxspring baled out slightly injured landing in an orchard. Based Gravesend.   Cat 3

1324.   Me109E4, 1988 **5/JG54**
Lydd, Scotney Court, Wall House Fm. (This location may be in Kent or Sussex. Scotney Court in Kent, Wall Fm (?) in Sussex.) Force landed after combat with the R.A.F. whilst escorting Jabo raid to London. Damage caused the engine to overheat. Oblt Schypek unhurt and POW. (May have been intercepted near Tunbridge Wells.) Based Guines.

1325.   Me109E1, 3548, 4+ **7/JG51**
Marden, Stonewall Fm, Hunton. Shot down in a dogfight with 501Sq Hurricanes. Fw Birg made a POW. Based St Omer-Longuenesse.

1326.   Hurricane I, P3615 **249**
Maidstone, Rankins Fm, Linton. This aircraft was hit from astern whilst acting as a weaver for the squadron patrolling Maidstone. It had turned southward at 18000ft when a lone Me109E approached unseen. Sgt J. Bentley-Beard baled out with slight burns and landed at Paddock Wood and hospitalised.

The site was dug in 1986 by Mid-Kent Aircraft Preservation Society and the pilot was invited to take part. Various pieces of wreckage were found proving conclusively that it was P3615.

Sgt Bentley-Beard who now runs an engineering firm in Warwickshire had a score of 2 × Me110's and 3 × Me109's between 18-28.9.40.

1327. **25.10.40**   Hurricane I, V7409 **249**
Rochester a/f. Force landed after combat as above. Adj H. Bouquillard (FFAF) wounded and hospitalised. Based North Weald. Cat 2

1328.   Me109E4, 5815, 7+1 **8/JG26**
Yalding, Congelow Fm. Whilst this aircraft was on a free-lance sortie it was shot down by 92Sq (F/O F. Villa). Fw J. Gaertner baled out and was made a POW. Based Caffiers.

76

1329. Spitfire I, X4480 **92**
Penshurst ALG. Force landed after combat with Me109's. P/O J. Mansell-Lewis unhurt. Based Biggin Hill. Cat 2

1330. Me109E, 5795 **8/JG26**
Sevenoaks, Riverhill House. Shot down by 92Sq (P/O Sherrington). Lt Ripke fell five miles from his wrecked aircraft with an unopened parachute. (Also claimed by McMullan of 222Sq.) Based Caffiers.

1331. Me109E4, 5178 **5/JG54**
Dungeness, Galloways. Attacked by the R.A.F. whilst part of a Jabo escort. It escaped into cloud but became disorientated and crashed. Lt E. Wagner unhurt and made a POW. Based Hermalinghen.

1332. Hurricane I, V6741 **257**
Penshurst ALG. Ran off the strip due to brake failure following combat with Me109's over the Channel. Sgt H.F. Shead unhurt. Based North Weald. Cat 2

1333. Me109E4, 3737 **Stab/JG51**
Marden, Millbush Inn. Blew up during an engagement with the R.A.F. Hptm Asmus baled out wounded and made a POW. Based Pihen or Wissant.

1334. Hurricane I, P5193 **501**
Cranbrook, Tolehurst Fm, Brewers Wood. Shot down by Me109's over the town. Sgt S.A. Whitehouse baled out unhurt. Based Kenley. Cat 3

1335. Hurricane I, N2438 **501**
Brenchley, Hatmill Lane, in a wood. Shot up by Me109's over Cranbrook. P/O V.R. Snell baled out unhurt. Based Kenley. Cat 3

1336. Hurricane I, P2903 **501**
Marden, Bridgehurst Fm. Collided with V6806 whilst they were involved in a dogfight over Tenterden. P/O V. Goth killed. Based Kenley. Cat 3

1337. Hurricane I, V6806 **501**
Staplehurst, Clapper Lane. Involved in the above collision. P/O K.W. McKenzie baled out unhurt. Based Kenley. Cat 3

1338. Spitfire IIA, P7371 **41**
Hawkinge a/f. Force landed with a 20mm cannon shell through the starboard cam shaft casing after combat with a Me109E off Dungeness. Sgt R.A. Beardsley unhurt. Based Hornchurch. Cat 2

1339. **26.10.40** Me109E7, 6180 **4/JG53**
Channel. Crashed in the sea after being in combat with the R.A.F. The pilot was picked up unhurt by Seenotflkdo. Based Dinan.

1340. Me109E7, 5929, 6 + **1/JG52**
off Littlestone. Shot down by (?) 92Sq (Holland). Obfw Strack killed. Based Coquelles.

1341. Me109E1, 6391, 8 + **6/JG53**
Pembury, Chalket Fm. Shot down by Sgt Fokes (92Sq) over Tunbridge Wells. Uffz Geiswinkler killed. Based Sempy.

1342. Hurricane I, P2916 **605**
Staplehurst, Baileys Fm. Shot down in flames after attacking a formation of Me109's. F/L J.C. Hayter baled out from 25000ft and landed unhurt. Based Croydon. Cat 3

1343. Hurricane II, Z2345 **421Flt**
Horton Kirby - S. Darenth. Force landed through H.T. cables. Sgt F.S. Perkins unhurt. Based Gravesend. Cat 2

1344. **27.10.40** Spitfire IIa, P7539 **66**
Hildenborough, Half Moon Lane. Crashed and burned out. Likely cause, P/O J.R. Mather suffered from anoxia, and was killed. Based Gravesend. Cat 3

1345. Me109E4, 5243 **4/JG53**
(?) Rochester, 2 miles S. Failed to return from a sortie over Kent. Uffz Schlitt missing. (?) Shot down by 54Sq (Nelson) or 66Sq (Cook). Based Sempy.

1346. Spitfire, P7368 **74**
West Malling. Force landed with combat damage sustained over Maidstone. S/L A. Malan unhurt. (There is doubt about the location.) Cat 2

1347. Spitfire IIa, P7526 **74**
Ashford, Dundas Fm, Elmstead. Shot down by Me109's over Maidstone. Sgt J.A. Scott killed. Based Biggin Hill. Cat 3

1348. Me109E4, 1603 **8/JG27**
Lenham, nr Hooks Wood. Shot down by 74Sq (Nelson) whilst on a free lance sortie. Oblt Pointer (Staffel Kapt) baled out unhurt. Based Guines.

1349. Me109E4, 3525, 4 + **3/JG52**
Penshurst ALG. Force landed after combat with 74Sq Spitfires. Fw Schieverhofer unhurt and POW. Based Coquelles.

1350. Me109E4, 2798 **3/JG52**
Upstreet Chislet Marshes. Whilst on an escort mission for Jabos to London was shot down by 74Sq. Oblt Steinhilper baled out unhurt and was made POW. Based Coquelles.
(The pilot appeared in BBC TV programme 'Churchill's Few' in 1986.)

1351. Me109E1, 3576 **7/JG54**
Lydd, on beach nr Water Tower. Had its engine severely damaged in combat over Kent and had to belly land. Uffz Zimmermann unhurt, POW. Based Guines.

1352. Me109E7, 4124 **I/JG3**
W. Wickham, Fishers Farm, between Court Hotel and Layham Road. Shot down by the R.A.F. whilst on a free lance sortie. Lt Busch (Gruppe Int Off) baled out wounded and POW. Based Colombert.

1353. Spitfire IIa, P7439 **603**
Canterbury, Waltham. Shot up in a surprise attack by a Me109E near Maidstone. F/O C.W. Goldsmith severely wounded and died the next day. Based Hornchurch. Cat 3

Incident No. 1351. Me109E of 7/JG54 had its engine severely damaged in combat and crash landed near the water tower on the beach at Lydd.

1354.   Spitfire IIa, P7365 **603**
Canterbury, Appletree Corner, Chartham Hatch. Shot down by III/JG27. P/O R.B. Dewey killed.   Cat 3

1355.   Spitfire IIa, P7286 **603**
Faversham, Bethel Row Throwley. Force landed after above attack. P/O D.A. Maxwell unhurt.   Cat 2

1356.   **28.10.40**
            Do17Z2, 2544, 5H+CH **I/KG3**
Maidstone, Judges Fm, Grafty Green. Suffered engine failure whilst on night ops. and had to crash land. Fw Vosshagen badly wounded and POW, Fw Nitsche and Schreiber + Uff Hausdorf all killed. Based Lille-Vendeville.

1357.   Me109E7, 4906, 2+ **5/JG27**
Maidstone, Pinewood Garage, London Rd. Shot down by 603Sq (Gilroy). Uffz Gonschorrek baled out, POW wounded. Based St Omer.

1358.   Me109E4, 5095 **II/JG51**
Dymchurch - New Romney, Fielding Lane. Shot down by the R.A.F. whilst on patrol over the South Coast. Lt Knittel (Gruppe Adj) killed. Based Desevres or Wissant.

1359.   **29.10.40**   Hurricane I,   **46**
Ashford, Hothfield Park. Shot down by Me109's. Sgt H.E. Black badly wounded and burnt. Died in hospital 9.11.40. Based Stapleford Tawney.   Cat 3
(A/c No. not in F.541.)

1360.   Spitfire **92**
Biggin Hill (Base). Collided with another Spit. whilst taxying. Sgt H. Bowen-Morris unhurt.   Cat 2
(A/c No. not in F.541.)

1361.   Spitfire **92**
Involved in the above. Sgt D.E. Kingaby unhurt.   Cat 2

(Further examples of incomplete records.)

1362.   Spitfire IIa, P7385 **74**
Rolvenden. Force landed during a routine patrol. Causes not known. Sgt H.T. Soars unhurt. Based Biggin Hill.   Cat 2

1363.   Hurricane I, V7383 **615**
W. Malling, Teston. Reported as being wrecked when it landed amongst trees. The forced landing due to overheated engine. Adj Lafont (FFAF) unhurt. Based Heathrow/Northolt.   Cat 3

1364.   Hurricane I, V6785 **615**
Romney Marsh. Shot up by Me109's and a 20mm cannon shell exploded in the cockpit. P/O E.R. Edmunds seriously wounded. Based Northolt.   Cat 2

1365.   Spitfire I, P9318 **222**
Lenham on a dummy airfield. Force landed with damage to the coolant system, caused when shooting down a Me109E of Epro-Gr210 over Pluckley. Sgt J.H. Burgess unhurt. Based Hornchurch.   Cat 2
(Also reptd as shot down by another Spitfire.)

1366.   Me109E4, 2024, 6+ **3/EproGr210**
Pluckley, Sheerlands Fm. As above. Oblt Hintze baled out and was made a POW. The victor may have been P/O Barton of 229Sq. Based Calais-Marck.

1367.   Me109E1, 4816 **3/JG51**
Elham, west of Gate Inn. Claimed by the R.A.F. whilst it was on a sortie over Dover. Fw Bubenhofer baled out unhurt landing at Rhodes Minnis. Based Pihen.

1368.   Me109E4, 5153, 5+ **9/JG3**
Sheperdswell, Wootton crossroads. Force landed after combat with the R.A.F. Oblt Troha (Staffel Kapt) unhurt. POW. Based Deservres.

1369.   Me109E4, 5370 **4/JG51**
Tunbridge Wells, Dodds Fm, Langton, Speldhurst. Shot down by 74Sq (P/O Nelson). Lt Tornow killed. Based Pihen.

1370.   **30.10.40**   Me109E, 5912 **8/JG26**
off Hythe. Shot down by the R.A.F. and the pilot picked up from the sea unhurt. Based Caffiers.

1371.   Me109E4, 5242 **7/JG26**
Marden, Brook Fm. After combat with the R.A.F. (?) 41Sq (McKenzie) exploded in the air. Uffz Toepfer killed. Based Caffiers.

1372.   Hurricane I, V7536 **249**
Channel. Failed to return from action with the Lw. P/O W.H. Millington missing. Based North Weald.   Cat 3

1373.   Hurricane I, V7301   **253**
Southfleet, Newbarn Fm. Crash landed after
a dogfight with enemy fighters. Sgt P.J.
Moore slightly injured. Based Kenley.   Cat 2

1374.   Spitfire IIa, P7282   **41**
nr Hythe, New Barn Fm, Postling. Shot up
over Ashford. P/O G.G. Draper slightly injured and admitted to hospital. Based Hornchurch.   Cat 3

1375.   Spitfire IIa, P7375   **41**
nr Hythe, Church Fm, Stanford. As above,
Sgt L.A. Garvey killed.   Cat 3

1376.   Me109E4, 6360   **6/JG3**
Meopham, Leylands. Shot up over N. Kent
by (?) 17Sq (Czernin) and crashed in flames.
Uffz Fahrian injured. Based Colombert.

1377.   Spitfire, X4269   **602**
Newchurch, Mullbank Fm. Damaged in a
surprise attack by Me109E's over Dungeness. P/O D.H. Gage unhurt. Based
Westhampnett.   Cat 2

1378.   Spitfire, X4542   **602**
off Greatstone. Shot down by Me109's as
above. Sgt W.B. Smith wounded.   Cat 3

1379.   Me109E4, 1474, 1+   **6/JG3**
East Farleigh, Court Lodge Fm. Crash landed
during a fighter engagement. Gfr Schuller
wounded and POW. Shot down by (?) 17Sq
(Griffiths). Based Colombert.

1380.   Spitfire IIa, P7446   **66**
W. Malling (Base). Nosed over on landing.
Sgt W.J. Corben unhurt.   Cat 2

1381.   Defiant I, N1566   **141**
Biggin Hill. Stalled on a night approach with
instruments frozen. Sgts Chard and Laurence unhurt.   Cat 3

1382.   **1.11.40**
                  Ju87B1, 5227, 6G + KS   **5/StG1**
off Whitstable (?). Shot down by (?)92Sq
whilst it was on an anti-shipping strike. Gfr
Karrach and M. Aulehner missing. (There is
some disagreement about the unit and
aircraft code.).

1383.   Spitfire, X4555   **92**
Hersden, Chislet Colliery. 92Sq were ordered
off against a raid of 50 × Ju87's and Me110
escort when this aircraft's R/T failed. F/O
M.C. Kinder and another (his wing man?)
dived down to attack the Stuka formation at
1500ft, dive bombing a convoy in the Estuary. He shot one down in flames but in turn
was shot up by a Me109. The pilot had both
wrists broken and an artery severed together
with shell splinters in his buttocks. Despite
this he shot down his attacker.
   However he was unable to make base and
had to force land beside the Canterbury to
Ramsgate road, to be collected by an ambu-
lance. Based Biggin Hill.   Cat ?
(No a/c No. given in the Form 541.)

1384.   Spitfire, X4487   **92**
Eastchurch. Damaged in the above action

and had to crash land. The pilot (Saunders)
was unhurt, despite a bullet crease in his
helmet and smashed goggles. Based Biggin
Hill.   Cat 2?

1385.   Hurricane, V6879   **605**
Canterbury in woods at Adisham. Shot up
over the city. S/L McKellar killed. (In recent
times a small piece of his aircraft was recovered from the top of a tree.) Based Croydon.   Cat 3

1386.   Me109E
off Ramsgate. Shot down by 605Sq. No further data.

1387.   Spitfire IIa, P7312   **74**
off Dover. Shot down by Me109's. P/O Nelson missing. Based Biggin Hill.   Cat 3

1388.   Hurricane I, V7616   **46**
Swingfield. Shot down by Me109's. Sgt R.
d'Hamale killed. Based Stapleford Tawney.
                                          Cat 3

1389.   Me109E
off Whitstable. Part of an escort for Ju87's.
Shot down by F/L Kent. (This was 92Sq's
100th victory claim. There were 4 more possible claims for this aircraft.)

1390.   **2.11.40**   Me109E4, 1624   **4/JG54**
Dungeness area. Cause of crash not known.
Lt Grote missing. Based Wissant (?).

1391.   Hampden P1176   **49**
W. Malling. F/L R.A. Learoyd, V.C. and his
crew were in circuit at Hawkinge en route to
a presentation at New Romney, his home
town, when the aircraft was hit by A.A. fire
and had to break off and force land at W.
Malling. The crew was unhurt if not best
pleased. Based Scampton.   Cat 2

1392.   Hurricane I, L1842   **310**
Isle of Sheppey. Caught fire and crashed,
the pilot, Sgt Kominek, baled out. Based
Duxford.   Cat 3

1393.   Ju88A1, 4159   **II/KG76**
Southfleet, New Barn Road. Crashed. 3 of
crew killed.

1394.   Me109E, 6+   **8/JG53**
Canterbury, Street End, Lower Hardres. 74
and 92Sq were patrolling Biggin Hill when
they sighted 60+ Me109's 4000ft below,
over Sheppey. They dived to attack and P/O
R.L. Spurdle shot one down and it crashed in
a field near Ashford. Fw X. Ray made POW.

1395.   **3.11.40**
                  Do17Z, 2573, 5K + CS   **8/KG3**
Bexley, Dartford and Wansunt Road. Inter-
cepted nr Gravesend by 41Sq also hit by
A.A. Claimed by P/O's Ambrose and
LeFevre. It had a bomb hung up when it
crashed. Lt W. Sonnenbere, Fw J. Kleditzsch,
Gfr W. Krohn and F. Zumbrock killed. Based
Evere or St Trond.

1395A.   **5.11.40**   Me109E1   **5/JG51**
off Dungeness. Shot down by the R.A.F. Lt F.
Jäger killed. Based Pihen (?).

Incident No. 1395. Do17Z 2373 of 8/KG3 was intercepted by 41 Squadron over Gravesend and crashed in Bexley. All the crew were killed. (Bexley Libraries)

1396. 4.11.40   Defiant I, N1561 **141 Chatham,** Gordons Fm. Suffered radio failure and was unable to find base whilst on a night sortie, and force landed. P/O Marsland and gunner were unhurt. Based Gravesend.
Cat 2

1397. 5.11.40   Me109E4, 2740 **9/JG26 Wittersham.** Collided with another Me109E flown by Uffz Braun and crashed. Oblt H. Ebeling became a POW. Based (?) Abbeville.

1398.   Me109E4, 3259 **9/JG26 Stone** cum Ebony. As above, Uffz E. Braun made a POW. Based Abbeville (?).

1399.   Me109E4, 1374 **I/JG26 Birchington,** Albion Road. Fw E. Schmidt shot down, and POW. Based Caffiers.

1400.   Me109E
off Herne Bay. 19 and 242Sq were on patrol at 37000ft over Gravesend when 10-30 Me109's were sighted. P/O Knight attacked one causing visible damage. When he flew alongside and waggled his wings the German pilot baled out. His fate is not known. (It is possible that Incidents 1399 and 1400 are one and the same.)

1401.   Hurricane I, V7588 **310 Sittingbourne** - Graveney. Had to force land after being damaged by own A.A. Based Duxford.   Cat 3

1402. 6.11.40 Whitley V, P5001, ZA-S **10 off N. Foreland.** Ditched after returning from ops. on Milano. P/O Jones, Sgt Smith, Harding, Walker and Watt were picked up by PTB 234. Based Leeming.   Cat 3

1403. 5.11.40   Hurricane I, P2806 **242 Sheerness** - Herne Bay, Neats Court. Shot down by enemy aircraft. P/O Hart killed. Based Duxford.   Cat 3

1405.   Spitfire, X4485 **92 nr Gravesend.** The squadron was patrolling on a bright clear day over the town when Sgt Ellis' aircraft was shot up by a Me109E and badly damaged. He had to force land at Gravesend a/f. Based Biggin Hill.   Cat 2

1406. 6.11.40
          Hurricane I, 323 or L1886 **615 Sevenoaks,** Noah's Oak. Crashed and burned near the railway line. Sgt J. Hammerton was killed. Based Northolt.   Cat 3
(This would appear to be another a/c borrowed from 1RCAF.)

80

Incident No. 1417. He111H of KG1 crashed into two houses in Bromley causing civilian casualties. (Bromley Libraries)

1407. **7.11.40** Hurricane I, V7507 **249**
Chatham. G/C V. Beamish was flying with 249Sq and was endeavouring to catch up with the flight when he was in collision with another Hurricane which crashed. He was able to force land unhurt. Based North Weald. Cat 2

1408. Hurricane I, V7627(?) **249**
off Chatham. As above. P/O T.F. Neil after attacking Ju87's and escort. Cat 3

1409. Me109E4, 4677 **3/JG26**
Thames Estuary, off Foreness. Was missing over the Estuary for unknown reasons. Obfw Muller missing. Based Caffiers.

1410. **8.11.40** Ju87B, 239, S1 + EL **I/StG3**
off N. Foreland. Shot down by the R.A.F. whilst it was attacking a convoy in the Estuary. Lt W. Kummer and Uffz U. Hoffenden killed. Based Caen-Carpiquet.

1411. Ju87B, 315, S1 + ML **I/StG3**
As above Uffz Imspringt and F. Krohn killed.

1412. Hurricane, V6870 **257**
Stelling Minnis, Hythe Road. Had its tail assembly shot off by a Me109E. Sgt A. Page killed. Based Martlesham Heath. Cat 3

1413. Hurricane I, V6860 **302**
Detling. Force landed after combat with Me109's. F/O Wezelik unhurt. Based Northolt. Cat 2

1414. Hurricane I, P3538 **302**
Detling. Force landed after combat with Me109's. Sgt Kosarz unhurt. Cat 2

1415. Magister I, R1917 **500**
Wrotham, Ightham. Crashed attempting a force landing, reason unknown. P/O's Chaffey and Mallalieu killed. Based Detling. Cat 3

1416. Hurricane I, N2649 **605**
Staplehurst, Huggins Fm, Harts Heath. Crashed. The pilot may have been Tarkowski or F/L Farley (46Sq). Based Croydon. Cat 3

1417. **9.11.40**
He111H, 3335, V4+JK **I/KG1**
Bromley, Johnson Road. Shot down demolishing 2 houses with at least one civilian death. A wing was found at Chislehurst. Lt Probst, Fw Gey, Gfr Geisinger and Uffz Kruger, the crew, 1 was a POW, others killed. (There were normally five in this aircraft type.) Based Rosieres en Santerre.

1418. Ju88A1, 2204, V4+HS **7/KG1**
Horsmonden, Elphicks Fm. Had been on a raid to London and crashed. Lt G. Finke, Fw Spehr, Uffz W. Klemm and W. Gottschalk all POW's. This bomber was shot down by 2 Spitfires. Based Rosieres. Some confusion over which a/c crashed here.

1419.   Hornet Moth   (?)24
Maidstone, Sutton Road in a field near Kent
Police H.Q. Force landed, pilot unhurt.
                                    Cat 2(?)

1420.   **10.11.40**
          2 × Spitfires, X4418 & X4420   **92**
Biggin Hill. Destroyed on the ground by a
night air-raid, and four others damaged.

1421.   **11.11.40**   Hurricane I, P2794   **17**
Manston, Monkton Church. Shot down
whilst attacking Ju87's and Me109E's on a
convoy attack. Sgt Hogg killed. Based
Martlesham Heath.   Cat 3

1422.   **13.11.40**   Beaufighter I, R2071   **219**
Edenbridge. Thought to have been shot
down by another night fighter. P/O Birkett
and Sgt Castle killed. Based Redhill.   Cat 3

1423.   **14.11.40**   Me109E4, 4096   **9/JG51**
off Dover. Shot down by the R.A.F. The pilot
Oblt Schnell rescued by SeeNotFlKm. Based
St Omer or St Quentin.

1424.   Spitfire IIa, V7386   **74**
Sandwich. Shot up by Me109's over Dover.
P/O W. Armstrong baled out. Based Biggin.
                                    Cat 3

1425.   Me109E   **1/JG51**
Broadstairs. Damaged by 249Sq and chased
by F/O Smythe to Manston where he shot it
down whilst it was attempting a landing. Fw
E. Wortbach killed. Based as above.

1426.   Ju87B, 436, J9+ZL   **9/StG1**
S. Foreland - Dover. Shot down by 74Sq.
Obgfr Fietmeyer POW, Obgfr Schmitt dead.
Based Guines (?).

                    Ju87B   **9/StG1**
off S. Foreland. Shot down by the R.A.F.
Uffz Muller made POW other crew member
missing.

        Ju87B, 5641, J9×BL   **9/StG1**
S. Foreland. Probably shot down by F/O
Park, 74Sq. Oblt Blumers and Gfr Koch both
POW.

1428.   **15.11.40**   Me109E, 1250   **3/JG26**
Eastchurch. Shot down by 605Sq(?) over the
Estuary. Lt R. Schiffbauer made POW.

1429.   Hurricane I, P2560   **605**
Eythorne - Dover. Shot down by Me109's
during a hit and run raid. P/O R.E. Jones
bailed out. Based Croydon.   Cat 3

1430.   Lysander II, R9079   **4**
Straits of Dover. Shot down whilst on an
A.S.R. mission. P/O Empson and Sgt Gethin
killed. One of a small flight of a/c detached
from the main unit based at R.A.F. Linton on
Ouse in Yorkshire.

1431.   **16.11.40**   Blenheim IV, R3687   **21**
Hartley - Fawkham, Longfield. Hit trees at
night attempting a force landing and
crashed. All the crew were injured. Based
Watton.   Cat 3

1432.   He111H, 6892   **1/KG1**
Woodnesborough, Palm Tree X roads. Shot
down during night ops. on London. Lt H.G.
Prampesburger, Uffz Mileska, Uffz Wendtland, Fw L. Mugge all killed.

1433.   **17.11.40**
                Me109E, 1528 or 4898   **1/JG3**
Ivychurch. Shot down by the R.A.F. and
crashed. Lt R. Riedel killed. Based Coulommiers or Guines.

1434.   **19.11.40**   Spitfire   **421Flt**
Hawkinge (Base). Overshot on landing and
damaged two other aircraft. P/O Lawrence
safe.   Cat 2(?)

1435.   Hurricane I, V6928   **46**
Wye. Ran out of fuel and had to force land.
P/O Mrazek unhurt. Based N. Weald. Cat 2(?)

1436.   Hurricane I, V6952   **46**
As above, Pilot Sgt Parrott.   Cat 2

1437.   **21.11.40**   Hurricane I, P5201   **615**
nr Tunbridge Wells - Hawkenbury, Little
Bayhall Farm. Force landed safely in a field.
P/O Millard unhurt. Based Northolt.
                                    Cat 2

1438.   He111H3, 3145, A1+GM   **4/KG53**
Teynham, Buckland Cross. Crashed. See No.
1439. Gfr Hagabiel, W. Tilger, B. Valkmann,
R. Deutsch and H. Loffler crew killed. Based
St Trond (?).

1439.   Spitfire IIa, P7387   **603**
Faversham, Teynham. This aircraft reported
to have rammed a He111 and both crashed.
Sgt Plant killed. After about an hour the
combined wreckage exploded killing 2
firemen. A further two were injured. Based
Hornchurch.   Cat 3

1440.   **23.11.40**   Me109E, 3868   **2/JG51**
Ivychurch. Crashed. Cause not known. Pilot
was Obgfr G. Loppach. Based St Omer.

1441.   Me109E, 4010   **5/JG53**
nr Smeeth Rly Stn. Damaged in combat with
the R.A.F. and hit a tree whilst attempting a
force landing. Lt O. Zeuner unhurt POW.
Based Peuplingues.

1442.   Fiat CR42, MM5694
                18°Gruppo 83Sqdl
1½ miles **off Folkestone.** 29 × CR42's were
on a sweep Dunkerque-Margate-Folkestone-
Calais, led by Maggiore F. Vosilla when at
1405hrs they were intercepted by 603Sq.
Ten. G. Mazza was attacked and shot down.
603Sq claimed 7 shot down.

                Fiat CR42, MM5665   **83Sqdl**
As above. Flown by Sgte Magg. G. Grillo
also shot down. The bodies of these two
pilots were not recovered. Based Ursel.

Incident No. 1441. Me109E of 5/JG53 hit a tree whilst forced landing, after being damaged in combat. Lt O. Zeuner was made a P.O.W.   (SE News)

Incident No. 1442. Ground crew manhandling a Cr42 at Ussel in Belgium.   (via Nicola Malizia)

The Corpo Aereo Italiano (C.A.I.)
Was a little known force formed in Northern Italy, and sent by Mussolini to take part in the conquest of Britain in September 1940.

It was composed of two Stormi of bombers, some 120-150 Fiat BR20M's, supported by two Stormi of fighters, about 100 in number. Half of these were Fiat CR42's roughly comparable to Gladiators, and quite inadequate for the task and half Fiat G50 bis, slightly inferior to the Hurricane.

In addition to the fighting force a squadriglia of Cant Z1007's was to act as a reconnaissance unit, and for logistical purposes the force had a considerable number of transport aircraft. The whole was commanded by Gen. S.A. (Air Marshal) Reno Corso Fougier.

The force was based on various Belgian air fields and came under the operational control of the Luftwaffe. To facilitate administration and control each unit was given a German designation.

    13° Stormo BT — KG13
    18° Gruppo CT — 18/JG56
    20° Gruppo CT — 20/JG56
    43° Stormo BT — KG43
    172ª Sqdl (Recce.) — AufKl (F) 172

The bomber force carried out a number of night and day raids on the coastal towns of Essex and Suffolk, and on 29.10.40 15 × BR20M's supported by 39 CR42's and 34 G50bis's plus a Jagdgruppe of Me109's attacked Ramsgate Harbour. They had 5 × BR20's damaged by A.A. fire one of them crashing on return to Belgium.

The fighter sweep of 23.11.40 resulted, in the losses off Folkestone, and a further two CR42's so damaged that they crashed in Belgium, severely wounding one of the pilots.

Early in 1941 all the Italian force had returned home. Obsolescent aircraft, poor training and lack of experience of Northern European winter weather had reduced their effectiveness.

1443.   24.11.40   Me109E
off Dungeness. This aircraft was shot down by P/O Baker and another unknown pilot.

1444.   Whitley V, T4160, KN-L   **77**
off Dungeness - Littlestone. Returned from operations on Italian targets and ditched, probably short of fuel. F/O Dyn, P/O Bagnall were picked up by a Hythe fishing boat; Sgts Gray, Parton, Moore and Sullivan missing. Based Topcliffe.   Cat 3

1445.   25.11.40   Do17Z
off Dover. Shot down by F/L Green (421Flt) and crashed in the sea. Crew presumably missing.

1445A.   26.11.40
    He59, 539, NO+FT   **Seenotflkdo 3**
Dungeness, 7 miles SSE. Shot down by a single burst of fire from a 421 Flt Spitfire and witnessed by 961 (Balloon) Sq. Crew

Obfw H. Beneke, Uffz J. Lange, Uffz W. Waldheim and Fw Friebe. Based Boulogne Harbour (?).

1446.   27.11.40   Spitfire IIa, P7306   **74**
Chatham. Shot down by enemy fighters and crashed. May have been due to A.A. fire. P/O Chesters wounded in the leg. Based Biggin Hill.   Cat 3

1447.   27.11.40   Me109E, 1634   **3/JG51**
Crundale. Shot down in combat by 41Sq (P/O Wells). Uffz Benzinger was killed. Based Pihen or Wissant.

1448.   Me109E, 6218   **3/JG51**
Benenden, Iden Green. Crashed for unknown reasons. Pilot killed.

1449.   Spitfire IIa, P7499   **421Flt**
Alkham, Collingham Fm. Had been on a met. recce. when it was shot down by a Me109E. The Spitfire broke up and P/O K.A. Lawrence found himself falling through space, but managed to open his 'chute before hitting the sea. He released a dye marker and was picked up by a minesweeper. He was later found to have a broken leg and dislocated shoulder. Based Hawkinge.   Cat 3

1450.   Me109E
off Dover. Shot down by Sgt D. Mackay (421 Flt). Name and state of pilot not known.

1451.   Me109E, 1653   **3/JG51**
Hawkinge, Monks Horton Park. Crashed on forced landing but only slightly damaged. Fw W. Erdniss made a POW. Based (?) Wissant.

1452.   Me109E, 4101   **2/JG51**
Manston. Had battle damaged coolant system as a result of an attack by 66Sq Spitfire (F/L Christie). Pilot was Lt Teumar. Based Peuplingues.
This a/c belly landed with a seized engine and is now on display at the R.A.F. Museum, Hendon.

1453.   Me109E
nr Dymchurch. 41Sq flying at 25000ft found 4 × Me109's. P/O E.P. Wells with a deflection shot sent this one down in flames.

1454.   28.11.40   Me109E, 3755   **1/JG26**
Channel. Shot down by the R.A.F. after a sweep in the Dungeness area. Fw Kaminski killed. Based Caffiers.

1455.   Defiant I, N1800   **141**
Gravesend (Base). Collided with another whilst taxying after landing. S/L Wolfe and gunner unhurt.   Cat 2

1456.   Defiant I   **141**
Involved in the above accident. Not recorded in the F.540.   Cat 2(?)

1457.   Hurricane I, R4194   **615**
Detling. Force landed with engine trouble. Adj la Font (FFAF) unhurt. Based Northolt.   Cat 2

1458. Spitfire IIa, P7492 **66**
Chiddingstone. Collided with another over Edenbridge. Sgt Willcocks killed. Based West Malling. Cat 3

1459. Spitfire IIa, P7491 **66**
Edenbridge. Involved in the above collison. P/O H. Allen baled out and landed at Dutton Homestead. Cat 3

1460. Spitfire I, K9950 **64**
(?) **Chiddingstone.** Caught fire in the air and was abandoned over Tunbridge Wells. P/O Salmond baled out with a fractured leg. Based Hornchurch. Cat 3

1461. Hurricane I, V6729 **249**
E. Peckham. Bounced by Me109's. P/O P. Wells baled out with burns and a dislocated shoulder. Based North Weald. Cat 3

1463. Me109E, 1289 **2/JG26**
Romney Marsh. Crash landed. Uffz H. Wolf was made a POW. Based Caffiers (?) in Sussex)

1464. 29.11.40 Hurricane I, V6692 **249**
Horsmonden. Whilst in company with another 249Sq aircraft was attacked by Me109's. P/O R.G. Barclay baled out wounded, whilst Sgt Davidson made good his escape. Based North Weald, Adv. Rochford. Cat 3

1465. Spitfire IIa, P7449 **603**
Leeds, Broomfield. Dived into the ground. Cause not known. P/O Rafter killed. Based Hornchurch. Cat 3

1466. Defiant I, N1564 **141**
Gravesend (Base). Returning from a night patrol, landed in poor visibility, undercarriage retracted. F/L FitzGerald and Sgt Allen safe. Cat 2

1467. Spitfire, P7498 **421Flt**
Hawkinge (Base). A/C Amer (ground crew) attempted to take off in this aircraft and it was written off. When arrested he said that he wanted to be a pilot. He was uninjured. Cat 3

1468. Me110, 2301 **Stab/StG1**
off Dover. Shot down after a sortie over the Estuary. Oblt Freyer and Obfw Buttlik. It is puzzling why this aircraft was on a Stukagruppe and why it was over the U.K. Based St Pol.

1469. 30.11.40 Me109E, 1145 **5/JG53**
Ruckinge. Uffz Wagelein baled out of his aircraft that had been damaged by 74Sq (Park and Stephens) but his 'chute had been holed and he was killed. The wreckage fell on the bank of the Royal Military Canal. This was the 600th *claimed* victory for the Biggin Hill squadrons. Based Etaples or Bercke.

1470. Me109E, 5052 **9/JG53**
off Dungeness. Lost after a sweep in this area. Pilot's name and state not known. Based Bercke St Mer.

1471. Me109E, 4900 **6/JG53**
Old Romney, Wheelstead Fm. Shot down by the R.A.F. Obfw Schmidt fate unknown. Based Dinan,

1472. Hurricane I, P3429 **46**
Ashford area. Abandoned after the controls failed. P/O Ambrose baled out unhurt. Based North Weald. Cat 3

1473. 1.12.40 Me109E, 4852 **9/JG51**
off Dymchurch. Shot down by P/O P. Hartas (421 Flt). Uffz W. Miesala killed.

1474. Hurricane I, V7609 (?) **605**
nr Maidstone. Shot down by Me109's. F/L Ingle slightly injured and baled out. Based Croydon. Cat 3

1475. Hurricane I, V7055 **605**
As above. P/O Passey force landed slightly wounded. Cat 2

1476. Hurricane I, V6844 **605**
Gravesend a/f. Belly landed with combat damage. Sgt Howes unhurt. Based Croydon. Cat 2

1477. Hurricane I, V6881 **253**
Ashford area. Crash landed with wheels up. F/L Watts safe. Based Kenley. Cat 2

1478. 2.12.40
Me109E, 5328, White 8 **1/JG53**
4 miles off Seabrook. Following combat with 74Sq Spitfire (S/L Malan) over Dover this aircraft crashed into the sea. Pilot Lt S. Fischer or Flischer missing.

1479. Spitfire I, X4618 **92**
Gravesend. Whilst patrolling North Kent was attacked by Me109's and had to force land. P/O Wade was safe. Based Biggin. Cat 2

1480. Spitfire, X4656 **92**
W. Malling. Crashed after a two hour patrol, cause not known. Sgt le Cheminant (FFAF) unhurt. Based Biggin Hill. Cat 2

1481. 4.12.40 Blenheim IV, T2161 **82**
Canterbury, Waltham. Crashed on return from ops. on Essen. Sgt Cartwright was diverted to Manston. Sgts Benbow, Cartwright and Crawford all killed. Only one a/c located the target. Based Bodney.

1482. 5.12.40 Hurricane I, V7617 **46**
Sevenoaks, Daughton House. Crash landed with F/O Young unhurt. Based North Weald. Cat 3

1483. Me109F7, 5968, White 4 **1/JG26**
off Dover. Shot down by F/O O'Meara (421 Flt) when this and other aircraft were attacking a minesweeper. Lt H. Heinemann killed. Based Caffiers.

1484. 6.12.40 Hurricane I **85**
Gravesend (Base). Crashed with undercarriage up. F/O Carnaby safe. Cat 2(?)

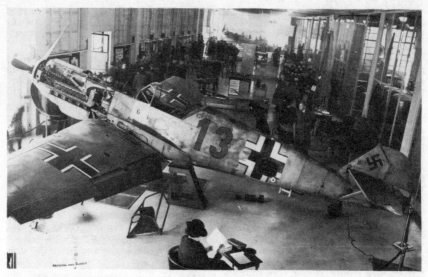

A Me109E of I/JG77 on show in the showroom of Rootes Group in Maidstone, 25.10.40. (Does not appear in text as it was shot down near Brighton.)

1485. **7.12.40**   Blenheim IV, T2395   **53**
Deal. Crashed after returning from a maritime recce. off the Hook of Holland. Cause of crash not known. P/O Steel and Sgt Hemsley killed; Sgt Robson injured. Based Thorney Island.   Cat 3

1486.   Spitfire, -L   **421Flt**
Hawkinge (Base). Crashed just short of the runway due to lack of fuel. F/S J. Gillies unhurt.   Cat 2

1487. **9.12.40**   Hurricane I   **85**
Gravesend (Base). Overshot on landing. Sgt Calderwood unhurt.   Cat 2

1488. **11.12.40**   Spitfire I X4658   **602**
Folkestone. Shot up by Me109's losing about a metre off one wing tip. F/O Edy had to belly land at about 130 mph. Based Westhampnett.   Cat 2

1489.   Me109E, 5941, Green D   **StabII/LG2**
Faversham, Forge Lane, Baddlesmere. Shot down in the early morning. Oblt V. Kraft baled out and made POW. Based Calais-Marck.

1490. **12.12.40**   Me109E, 3708   **7/JG26**
Leeds Castle, Abbey Fm. Shot down by 229Sq (Bright). Uffz Lindemann wounded and POW. Based Porte le Grand.

1491.   Hurricane, V7123   **615**
W. Malling. As a result of a damaged runway this aircraft tipped on its nose. F/O Foxley-Norris unhurt. Based Northolt.   Cat 2

1492.   Hurricane, V7598   **615**
W. Malling. This aircraft was also damaged by the unserviceable runway. Adj Mouchotte (FFAF) unhurt. Based Northolt.
                                            Cat 2

1493. **18.12.40**   Do17Z
off Dover. Shot down by 421 Flt (Hartas and Forest) and witnessed by personnel of 961 (Balloon) Sq.

1494. **22.12.40** Hurricane I, V6679, VY-F   **85**
Cuxton. Abandoned when the pilot lost control due to icing and damage caused by own A.A. Sgt Howes killed. Based Gravesend.
                                            Cat 3

1495. **27.12.40**   Spitfire II, -R   **421Flt**
Hawkinge (Base). Crashed when its engine cut out on finals and it went through the perimeter fence. F/O O'Meara unhurt. Cat 3

1496. **29.12.40**   Defiant I, N1806   **141**
Gravesend (Base). Hit trees on take off and crashed. Sgt Laurence injured, Sgt Chard not.   Cat 3

1497. **31.12.40**   Spitfire II, -F   **421Flt**
nr Biggin Hill. Crashed trying to land in very bad weather conditions. Sgt M.A. Lee killed. This was the third time he had to force land in just over a fortnight. An indication of the need to keep this unit flying and reporting. Based Hawkinge. (Addington, Surrey) Cat 3

IMPRECISE REPORTS

The following pages include information concerning crashed aircraft that is incomplete.

It varies from reports that lack only one major factor to those where nothing is known other than that an aircraft crashed at a certain place on a certain day. This especially applies where losses occurred around midnight and the subsequent report was made out the following day..

The following abbreviations are used more frequently in this section.

A.A.	Anti aircraft artillery
a/c	Aircraft
C.D.	Civil Defence
C.G.	Coast Guard
e/a	Enemy aircraft
L.B.	Lifeboat
Lw	Luftwaffe
Met.	Meteorological or weather
Ops.	Operations, sorties or missions
recce.	reconnaissance missions
Rly.	Railway
s.e.f.	single engined fighters
Stn.	station
u/i	unidentified

23.11.39   u/i
Isle of Grain. a/c reported down in the sea. 500Sq searched unsuccessfully.

17.12.39   u/i
E. Tongue Light. An explosion heard and large patch of oil seen on the sea. L.B. crew heard an aircraft just before the explosion. Possibly a mine laying accident?

25.5.40   Anson, N9731, MK-U   **500**
Ditched in sea, reason not known, P/O Grisenthwaite, P/O McLundie, LAC Bowers and A/C Hopwood all rescued by Destroyer. Based Detling.   Cat 3

27.5.40   Me110   **2(F)122**
S.E. England. Failed to return from a recce. mission. Crew missing.

29.5.40   u/i
2 NE Broadstairs. Reported by C.G. that an a/c was in the sea. L.B. searched but later told by C.G. to abandon.

     Anson, K8771, ML-L   **500**
? Ditched. P/O's Dews and Draw; LAC Hawke and A/C Mansfield missing.

12.6.40   u/i (? Me110)
7 NE Margate. 2 a/c in combat, 1 dived into the sea. Shore boat picked up 2 Lw airmen. ? No. 92 or 93? Plot

29.6.40   u/i
6 miles off Dungeness. L.B. launched and searched for a/c in the sea. Nothing found.

30.7.40   ?
off Margate, Kingsgate. 'Chute reported falling into the sea. L.B. and H.S.L. searched until dark.

10.8.40   ?
½ mile off Margate. Pilot picked up from the sea by L.B. Not in his dinghy, during an air raid.

12.8.40
off Margate. 'Chute reported in the sea, no trace found.

14.8.40   u/i
Margate, 3 miles N. Seen to crash and L.B. picked up pilot whose 'chute had partially opened. Dead on arrival at hospital.

15.8.40
Brenchley, Castle Hill.   e/a

Canterbury, Frognall.   e/a

16.8.40
Northbourne.   R.A.F. + u/i e/a

18.8.40   He111
Dunkirk. Faversham.

Boxley.   R.A.F.

Chatham.   e/a

Whitstable, Radfall G.C. Crashed and burned.   e/a

Orpington.   e/a bomber

Goodnestone, House Fm.   Me109

22.8.40
Hythe. Shot down by A.A.   u/i

Hythe. As above, but pilot baled out.   u/i

24.8.40
Elham, Newington.   e/a

25.8.40
Ivychurch. Pilot injured.   Me109

Southfleet - Dartford.   e/a

Ospringe.   R.A.F.

Medway area, force landed (night flight).   Hurricane

26.8.40
Brookland.   e/a

Broadstairs, Grove.   R.A.F.

Broadstairs, Percy Avenue.   e/a

Above two incidents at about the same time.

Wickhambreux. R.A.F.

Dover, South Road. u/i

Canterbury. Behind Newhouse Farm, Thannington. R.A.F.

28.8.40

Ashford, Kingsnorth. R.A.F.

Sellindge, Hodeford Mill or Partridge Fm. R.A.F.

Bridge Blean, Swartling Manor. Lw

Elham. R.A.F.

Sturry, Giles Fm. R.A.F.

Eastry. e/a s.e.f.

W. Blean or Sturry, Champion Fm. Defiant

Sturry, Broad Oak, Mayton Fm. R.A.F.

Dover area, crew safe. e/a bomber

Westbere, in R. Stour. Me109

St Nicholas at Wade. Fell close to another on this site. Me109

30.8.40.

Minster, in the sea. e/a s.e.f.

Tunbridge Wells. Exploded in the air. u/i

Isle of Grain - Nore. e/a

Bethersden, Honeyfield Wood (also reptd 1½ miles E. High Halden). R.A.F.

31.8.40

Reculver 1 NE. No trace. u/i

Rochester, Strood. e/a

Dartford, Darenth. R.A.F.

Seasalter. R.A.F.

High Halden 1 mile NE. (The same location as 30th ?) Spitfire

Headcorn, Kelsham Fm. Me109E

Maidstone, 4 miles SW Huddles Fm. Me109

Dover. Claimed shot down by small arms fire from balloon crew, 961Sq/A4. Me109

1.9.40 Spitfire, R6778 **616**
? Reported hit in oil tank and wing after attacking Do215's over Kenley. (F.541 has no information. AB Serials say hit by Do17Z. Was reported to M.U. at Stelling Minnis 2.9.40.) P/O Casson unhurt. Cat 3

Seal Chart, Kemsing. R.A.F.

Sevenoaks, Brasted. R.A.F.

EXTRA IMPRECISE REPORTS

2.9.40 Me109R, 3714 **1/JG51**
Channel. Crashed during return flight, Fw Bar rescued unhurt by Seenotdienst. Based Wissant.

2.9.40 Ju88A1, 0276, F6+DK **2(F)122**
Failed to return from long range recce sortie and presumed crashed in sea. Oblt Schmid, Fw Jahnke, Obgefr Rockstrol and Gefr Kronberg all missing.

2.9.40

Sandwich, Worth Bay. e/a

off Margate. u/i

Faversham. e/a

Kennardington, nr Snargate boundary. e/a

Bilsington. (? Me109 at Bridge Fm). e/a

Elham. R.A.F.

off Hythe. e/a

3.9.40

Folkestone, 5 miles off. R.A.F.

Eastry, E of Walton. R.A.F.

Herne Bay. R.A.F.

4.9.40

Eastry. R.A.F.

Me109 **II/JG2**
? Failed to return from a sortie to the SE. Oblt Muller missing.

5.9.40

Denge Marsh, 4 miles W. L.B. launched. u/i

Canterbury, Upper Hardres. R.A.F.

6.9.40

Margate. Wreck brought ashore after 2 a/c rptd in the sea. Lw

Sevenoaks Weald. R.A.F.

Marden. u/i

off Hythe. e/a

7.9.40 Ju88A1, 6032 **II/KG54**
Failed to return from operations. Obfw Schmitz, Obfw Brehmer, Fw Kalucza all killed, Fw Liebernecht missing. Based St Andre.

7.9.40

East Last Buoy. L.B. found injured Lw pilot. Lw s.e.f.

Reculver, 1 mile N. Shoreboat found wreck of a/c. u/i

Margate, 4 miles NW. No trace found (? Incident 1317). Lw s.e.f.

Thames Estuary. C.G. reported a/c seen in sea off Last Buoy and one crewman picked up. e/a

Dover. Received direct hit from A.A. shell. Reptd by 961 (Balloon) Sq. He111

9.9.40
Sheerness.   R.A.F.

Benenden (Could be a Me109 shot down
here, Plot 905.)   R.A.F.

Dungeness, 7 miles WSW. Crew of 4 picked
up by a fishing boat.   u/i

Ivychurch.   R.A.F.

10.9.40
Ightham.   R.A.F.

Wrotham.   e/a

11.9.40
Shoreham - Eynsford.   R.A.F.

11.9.40   He111H5, 3545   **II/KG26**
East of London. Shot down by 249Sq. Uffz
Meusel killed, Lt Wesemann, Fw Giess and
Gutacker POW's.

14.9.40
Hythe (Could be He111 5357 off S. Coast.)
                                                    e/a

Staple, nr Wingham.   R.A.F.

15.9.40
nr Rochester a/f.   e/a

Dungeness, E. of.   e/a

Leysdown (1 or 2 incidents ?).   e/a

                                      Do17Z   **III/KG2**
? Shot down by (?) 242Sq whilst it was
attacking London. Fw Simon dead; Uffz
Hirsch and Fleming missing and Gfr Sandmann.

17.9.40
Cranbrook.   R.A.F.

Brenchley.   R.A.F.

18.9.40
Dover, Ripple.   R.A.F.

Canterbury, Hackington.   R.A.F.

                                      Ju88A1   **7/KG77**
? Failed to return from ops. on Tilbury. (?)
Shot down by A.A. Other aircraft of this unit
shot down over Kent.

19.9.40   Ju88A1, 7058   **I/KG51**
Channel. After a sortie to London shot down
by R.A.F.

                                      Ju88A1, 6141   **1/KG77**
? Crew Gfr Mökel killed; Obfw Strahl, Fw
Winkelmann and Uffz Kunz missing.

(One of the above Ju88's may have crashed
3 miles E of Deal Castle.)

26.9.40   R.A.F.
Galloway, 5 miles WSW. 2 shoreboats
picked up a pilot. All the boats in danger of
air attack. (Incident 1103 would fit but there
P/O Samolinski rptd killed.)

28.9.40
Dunkirk, nr boundary with Selling.   R.A.F.

29.9.40
Faversham, in a wood.   R.A.F.

30.9.40
Higham.   e/a

                           Hurricane, P3217(?)   **303**
? Shot down in combat with Me109's
possibly over Dungeness. Sgt Belc baled
out.

5.10.40   Do17Z
Folkestone. Crashed reported by 961 (Balloon) Sq.

11.10.40
Aylesford.   R.A.F.

Ashford, Smeeth.   R.A.F.

Canterbury.   Lw

12.10.40
Romney Marsh. Rptd by 961Sq.   Me109

15.10.40
High Halden.   R.A.F.

mid Channel. Shot down. Reported by
961Sq.   Me109

22.10.40   Lw
Dungeness. a/c reptd in sea. No trace found.

25.10.40   Ju88A, 4135   **II/KG77**
? Failed to return from a raid on London. ?
shot down by A.A. Obfw A. Hohn, Fw R.
Muller and Carnot + Gfr Tschentke
missing.

                   Ju88A, 6140   **III/KG77**
? on above night raid. Uffz Hekers and Pirschan, Obgfr Gurnkrantz (or Firnkrantz) and
Hoffmann all missing.

26.10.40   He111H, 3637   **2/KG53**
? Failed to return as above. (?) Shot down by
A.A. Lt Hanau Fw Brandt, Lt H. Gichi, Gfr
Heucht and Uffz Schubauer missing.

                   Spitfire, R6839   **602**
SE of London, in a hop garden. Sgt Elcome
killed as a result of anoxia (?).

31.10.40
Adisham.   R.A.F.

2.11.40   Ju88A1, 4159, F1+DN   **II/KG76**
Failed to return from sortie over south east
coast. Uffz E. Stumpf, Obfw O. Grunke,
Obfw A. Vogel and Uffz M. Biller all missing. See plot 1393.

2.11.40 Do17Z, 3387, 5K + BM **4/KG3**
Failed to return from operations, reasons unknown. Lt Breuer, Uffz H. Ruhn, Obgefr H. Greil, Gefr W. Grafer all missing.

2.11.40 Ju88A1, 7089, 5J + TS **8/KG30**
Missing, reason not known. Fw W. Wowereit, Obfw Schutegh-Mader, Uffz Rudermond and Uffz Pohling all missing.

2.11.40
Dungeness, 6 miles NNE. Fishing boat searched for a/c rptd in sea. u/i

Northfleet. Downs Road. 3 crew killed.
Ju88A1

Hythe. e/a

Dymchurch in sea, pilot dead. Me109

Me109, 5171 **7/JG53**
As above. Oblt F. Hoffmann missing.

Me109, 5933 **II/JG52**
? as above. Fw D. Junger missing.

Me109, 3784 **II/JG52**
As above. Hptm W. Ennslen dead.

5.11.40 Spitfire
Sheppey. Force landed. Pilot unhurt.

Sheerness. Spitfire

Faversham, 3 miles W. Norton.
Hurricane, V6619

8.11.40
Eastry, Lt Mongham - Ripple Cross. R.A.F.

9.11.40 Lw bomber
off Dungeness. Only oil slick found.

Dungeness, 3 miles S. Do17Z

Ringwould, in sea. R.A.F.

Ju88, 4184 **I/KG77**
? Missing after ops. on London. Lt Waltermann, Uffz Klaus, Leichsnering and Gefr Woite missing. Possibly plot 1418.

Ju88 **I/KG77**
? A.A. as above. Lt Vaupel, Uffz Bersch, Obgfr Bartling and Schindlhauer missing.

14.11.40
off Dungeness. No trace found. u/i

Hurricane, R4220 **615**
Biggin Hill. Crashed. P/O Millard unhurt.

15.11.40
Sheppey. Me109

Sheerness, N. of. Me109

Eastchurch. Me109

(Above three at 3 different times.)

Luddenham in the river. e/a

Sheerness - Nore. e/a bomber

15 or 16.11.40 Hurricane
Dover, Shakespear Cliff. Shot down in flames.

16.11.40
Margate, Cliff Point. A/c in sea, crew ashore in dinghy. u/i

Ivychurch. e/a

Dungeness, 4 miles NE. L.B. search unsuccessfully. 2 × u/i

Folkestone, 1 mile SE. Reported in distress. An unsuccessful search made. u/i

27.11.40 Me109
Dover. Rptd shot down by light A.A. (961Sq report).

Me109, 6218 **3/JG51**
? Missing after action over the SE.

30.11.40
Ashford, Smeeth. R.A.F.

27.12.40 Ju88
off Sheerness. A/c lost.

late 1940 Wellington
Wittersham, Lambsland Fm. Flew into the ground with crew aboard. Debris still found in the field in 1985.

Notes Most of these reports are from Civil Defence records. Because of the personnel manning this reporting service being part-time volunteers, aircraft recognition was not too reliable and this should be borne in mind when trying to identify individual crashes.

Changes of watches and crashes around midnight make dates not as certain as might be.

Reports from other sources including 49 Maintenance Unit and Air Britain Serial Lists.

27.5.40 Spitfire I, N3289 **610**
Missing after a Dunkerque patrol. Sgt Medway pilot. May have been on 29th and a/c No. N3284. Cat 3

Spitfire I, L1016 **610**
As above. P/O A.R. Medcalf. Cat 3

8.7.40   Spitfire I, L1001   **74**
Manston. Damaged. Pilot Sgt Skinner.   Cat 2

11-13.7.40   Blenheim IV, R3610   **53**
Detling (Base).   Cat 2

13.7.40   Blenheim I, L8715   **604**
Gravesend. F/O Heal, Sgts Crump and
Guthrie unhurt.   Cat 2

               Spitfire I, P9512   **610**
Hawkinge. Damaged on ops.   Cat 2

20.7.40   Hurricane I, N2671   **32**
Lydden   Cat 2

21-23.7.40   Spitfire I, R6767   **64**
Hawkinge.   Cat 1

               Spitfire I, L1039   **64**
Hawkinge.   Cat 2

31.7.40   Spitfire I, R6990   **64**
Hawkinge. Battle damaged.   Cat 2

5-7.8.40   Magister, P6344   **74**
Deal. Force landed.   Cat 2

7-9.7.40   Hurricane I, P3028   **56**
Manston.   Cat 2

9.8.40   Lysander, P1714   **26**
W. Malling. P/O Davies and Sgt Bott unhurt.
                             Cat 2

10/11.8.40   Lysander, N1295   **4**
W. Malling.   Cat 2

12.8.40   Spitfire I, P9330   **610**
Hawkinge.   Cat 2

14/15.8.40   Spitfire I, P9540   **257**
Ashford.   Cat 2

15.8.40   Hurricane I, P3651   **501**
? Missing.   Cat 3

18.8.40   Hurricane I, ? P3397   **501**
? Aircraft lost. F/Sgt Morfill baled out.   Cat 3

Reports (unconfirmed) from 961 (Balloon)
Sq, Dover

14.9.40   Me109E
Lympne. Crashed.

5.10.40   Do17Z
Folkestone. Crashed.

12.10.40   Me109E
Romney Marsh. Crashed.

15.10.40   Me109E
Dover - Calais. Shot down.

27.11.40   Me109E
Hawkinge. Shot down by Dover L.A.A.

ADDITIONAL LIST

Details in this list do not appear in the Index. Information received after the format was established.

25.11.39   Hurricane I, L1906   **79**
Manston (Base). Crashed on take off due to engine failure. Sgt G. Spencer slightly injured.   Cat 3

14.4.40   Blenheim IV, L9207   **40**
Thames Estuary. Crashed in sea on an unauthorised flight. Based Wyton.   Cat 3

23.5.40   Blenheim IV, L9403   **15**
Hawkinge. Was reported missing at Arras on 23rd but was inspected by a Maintenance Unit at Hawkinge on the 27th.   (?)Cat 3

26.5.40   Blenheim IF, L6607   **604**
Manston (Base). Crashed. Based Wyton.
                             Cat 3

27.5.40   Spitfire I   **610**
Hawkinge. Force landed after damage sustained in combat over Dover. Based Gravesend.   Cat 2

30.5.40   Lysander, P1723, KO-A   **2**
Hawkinge. Force landed flak damaged whilst over Dunkerque. Based Bekesbourne.
                             Cat 2

31.5.40   Hurricane I, P3553   **229**
Hawkinge. Shot down over Dunkerque, but also reported as being inspected by 49M.U. at Hawkinge. (No information on this point in the unit's F.541.)

1.6.40   Spitfire I, K9836   **19**
Channel. Ditched. Based Hornchurch. Cat 3

                 Hurricane I   **17**
Hawkinge. Damaged by gunners of a Ju88 over Dunkerque. (Not in the Form 541.) Based Hawkinge.   Cat 3

5.6.40   Mentor I, L4425   **16Gp Comm Flt**
Rochester. Crashed.   Cat 3

19.6.40   Whitley V, N1373   **102**
Manston. Force landed cause unknown. P/O's W. McArthur and D. Lowson + Sgts A. Jepps, A. Stokes, E. Pike, all unhurt. Based Driffield.   Cat 2

23.6.40   Hurricane I, P3577   **245**
Hawkinge (Base). Damaged, cause unknown. P/O R. Chaffe unhurt.   Cat 2

27.6.40   Blenheim IV, R3811   **40**
Hawkinge. Force landed after being battle damaged by Lw fighters. F/O Bromley and Sgts Gamble and Little unhurt. Based Wyton.
                             Cat 2

29.6.40   Wellington I   **9**
nr Sandwich. Had engine trouble on returning from operations and had to force land. P/O Bull and crew unhurt. Based Honington.
                          Cat 2

3.7.40   Spitfire I, L1076   **610**
Hawkinge. Damaged. Sgt Ramsey unhurt. Later inspected by 49 M.U. (Not in unit's F.540.)   Cat 2

8.7.40   Anson I, K6249
      School of General Reconnaissance.
Channel. Ditched.

20.7.40   Hurricane I, P3679   **32**
Biggin Hill (Base). Attacked by Me109's over Dover (possibly Hptm Tietzen of II/JG51). Sgt W.B. Higgins slightly wounded by 20mm shell splinters.   Cat 2

25.7.40   Spitfire I, N3231   **64**
Hawkinge. Crash landed owing to battle damage received over Dover. F/O H.J. Woodward unhurt. Based Kenley.   Cat 2

27.7.40   Blenheim IF, L8451   **600**
Manston (Base). Crashed cause not known.
                          Cat 3

             Spitfire I, R6706   **74**
Manston. Force landed with battle damage. P/O Freeborn unhurt. Based Hornchurch.
                          Cat 3

11.8.40   Spitfire I, L1037   **610**
off Calais. Shot down by Me109's. Sgt J.H. Tanner missing. Based Gravesend.   Cat 3

            Spitfire I, R6630   **610**
As above, Sgt W.J. Neville missing.   Cat 3

13.8.40   Anson, N5229   **500**
Detling (Base). A wheel went into loose soil filling a bomb crater on take off. P/O Peters. Sgts Collorossi, Newton and Stanley all safe.
                          Cat 2

13.8.40   4 × Ansons
Detling. The following were damaged during an air-raid. No aircrew involved. N9898, R3349, R9633, R9664.   All Cat 2

26.8.40   Do17Z   **2/KG2**
Dover, nr Kearsney Rly Stn, Temple Ewell. Blew up. Hptm Bose and crew (?) killed. Based Cambrai.

31.8.40   Hurricane I, V7260   **601**
Thames Estuary. Shot up by Me109's and P/O H.T. Gilbert baled out. Based Tangmere.
                          Cat 3

          Hurricane I, R4215   **601**
As above. F/O M.D. Doulton missing.   Cat 3

          Hurricane I, P3735   **601**
nr Gravesend. After shooting down a Me109 was forced to crash as a result of a hit in the fuel tank, burning out. Sgt R.N. Taylor baled out.   Cat 3

1.9.40   Spitfire I, L1020   **603**
Gravesend. Force landed during an operational sortie. Reasons not known. Pilot was P/O Cardell.   Cat 3

4.9.40   Hurricane I, R4214   **601**
Lympne. Force landed with damage sustained in combat with Me109's over Worthing (?). F/O J.S. Jankiewicz wounded.
                          Cat 2

23.9.40   Hurricane I, P3643   **257**
Hollingbourne. Crashed. Pilot (?) Sgt Hulbert.

5.10.40   Spitfire I, K9963   **603**
Bilsington. Name of pilot and cause of crash not known.   Cat 3

8.10.40   Spitfire PR I, R6894   **P.R.U.**
Adisham. Crashed.

ADDENDUM

28.5.40 Spitfire I, L1011 **610**
East Langdon, nr Dover. Force landed, reason not known. F/O W.H.C. Warner unhurt. Based Gravesend. Cat 2

12.8.40 Spitfire I, P9330 **610**
Hawkinge. Damaged by Me109 near Dover and force landed. Pilot unhurt. Based Biggin Hill. Cat 2

14/15.8.40 Spitfire I, P9540 **257**
nr Ashford, Kent. Force landed, reason not known. Pilot unhurt. Based Northolt. Cat 2

16.8.40 Spitfire I, X4030 **266**
Manston. Severely damaged by Me109's over Canterbury and force landed, Sgt A.W. Eade unhurt. Based Hornchurch. Cat 2

16.8.40 Blenheim I, L6617 **600**
Manston. Damaged in strafing attack on aerodrome. No personnel casualties. Based Manston. Cat 2

16.8.40 Blenheim I, L8760 **600**
Manston. Badly damaged in strafing attack on aerodrome and SOC on 27.8.40. Based Manston. Cat 3

30.8.40 Hurricane I, N2540 **32**
Biggin Hill. Destroyed in air attack on airfield, no personnel casualties. Based Biggin Hill. Cat 3

31.8.40 Spitfire I, R6928 **72**
Biggin Hill. Destroyed in air raid on airfield, no personnel casualties. Based Biggin Hill. Cat 3

31.8.40 Spitfire, P9424 **72**
NE of High Halden. Force landed after combat. Sqdn Ldr Collins unhurt. Based Biggin Hill. Cat 3
Was in fact salvaged and repaired.

9.7.40 Spitfire I, R6619 **65**
Manston. Aircraft damaged but reason not recorded, P/O Smart unhurt. Based Hornchurch/Manston. Cat 2

15.8.40 Hurricane I, R4101 **501**
nr Folkestone. Force landed after combat, F/L G.E.B. Stoney unhurt. Based Gravesend. Cat 2

1.9.40 Spitfire I, K9958 **72**
Hawkinge. Force landed reason not known. P/O Winter unhurt. Based Croydon. Cat 2

2.9.40 Spitfire I, X4105 **610**
Hawkinge. Damaged on operations, pilot unhurt. Based Biggin Hill. Cat 2

5.9.40 Hurricane I, P2924 **17**
Higham, Gravesend/Rochester. Aileron and rudder badly damaged in combat over Gravesend and force landed. Sgt L.H. Bartlett unhurt. Based Debden. Cat 2

5.9.40 Hurricane I, P3204 **73**
Gravesend. Shot down in combat and F/L R.E. Lovett bailed out. Based Debden. Cat 3

5.9.40 Spitfire I, N3043 **66**
Staplehurst. Damaged by Me109, lost aileron and force landed. P/O H.R. Allen unhurt. Based Kenley. Cat 2

4.9.40 Spitfire I, N3044 **66**
nr Hawkinge. Force landed following combat, F/L F.P.R. Dunworth slightly wounded. Based Kenley. Cat 2

6.9.40 Hurricane I, V6542 **43**
nr Dover. Damaged in combat and crash landed. F/L T.F. Dalton-Morgan wounded in knee. Based Tangmere. Cat 2

6.9.40 Hurricane, P2875 **73**
Maidstone. Shot down in combat with enemy fighters over the Thames Estuary. P/O H.W. Eliot bailed out wounded and with burns. Based Debden. Cat 3

7.9.40 Spitfire I, N3266 **41**
nr Littlebourne. Force landed after combat, Sgt R.C. Ford unhurt. Based Hornchurch. Cat 2

11.9.40 Spitfire I, R6710 **72**
Yalding. Damaged during interception of enemy aircraft over Gravesend and force landed. P/O B. Douthwaite slightly wounded. Based Croydon. Cat 2

15.9.40 Hurricane I, V6576 **242**
nr Maidstone. Force landed following combat over London. F/L G.E. Ball unhurt. Based Coltishall. Cat 2

23.9.40 Spitfire I, X4010 **66**
Gravesend. Damaged, details unknown and pilot unhurt. Based Gravesend. Cat 2

28.9.40 Spitfire II, P7432 **19**
Hawkhurst. Flying accident, details unknown and pilot unhurt. Based Fowlmere. Cat 3
Was then re-classified Cat 2 and repaired.

12.10.40 Hurricane I, V7251 **145**
Dungeness. Severely damaged by Me109's off Dungeness and force landed. P/O P.W. Rabone unhurt. Based Tangmere. Cat 2

17.10.40 Spitfire II, P7292 **74**
Biggin Hill. Cause of damage unknown, F/L Freeborn unhurt. Based Biggin Hill. Cat 2

27.10.40 Spitfire II, P7494 **74**
Biggin Hill. Crashed on landing, P/O Chesters unhurt. Based Biggin Hill. Cat 2

1.11.40 Spitfire II, P7501 **74**
Biggin Hill. Damaged by enemy aircraft over Dover but returned to base. F/Sgt Burnard wounded. Based Biggin Hill. Cat 2

10.11.40 Spitfire II, P7493 **66**
Biggin Hill. Damaged by enemy aircraft. P/O Appleford unhurt. Based Biggin Hill. Cat 2

8.11.40   Spitfire II, P7524 **66**
Biggin Hill. Damaged, reason unknown, Sgt
Cook unhurt. Based Biggin Hill.   Cat 2

8.11.40   Spitfire I, X4478 **66**
Biggin Hill. Tipped on nose due to wheel
running into soft soil of filled in bomb
crater. P/O Baker unhurt. Based Biggin Hill.
                                              Cat 2

8.11.40   Spitfire II, P7361 **74**
Biggin Hill. Damaged on operations, Sgt
Parkes unhurt. Based Biggin Hill.   Cat 2

9.11.40   Spitfire **66**
Biggin Hill. Tipped on nose due to wheel
running into soft ground of filled in bomb
crater. P/O Pickering unhurt. Based Biggin
Hill.   Cat 2

10.11.40   Spitfire II, P7492 **66**
Biggin Hill. Collided with a lorry while taxying. P/O Baker unhurt. Based Biggin Hill.
                                              Cat 2

10.11.40   Spitfire II, P7433 **66**
Biggin Hill. Collided with a petrol tanker
while taxying. F/L Cooke unhurt. Based
Biggin Hill.   Cat 2

10.11.40   Spitfire I, N3106 **92**
Biggin Hill. Badly damaged by fire during
night raid and SOC 18.12.40. No personnel
casualties. Based Biggin Hill.   Cat 3

11.11.40   Spitfire II, P7536 **74**
Biggin Hill. Damaged on operations but
returned to base. P/O Churches unhurt.
Based Biggin Hill.   Cat 2

13.11.40   Spitfire II, P7383 **421Flt**
Biggin Hill. Damaged, reason not known.
Pilot believed to be F/L Green unhurt. Based
Hawkinge.   Cat 2

14.11.40   Spitfire I, X4024 **92**
Biggin Hill. Flying accident, no details but
pilot unhurt. Based Biggin Hill.   Cat 2

14.11.40   Spitfire II, P7557 **74**
Manston. Damaged on operations and force
landed. Sgt Morrison unhurt. Based Biggin
Hill.   Cat 2

14.11.40   Spitfire II, P7437 **66**
Stallisfield. Force landed after combat, P/O
Kendal unhurt. Based Biggin Hill.   Cat 2

14.11.40   Spitfire II, P7500 **66**
Hawkinge. Shot up by enemy aircraft and
crash landed. P/O Hayton unhurt. Based
Biggin Hill.   Cat 2

EXTRA ADDENDUM

23.9.40   Spitfire I, X4010 **66**
Gravesend. Force landed, reason not known,
P/O Bodie unhurt. Based Gravesend.   Cat 2

10.11.40   Spitfire I, X4420 **66**
Biggin Hill. Destroyed by fire in an air raid.
No personnel casualties. Based Biggin Hill.
                                              Cat 3

10.11.40 or 16.11.40 Hudson II, T9382 **206**
Birchington. Damaged by flak and abandoned, crew bailed out. F/L Dias, P/O
Warner, Sgt Chafield (?), Sgt Haywood
unhurt but the Air Gunner had sprained
ankle. Based Bircham Newton.   Cat 3
Squadron F540 gives date as 16.11.40 and
this may well be correct.

25.11.40   Lysander II, P9114 **110 RCAF**
Tonbridge. Force landed and damaged
beyond repair, crew state not known. Based
(?).   Cat 3

6.9.40   Spitfire I, X4260 **603**
off Manston. Thought to have been shot
down in sea but P/O J.R. Caister later found
to have bailed out and landed in France,
POW. Shot down by Hptmn Von Bonin of
I/JG54 in sporadic combat over the Straits
off Manston. Based Hornchurch.   Cat 3

18.8.40   Hurricane, P3678 **1**
Bilsington. Force landed after combat, P/O
Goodman unhurt. Based Northolt.   Cat 2

31.5.40   Anson, N5232 **500**
Detling (Base). Overshot on landing and
came to rest in hedge. Sgt D.C. Spencer and
crew unhurt.   Cat 2

5.6.40   Spitfire, P9460 **72**
Gravesend (Base). Was landing when another Spitfire came in on top of him cutting
off the aircraft's rudder. F/O R.A. Thomson
unhurt.   Cat 2

3.7.40   Do17Z, 2642, 3Z+GS **8/KG77**
Horsmonden, Baybrooks. Force landed after
being damaged by 32Sq Hurricanes (P/O
Gardner, Sgts Bayley and Higgins). Target
was Kenley. Oblt H-G Gallion, Uffz R.
Brandes POW injured, Obgefr E. Hoffman
and Uffz W. Theilig killed. See plot 107.

4.7.40   Hurricane, P2724 **32**
Hawkinge Aerodrome. Forced down by
Me109, P/O K.R. Gillman unhurt. Based
Biggin Hill.   Cat 2

13.8.40   Spitfire, R6759 **74**
Manston. Damaged by return fire from
Do17Z over Thames Estuary and glycol tank
punctured, force landed. F/L P. Kelly unhurt.
Based Hornchurch.   Cat 2

APPENDIX 'A'

NOTES ON THE LUFTWAFFE

HISTORICAL BACKGROUND

The R.A.F. was formed by the fusion of the R.F.C. and the R.N.A.S. and thus had a wide background and tradition. The Luftwaffe on the other hand was solely the child of the German Imperial Army in World War I, and was disbanded in 1918 not to be reformed until the 1930s. As a result it lacked the experience of the inter-war years, and even worse the middle rank officers who should have been the basis of an experienced General Staff.

When the High Command was formed it was necessary to transfer senior officers from the Wehrmacht with little or no experience of flying. This resulted in a heavy bias towards Army thinking and methods which produced an army close support Air Force.

The aircraft which equipped the Luftwaffe then were best suited to that role. The fighters were short ranged as were the medium bombers with little scope for development, no Fleet Air Arm and the failure to produce a practical heavy bomber, and an obsession with the desirability of a dive bombing ability.

During the Polish campaign and the battle for the Low Countries and later France the weaknesses did not really show, although the politically weakened Armée de l'Air, disorganised as it was, inflicted considerable losses. It was to be the Battle of Britain which was finally to highlight the inadequacies.

Strength	1939	7/40	9/40
Bombers	924	1330	439
Dive Bombers	327	280	193
Single engine fighters	818	760	532
Twin engine fighters	342	250	220

CHAIN OF COMMAND

COMBINED H.Q.

Luftwaffe High Command

Luftflotte		Luftflotte		Luftflotte
	FliegerKorps		FliegerKorps	
Geschwader	Geschwader		Geschwader	
Gruppe	Gruppe		Gruppe	
Staffel	Staffel		Staffel	

FUNCTIONS

Luftflotte Controlled all types of aircraft operating in a given geographical area. Some 200-1300 a/c depending on the importance.

FliegerKorps similarly controlling all types, normally for a special campaign. 200-750 a/c.

Geschwader Had usually 3 Gruppen, but later in the War up to 4 or 5 in bomber and Training Geschwadern.

The aircraft were not always of the same types and it is possible to find Gruppen of the same Geschwader flying He111's in the first Gruppe and Ju88's in the second.

Gruppen usually had 27 a/c divided between the three staffeln.

Staffel Commanded by a Staffel Kapitan, usually an Oblt.

Stab. In addition to the above each Geschwader and Gruppe had an H.Q.'s flight (called Stab in abbreviation). This was not only an Administrative plus Technical unit but also had operational aircraft, 4 for the Geschwader and 3 for the Gruppe. These were flown by the Staff officers, Adjutant, Intelligence, Engineering, on operations.

DESIGNATION OF UNITS

This is best explained by taking an example — I/KG76.

    KG identifies it as a bomber unit

    I/ identifies it as the first Gruppe

    76 identifies it as the 76th Geschwader

However 1/KG76 is the first staffel

    7/JG26 then is the 7th Staffel of the 26th fighter geschwader.

In all units I/ Gruppe is made up of 1 2 3 Staffeln

II/	4 5 6 Staffeln
III/	7 8 9 Staffeln
IV/	10 11 12 Staffeln

    The following are the geschwader type designations: KG bombers; JG fighters; ZG twin engine fighters; StG dive bombers; LG training.

KuflGr Coastal Recce. Gruppe; **EproGr** research and development gruppe (usually for one type of aircraft only); **Seenotflkdo** Air Sea Rescue Gruppe. These with a few others were independent gruppen eg. KG4 100.

Reconaissance Gruppe Divided into type according to range. e.g.

4(F)122   was a long range group as indicated by the (F)

2NaGr12   short range as indicated by the Na

Order of Battle

It is often not possible to trace the movement of units especially after September 1940. Some of the reasons for this are:

1.   The practice of operating units as small as single staffeln independently could mean that of one Geschwader one gruppe could be in Russia, another on the Western Front whilst the third could be in Africa.
2.   As explained earlier these smaller units were very mobile and were subject to frequent moves often over long distances.
3.   Designations of units were not infrequently changed and switching from one geschwader to another took place.

ORGANISATION OF FLYING UNITS IN THE LUFTWAFFE

Geschwader	**Personnel** — Geschwader
Stab	Kommodeur (OberstLt or Maj)
Gruppen I II III IV	Exec. Officer (Major Beim)
	Technical Officer (All aircrew flying Stab a/c)
125-150 officers	Operations Officer
150-250 N.C.O.'s	Intelligence Officer
1300-1500 other ranks	Security Officer
	Flight Surgeon
	Stab Feldwebel
Gruppe	
Stab	Gruppe Kommandeur (Major or Hauptmann)
Staffeln 1 2 3	Exec. Officer
Stab Section	Technical Officer
3-5 Officers	Operations Officer
3-6 N.C.O.'s	Met. Officer
40-60 other ranks	Flight Surgeon
Operational Section	StabFw
25-40 Officers	Security Platoon
40-50 N.C.O.'s	Radio Section
400-500 other ranks	Field Signals Section
Staffel	
Stab	Staffel Kapitan and StabFw
Operational Section	
6-8 Officers	Ground crews
6-10 N.C.O.'s	Staffel Tech. Officer
110-130 other ranks	Mechanics
	Cooks
	Airfield Security
	Motor Transport Section

When Gruppen and Staffeln operated independently as they frequently did, they would rely for some services, normally supplied by the parent Geschwader, e.g. major servicing of aircraft, equipment supply, intelligence, on nearby geschwadern or higher units.

LUFTWAFFE AIRCRAFT IDENTIFICATION MARKINGS

other than s.e.f.'s and ground attack aircraft.

How to read the markings

e.g. 3U + HR   3U = Geschwader in this case ZG26
               R = Staffel in this case 7th
               H = individual aircraft.
                     so this is aircraft 'H' of the 7th Staffel of ZG26

A1	KG53		S9	EproGr210
A2	ZG52		T1	AufKlGr10
A3	KG200		T6	StG2
A5	StG 1		U2	NaKlGr5
A6	AufKlGr120 or (F)120		U5	KG3
B3	KG54		U8	ZG26
B4	NJG Staffel Finland/Norway		U9	NSchlGr3
B7	Werka 1		V4	KG1
C1	Epro16		V7	AufKlGr32
C2	AufKlGr41		W7	NJG100
C6	KGzbV 600		Z6	KG6
C8	TG5		1A	Werka5
C9	NJG5		1G	KG27
D1	SeeaufKlGr126		1H	KG26
D3	NachtSlGr2		1K	NSchlGr4
D5	NJG3		1L	NJG10
D7	Werkal		1T	KGr126
D9	NJG7		1Z	KGzbV1-TG1
E8	NSchlG9		2N	ZG1
F1	KG76		2S	ZG2
F6	AufKlGr122		2Z	NJG6
F7	SeeAufKlGr130		3C	NJG4
F8	KG40		3E	KG6
G1	KG55		3K	MinensuchGr
G2	AufKlGr124		3U	ZG26
G6	KGzbV2 became TG4		3W	NSchlG11
G9	NJG1		3Z	KG77
H1	AufKlGr12		4D	KG25-30
H4	LuftlandG1		4E	AufKlGr13
H8	AufKlGr33		4F	KGrzbV400
J2	NaKlGr3		4N	AufKlGr22
J4	T Staffel5		4R	NJG2
J6	KGzbV500		4U	AufKlGr123
J9	StG1		4V	KGzbV172
K6	KuFlGr406		5D	AufKlGr31
K7	NachtaufKlGr		5F	AufKlGr14
L1	LG1		5J	KG4
L2	LG2		5K	KG3
L5	KGzbV5		5W	SeeNotStaff10
M2	KuFlGr106		5Z	Werka26-76
M7	KGr806		6G	StG51
M8	ZG76		6I	KuFlGr706
P1	KG60		6J	NSchlGr8
P2	AufKlGr21		6K	AufKlGr41
P7	Seenot Staff5&51		6M	AufKlGr11
R4	NJG2		6N	KGr100-KG100
S2	StG2		6R	SeeAufGr127
S3	TG30		6U	ZG1
S4	KuFlGr506		6W	SeeaufJlGr128
S5	KG506		7A	AufKlGr121
S7	StG3		7J	NJG102

7R	SeeaufKlGr125
7T	KGr606
7U	KGzbV108
8L	KuFlGr906
8T	KGzbV800-TG2
9K	KG51
9P	KGrzbV9
9V	FaufKlGr5
9W	NJG101

Other type ident.

AufKlGr	Recce.
KGbzV or TG	Transport
KustFlGr	Coastal
Luftland.	Gliders
Minensuch.	Aerial mine
	minesweeper
NJG	nightfighter
NSchlGr	night strike
SchlactG	strike
SeeaufKlGr	marine recce.
Werka Met.	recce. flight

Staffel letters

A	Stab
B	I/Gruppe Stab
C	II/Gruppe Stab
D	III/Gruppe Stab
E	IV/Gruppe Stab
F	V/Gruppe Stab
H	1/Staffel
K	2/Staffel
L	3/Staffel
M	4/Staffel
N	5/Staffel
P	6/Staffel
R	7/Staffel
S	8/Staffel
T	9/Staffel
U	10/Staffel
V	11/Staffel
W	12/Staffel
X	13/Staffel
Y	14/Staffel
Z	15/Staffel

In addition to the above codes on the rear fuselage, a/c often carried a unit badge (of Geschwader, Gruppe, or Staffel) on the nose.

Single engined aircraft (except dive bombers)
There was no letter code for these aircraft. However in the later forties a system of numbers was introduced but it only identified the aircraft in a Gruppe.
It consisted of a single or double number. Where a single number was used it was placed forward of the black fuselage cross. Where doubles were used there would be one before and one aft of the cross.
e.g. 5 + or 1 + 6
Another variation was to use a number painted in different colours, and these will appear in the text as 'green6' and so on.
Propellor nose cones were painted different colours in different theatres of war.
The Lw did not permit individual flights of fancy such as the U.S.A.A.F. nose art, but turned a blind eye to indications of success such as R.A.F. roundels to denote victories.

SINGLE ENGINED AIRCRAFT

Gruppen markings on the rear of the fuselage.
No markings   I/Gruppe

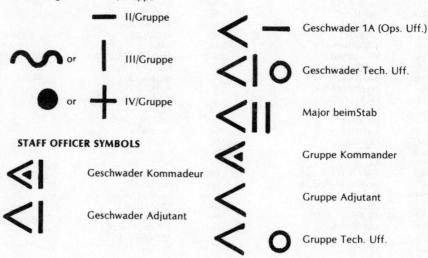

STAFF OFFICER SYMBOLS

II/Gruppe
III/Gruppe
IV/Gruppe

Geschwader Kommadeur

Geschwader Adjutant

Geschwader 1A (Ops. Uff.)

Geschwader Tech. Uff.

Major beimStab

Gruppe Kommander

Gruppe Adjutant

Gruppe Tech. Uff.

APPENDIX 'B'

COMPARATIVE RANKS IN THE AIR FORCES

Luftwaffe	R.A.F.	Others
Flieger	Aircraftsman	
Gefreiter	Leading aircraftsman	
Obergefreiter)		
Unteruffizer)	Corporal	
Feldwebel	Sergeant	
Oberfeldwebel	Flight Sergeant	
Stabsfeldwebel	Warrant Officer	Adjudnant (FFAF)
Leutnant	Pilot Officer	Midshipman (R.N.)
Oberleutnant	Flying Officer	Sublieutenant
Hauptmann	Flight Lieutenant	
Major	Squadron Leader	
Oberstleutenant	Wing Commander	
Oberst	Group Captain	

Ranks in the different air forces are not directly comparable. In general equivalent units in the Lw and R.A.F. would be commanded in the latter by higher ranking officers.

Staffel would have an Oberleutnant as a C.O. whilst an R.A.F. Fighter squadron (only slightly larger) by a S/Ldr and a Bomber squadron by a W/Cdr.

Gruppe by a Hauptmann or Major.

Geschwader by an Oberst, OberstLt or Major.

Whereas all R.A.F. Units had an establishment for all ranks, and personnel were promoted or posted in to fill this establishment, the Luftwaffe had an establishment for the whole force and promotions were on seniority in the rank.

As a result of this policy appointments such as Staffel Kapitan or Geschwader Komodore were not filled with a set rank, but the senior rank available so the C.O. of a Gruppe could be anything from Oberleutnant to Major, and a Geschwader Komodore a Major, Oberst Lt or Oberst.

Similarly in the R.A.F. the minimum rank for an aircrew member was sergeant) from mid-1940 onwards, with a time promotion to flight sergeant and warrant officer similarly from pilot officer to flying officer.

On the other hand in the Luftwaffe the commonest aircrew rank was unteruffizer and in these records are instances of the pilot of a fighter being a flieger.

Command of a multiplace aircraft also differed. In the Lw the commander of such an aircraft was usually the senior officer, whereas in the R.A.F. it was normally the pilot, regardless of rank.

APPENDIX 'C'
DEUTSCHEN SOLDATEN FRIEDHOF at Cannock Chase, Staffordshire

This is the main site for burial of German service men who died in the United Kingdom from 1938-1948, containing the remains of some 5,000 men.

The control of this cemetery is not vested in the Commonwealth War Graves Commission, but was set up and financed by a German group:

Volksbund Deutsche Kreigsgräberfursage E.V.
Werner Hilpert Strasse 2,
3500 KASSEL, W. Germany.

When the decision was made to centralise burial, the next of kin were approached to see if they would prefer to leave their dead in their original burial site, and some opted for this, so there are still many German graves in scattered locations. As an alternative it was possible for the remains to be returned to Germany, but in this case the next of kin had to face the high cost involved. For some reason not understood, the German government paid for the return of civilians who died here.

The area is divided into a number of large plots and an attempt was made to bury those killed in the same year in one plot. The headstones are usually shared by two dead and show the name, rank, branch of service, date of birth and death. Each has a three part serial number e.g. 23.5.346 where 5 is the plot number and 346 the grave.

Where bomber crews were interred it was not normally possible to identify the individual remains and so they are buried in a common grave for the four or five crew members with a horizontal stone.

There is an unmanned office which has details of all the burials. To obtain access to this it is necessary to contact the custodian/groundsman. It is better to 'phone in advance and make an appointment, for he is difficult to locate.

Close by are other burial sites, one for New Zealanders killed in WW1, another for Germans of that war including crew members of Zeppelins and Gothas shot down over Britain.

Service burials in Kent
For those interested in location of burial sites the War Graves Commission publish interment lists for the English counties.

The records of Burials in Kent have proved to be difficult to find. During the war each town had its own cemetery and its own method of recording. Some such as Hawkinge kept a separate register for servicemen including in it the rank, unit and place of death. Others simply kept a single register without the details.

There seems to be no logical pattern where the dead were buried so that in one cemetery there may be dead from sites many miles apart. Next of kin had the option of having dead returned to a local cemetery for burial, and many exercised this right.

We have found local government staff most helpful in trying to assist our research.

APPENDIX 'D'
AIR SEA RESCUE

This obviously falls into two parts:

Search principally airborne; **Rescue** mainly seaborne.

Between the Wars the R.A.F. had built up a Marine Craft Branch. Its functions were varied, target towing for gunnery and bombing practice; range surveillance; tenders for the considerable number of flying boat squadrons and rescue for ditched aircraft. These services continued until 1986 when the last of the high speed launches were replaced by helicopter units of the R.A.F. and Navy.

Over the years in parallel with the diversification of the aircraft types a similar change took place in marine craft. This was particularly noticeable in the rescue function. The launches had to become larger and faster, larger to accommodate their own crews and those rescued for longer journeys, faster to reach survivors as quickly as possible, for the North Sea in winter is no place for prolonged immersion. finally they were to be armed for self defence.

Marine craft in the S.E. England
No.27 M.C.U. and No.30 were based early in the war at Dover and Calshot respectively, with 29 M.C.U. at Littlehampton and 28 M.C.U. being located at Newhaven in early 1940.

27 M.C.U. had a detachment at Margate and also kept an H.S.L. on permanent standby under the lee of Dungeness in all but the worst weather conditions. Later in 1942 the Margate detachment was withdrawn and a new unit formed at Sheerness to cover the upper Thames Estuary.

The duties of the crews were no sinecure. High speed involved light construction and two very large engines occupying much of the hull space. The launches had to be able to plane on the hull step and in even a slight chop progression was achieved in a serious of gut shaking thumps. Additionally the actual rescue could involve the retrieval of seriously injured or burnt crew men or what was left of bodies after long periods in the water.

Later in 1940 they were also subjected to attacks by enemy fighters and E-boats, and on one day 27 M.C.U. lost three launches and their crews.

The launches and their crews were not as closely associated with their units as were air-crews and their squadrons and might be moved from one unit to another as operation conditions required, including postings overseas.

Provision of personal rescue equipment
Provision of these went ahead in much the same way as other flying equipment. The first, of course being the parachute. By the outbreak of War the inflatable life jackets, known to all as 'Mae West's' after a well developed female film star, and inflatable dinghies were issued. These were all intended to function for short periods, although accounts exist of crews spending days in the larger multi-place dinghies. The ultimate in airborne equipment came later in the War with the advent of the Lindholme dinghy, a metal lifeboat fully equipped for survival and self rescue which was dropped, usually by Warwick aircraft on a multi parachute suspension.

Search
Most of the above refers to the rescue function. The search side was more difficult and varied.

The location of a single crewman in a one man dinghy could be extremely difficult even in fine weather, and was vastly increased with any deterioration of visibility or surface disturbance.

Certain measures were instituted to reduce the difficulties as far as possible.

Normally the pilot of a single engined aircraft would not be operating alone. If he was in danger of force landing in the sea he would call his controller by R/T giving his approximate position and continue to transmit until he hit the water, whilst one or more of his fellow pilots would circle his position as long as fuel allowed, climbing if necessary to facilitate a gound station fix.

In a multi-place aircraft on being warned of a likely ditching the wireless operator would transmit a 'Mayday' until the last possible minute when he would screw down his radio key before taking up a ditching position.

Even when a reasonable fix had been obtained it could be some time before help was at hand and during this time wind and tide could have changed the position significantly. In this case a square search was made moving outward from the estimated position.

In the first few months of the War A.S.R. searches were carried out by civilians flying light aircraft. Afterwards the work was taken over by any aircraft available, with squadrons preferring to search for their own missing companions. This did not fit in well with operational requirements, and it then fell to some training units such as O.T.U.'s and Bombing and Gunnery Schools to incorporate these searches as part of the training course.

By 22.9.40 in the S.E. a detachment of Lysanders of 4 Sq. based at Clifton (York) were flying from Manston specifically for these duties.

Royal and Merchant Navies
Both of these services carried out many rescues, and were on the alert for crippled aircraft in the coastal waters.

R.N.L.I.
Not all the L.B. Stations were operational during the early part of the War, and in any case could only launch when given specific permission by the Senior Naval Officer in the area. Nevertheless the Kent Lifeboats carried out many successful rescues. However the Dover boat was taken over by the R.N.

Shoreboats
This term was used to describe anything from a single-handed rowing boat to inshore trawlers with several men in the crew and here again they were very active. One notable rescue was carried out by a lady at Hythe who went out in a canoe to pick up a crewman from a ditched Whitley.

BIBLIOGRAPHY

Air War over France 1939/40	R. Jackson	I. Allen
Air Battle over Dunkirk	N. Franks	Kimber
Aces High	Shores & Williams	N. Spearman
Action Stations No.8	B. Halpenny	P. Stevens
Action Stations No.9	C. Ashworth	P. Stevens
A Clasp for the Few	K.G. Wynn	
Battle of Britain	B. Collyer	Batsford
Battle for Britain	W/Cdr H.R. Allen	A. Barker
Battle of Britain Diary — East Kent	D.G. Collyer	K.A.H.R.S.
Battle over Britain	F.K. Mason	McWhirter
Battle of Britain, Then and Now	J. Ramsey	After the Battle
The Blitz Then and Now	J. Ramsey	After the Battle
Bomber Command War Diaries	Middlebrook & Everitt	Viking
Bomber Squadrons of the R.A.F.	P. Noyes	MacDonald
The Bader Wing	J.F. Turner	Midas Books
Civil Defence	T.H. O'Brien	HMSO
Croydon Airport and the Battle of Britain	Cluett, Bogle & Learmouth	Sutton Libraries
Commonwealth War Graves in Kent		War Graves Commission
Coastal, Support & Special Sqdns of the R.A.F.	J.D.R. Rawlings	Janes
Dowding & The Battle of Britain	R. Wright	MacDonald
Defence of the United Kingdom	B. Collier	HMSO
Duel of Eagles	P. Townsend	Wedenfeld & Nicholson
Eagle Day	R. Collier	Hodder & Stoughton
Fighter Aces of the Lw	Toliver & Constable	Aero Pubs.
Fighter Sqdns of the R.A.F. and Their Aircraft	J. Rawlings	Macdonald & Janes
Front Line County	A. Roots	Hale
Ginger Lacey — Fighter Pilot	R. Townsend-Bickers	R. Hale
The Hardest Day	A. Price	MacDonald & Jane
Harvest of Messerschmitts	D. Knight	F. Warne
Hawkinge 1912-1961	R. Humphreys	Meresborough
Hawker Hurricane	Mason	Aston
JG26	Priller	Motorbuch Verlag
JG51 — Mölders	Aderds & Held	Motorbuch Verlag
KG51 — Edelweis	Dierich	Motorbuch Verlag
Kent War Diaries	Archive Office	Maidstone
Kent Airfields in the Battle	K.A.H.R.S.	Meresborough
Kent's Own — 500 Sqdn	R.T. Brooks	Meresborough
The Last Enemy	R. Hillary	Macmillan
The Lonely Warrior	J. Offenberg	Granada
Luftwaffe Handbook	A. Price	I. Allan
Luftwaffe War Diaries	C. Bekker	G. Stalling Verlag
The Narrow Margin	Wood & Dempster	Hutchinson
Nine Lives	G/Capt A. Deere	Hodder & Stoughton
Paddy Finucane, Fighter Ace	Stokes	W. Kimber
R.A.F. Biggin Hill	G. Wallace	Putnam
R.A.F. 1939-45	H.S. Saunders	HMSO
Raiders Approach	S/Ldr H.T. Sutton	Gale & Polden
The R.C.A.F. and its aircraft	S. Kostenuck & V. Griffin	Canadian War Museum
R.A.F. Serials		Air Britain
The Rise and Fall of the German Air Force		Arms & Armour Press
The Right of the Line	J. Terraine	Hodder & Stoughton
The Reluctant Messerschmitt	D. Everson	Portcullis Press
Spitfire — The History	Morgan & Shacklady	Key Pubs.
Sky Tiger	N. Franks	W. Kimber
Squadrons of the R.A.F.	J. Halley	Air Britain
Squadron Histories	D. Lewis	Putnam
Sir Keith Park	V. Orange	Methuen
Squadron Codes — 1937-56	M.J. Bowyer & J.D. Rawlings	P. Stephens
Target England	D. Wood	Janes
Who Won the Battle of Britain	W/Cdr H. Allen	A. Barket

INDEX OF LOCATION OF INCIDENTS

East Farleigh — 1379
East Langdon (nr Dover) — 499 788 1077
Eastling — 854
East Malling — 1118
East Peckham — 892 1029 1176 1461
Eastry — 334 488 494 646 715 1064 1201 1221
East Seal — 420
East Sutton — 814 1147
Edenbridge — 27 442 900 919 1108 1422 1459
Elham — 130 310 476 519 652 775 784 785 803 852 1232 1269 1367
Elmley (Isle of Sheppey) — 1091
Elvington — 742
Eynsford — 771 844
Eythorne — 872 1429
Farnborough — 1185
Farningham — 889 890 1113
Faversham — 411 467 495 579 626 781 853 856 959 1034 1073 1140 1355 1439 1489
Flimwell — 903
Folkestone & Hythe — 23 26 69 119 120 121 122 142 151 152 157 163 171 172 173 205 235 236 244 269 303 342 344 345 348 362 366 368 371 374 391 392 445 522 565 575 585 607 620 630 712 723 724 754 756 875 1081 1104 1127 1128 1200 1212 1218 1255 1370 1374 1375 1442 1488
Foreness (nr Margate) — 465 554 571 647
Frant — 397
Frittenden — 982
Gillingham — 456 1150 1273
Godmersham — 359 582 1084 1122 1199
Goodnestone — 580
Goodwin Sands — 49 79 80 86 138 214 567 664
Goudhurst — 821 895 896 985 1014 (Bedgbury) 1178 1205 1304
Gravesend — 22 47 84 104 224 239 251 252 367 526 569 629 658 659 665 710 949 962 981 1045 1101 1155 1187 1188 1207 1224 1259 1280 1281 1282 1287 1301 1303 1405 1455 1456 1466 1476 1479 1484 1487 1496
Great Chart — 957
Greatstone — 1211 1378
Ham Street — 686 694
Harrietsham — 1030 1252
Hartley (nr Dartford) — 989 1164 1431
Hastingleigh — 917 1258
Hawkenbury — 1161 1437
Hawkhurst — 316 395 654 667 1006
Hawkinge — 35 38 55 82 88 90 92 111 112 123 147 148 162 165 175 181 200 202 240 245 255 261 262 281 287 288 299 301 302 307 333 353 354 356 357 376 378 380 385 409 471 474 479 480 482 487 493 538 550 552 569 597 609 734 824 848 849 935 1044 1172 1223 1233 1233 1276 1338 1434 1451 1467 1486 1495
Headcorn — 832 1208
Herne Bay — 2 44 515 545 546 563 589 747 769 789 971 1018 1400
Hextable — 809
Higham — 1068 1096
Hersden — 1383

High Halden — 655 1130
High Halstow — 1265 1274
Hildenborough — 680 933 1070 1344
Hoath — 535 540 857
Hollingbourne — 850 885 960 1041 1132 1145 1253 1284 1290
Hoo — 1271
Horsmonden — 107 923 1135 1418 1464
Horton Kirkby — 1203 1343
Hothfield — 834
Hougham — 178 718 878 1071 1279
Ide Hill — 1
Isle of Grain — 864 993 996 1079
Isle of Sheppey — 96 328 514 624 648 858 876 966 1001 1057 1058 1392
Ightham — 394 1162 1163
Ivychurch — 726 1433 1440

Kent Reach — 1275
Kingsdown (nr Dover) — 203 1089
Kingston (nr Barham) — 460
Knockholt — 894
Lamberhurst — 1153 1267
Leeds Castle — 448 689 707 888 1012 1465 1490
Leigh — 1165
Lenham — 429 434 739 827 1308 1348 1365
Leysdown — 331 469 470 765 780
Littlestone — 10 816 1317 1340
Location — nothing stated — 339 811 860 913 1005 1114 1158 1159 1173 1174 1295 1296
Lower Stoke (north of Rochester) — 1007
Lydd — 11 65 66 446 671 893 931 1115 1169 1171 1318 1321 1324 1351
Lydden — 239
Lyminge — 517 521 1069 1194
Lympne — 28 145 204 289 365 600 610 692 735 1016 1017 1074 1182 1183
Lynsted (nr Sittingbourne) — 1151
Maidstone — 360 570 773 802 843 915 963 1036 1129 1227 1298 1310 1326 1356 1357 1419 1474 1475
Manston — 9 16 21 31A 36 50 52 54 60 61 63 67 72 76 83 89 103 117 118 125 133 135 141 144 146 194 216 218 226 230 231 243 246 256 283 298 306 311 314 340 341 343 350 355 375 399 417 418 451 452 453 468 475 477 483 484 485 490 491 498 501 504 505 509 623 643 790 829 1076 1093 1180 1291 1314 1421 1452
Marden — 410 466 662 745 783 994 1325 1333 1336 1371
Margate — 14 17 25 85 93 94 95 109 186 189 190 192 193 265 266 278 279 280 305 312 324 382 486 496 510 561 587 744 749 750A 925 926 927
Meopham — 708 886 936 1376
Mereworth — 1119 1309
Milstead — 1124
Minster (Isle of Sheppey) — 590 641 642
Monks Horton — 732
Newchurch — 431 677 877 921 1235 1316 1377
Newenden — 946

New Romney — 284 285 313 1250 1302
Nore Light (Thames Estuary) — 714 794
  825 826 1062
North Foreland — 34 277 294 458 1402
  1410 1411
Oare (nr Faversham) — 411
Off Kent Coast — 319 402 503 506 912 965
  1243
Old Romney — 731 932 1471
Orlestone — 683 686 955
Orpington — 1137
Otford — 444
Over Kent — 97 768 792 793 830 1020
  1173 1174 1295 1296
Paddock Wood — 991
Pembury — 806 813 928 1009 1341
Penshurst — 20 729 730 761 1139 1329
  1332 1349
Petham — 574 581 1048 1134
Pluckley — 433 685 836 1152 1190 1292
  1366
Ramsgate — 74 105 114 256 258 259 292
  293 384 481 497 502 564 1038 1225 1386
Reculver — 18 383 547 779
Rochester — 77 263 617 891 1133 1202
  1217 1260 1278 1327 1345 (Strood) 1027
  1096 1168 1231 1257 1260
Rhodes Minnis — 518
Rodmersham — 161 1078
Rolvenden — 871 1283 1362
Romney Marsh — 1364 1463
Ruckinge — 461A 684 687 807 1469
St Margarets — 31 48 110 167 213 220
St Mary Hoo — 1090
St Nicholas at Wade — 315 324 531 586
  791 1136
Sandgate — 1210
Sandhurst — 914 1019
Sandwich — 129 358 559 663 1053 1126
  1141 1262 1268 1424
Seal — 820 887 980 1110
Seasalter — 325
Seabrook — 1478
Sellindge — 304 713 1054
Selling — 1146 1246
Sevenoaks — 377 427 454 842 873 902 983
  1138 1204 1214 1288 1330 1406 1482
Shadoxhurst — 751 1175 1319
Sheerness — 332 560 1063 1242 1403
Shepherdswell — 492 1368
Shipbourne — 695
Shorncliffe — 390
Shoreham — 940 975
Sidcup — 422
Sittingbourne — 7 435 512 640 740 866 901
  953 979 1004 1037 1067 1086 1123 1154
  1228 1294 1401
Smarden — 616 767 1000 1181
Smeeth — 941 1441 1222
Snargate — 424 615
South East Coast — 45 1158 1159
South Foreland — 1426
Southfleet — 898 1373 1393
Staple — 912
Staplehurst — 649 678 693 950 956 970
  972 1039 1237 1337 1342 1416

Stelling Minnis — 591 1026 1412
Stockbury — 588 1270
Stodmarsh — 326
Stoke Marshes — 822 996
Stone cum Ebony — 1398
Stone (nr Dartford) — 954
Stone (nr Faversham) — 954
Sturry — 430 741 984
Sundridge — 818
Sutton at Hone — 823
Sutton Valence — 847 865 879
Swanley — 1300
Swingfield — 15 1388
Tatsfield — 5 160 423
Temple Ewell — 551
Tenterden — 602 668 748 751 1003 1248
  1293
Teston — 393
Teynham — 1438 1439
Thames Estuary — 137 140 145A, 179 206
  268 270 271 274 276 321 363 419 681 778
  798 799 800 846 859 863 964 967 1008
  1011 1032 1033 1046 1082 1083 1085
  1107 1160 1219 1266 1409
Throwley (Faversham) — 578 1121
Ticehurst — 1153
Tilmanstone — 3
Tonbridge — 19 443 737 833 835 969 1166
  1306 1313 1315
Tongue Light — 587
Tunbridge Wells — 679 815 976 977 1209
  1234 1323 1369 1437 1461
Ulcombe — 675 725 1148
Upchurch — 1213
Upper Hardres — 605
Upstreet — 549 1350
Walderslade (Chatham) — 634 661 1052
Welling — 1307
Westbere — 428 594
Westerham — 922
Westgate — 264
West Kingsdown — 520 666 1239
West Malling — 102 320 379 398 438 618
  632 633 688 691 698 868 958 995 1008
  1010 1080 1118 1131 1144 1346 1363
  1380 1391 1480 1491 1492
W. Stourmouth — 753
Westwell — 627 805
West Wickham — 1112 1352
Whitstable — 6 330 404 414 425 450 462
  463 528 828 1382 1389
Wickhambreux — 408 867 1247
Wittersham — 254 1256 1397
Womenswold — 706
Woodchurch — 635 637 748
Woodnesborough — 403 488 1432
Woollage — 743
Wrotham — 614 657 862 884 930 1240
  1263 1415
Wye — 349 557 572 939 943 1120 1435
  1436
Yalding — 670 763 992 1043 1285 1328

INDEX OF ALLIED PERSONNEL

The ranks given are those held when the name first appears. Initials are included where known.

In some units' records, ranks have been omitted. This causes a possible complication. As pilots may have been posted from one squadron to another, if no rank or initials are given it is not possible to decide whether it is one or two individuals.

The first figure gives the number of the squadron and the following numbers are those of the incident in which the individual was involved.

In a few cases where imprecise information, lacking some major factor, exists 'Imp' followed by a date is used, e.g. Imp 25/7 (25th July).

Similarly where late information has been obtained and has been included in the Addendum 'Add 25/7' is used.

The state of each individual crew member is assumed to be safe unless the name is followed by (D) = dead; (M) = missing; (P) = POW.

F/O D.A. Adams   41 — 1200
P/O H.C. Adams   501 — 735 803
P/O E.S. Aldous   610/51 — 493 1152
P/O Aldridge   53 — 48 114
P/O K.R. Aldridge   501 — 520
P/O J.W. Alexander   151 — 582
P/O G. Allard   85 — 486 584 585 692 699
P/O D. Allcock   229 — 1090
Sgt Allen   141 — 1466
P/O H. Allen   66 — 1132 1233 1459
P/O J. Allen (D)   54 — 191
Sgt H.H. Allgood (D)   253 — 1227
P/O Allington   48 — 62
Sgt L.C. Allton (D)   92 — 1299
P/O C.F. Ambrose   46 — 738 741 1395 1472
A/C Amer   421Flt — 1467
F/O C.J. Andreae (M)   64 — 261 381
Sgt J. Anderson   253 — 954
P/O S.E. Andrews   257 — 1203
Sgt S. Andrews   46 — 888
Sgt Andrew   53 — 316
Sgt T. Andruszkow   303 — 1007
P/O E. Aries   602 — 862
P/O Arkill   500 — 13
P/O W. Armstrong   74 — 1424
Sgt S.J. Arnfield   610 — 94 287 488
Sgt Arrowsmith (M)   139 — 1092
F/L R. Ash (D)   264 — 502 579
P/O Asheton   222 — 622
P/O Ashton (D)   59 — 87
Sgt A. Aslin   257 — 1084
F/L Astley   48 — 57
P/O Aston   500 — 156

Sgt F.P. Atkins (D)   141 — 171
P/O R. Atkinson (D)   213 — 1292
Sgt C. Ayling (D)   421Flt — 1235
S/L J.C. Badger (D)   43 — 637
P/O Bagnell   77 — 1444
P/O J.R. Bailey   264 — 574
Sgt R. Baker (M)   264 — 501 545
Sgt R. Baker (D)   56 — 161 276
P/O H. Baker   41 — 1026 1443
F/L G. Ball   242 — 1126
F/O Balston   500 — 10
Sgt Bamberger   41 — 1077 1190
F/O A.J. Banham   264/229 — 501 545 1270
Sgt P. Banks   245 — 65
P/O R.G. Barclay   249 — 1144 1464
LAC (later Sgt) F.J. Barker   264 — 52 504 542
Sgt N. Barron   236 — 212
F/O N. Barry (D)   501 — 1161 1198
F/L A. Bartlett   53 — 114
S/L Bartlett   58 — 750A
F/O A. Bartley   92 — 1042
P/O A.R. Barton   32/253 — 300 301 356 1017 1069
P/O Barton   229 — 1366
P/O E. Barwell   264 — 63 70
Sgt S. Baxter   222 — 621

Sgt E. Bayley (D)   249 — 1226
F/L A.W.A. Baynes   17 — 926
F/L Basley   266 — 408
G/C V. Beamish   ? — 514 1407
P/O E. Beardmore   1RCAF — 1046
Sgt R.A. Beardsley   41/610 — 620 1172 1338
P/O H.J. Beazley   249 — 709
Sublt H.W. Beggs   151 — 339 390
Sgt M. Belc   303 — 1105 1183 Imp 30/9
P/O R.W. Beley (D)   151 — 293
F/O J.S. Bell (D)   616 — 540 618
F/O Bell-Salter   253 — 720
Sgt H. Bell-Walker   72 — 955 1045
Sgt Benbow (D)   82 — 1481
Sgt D. Bennett   609 — 68
P/O I. Bennions   41 — 219 230 822 1074
P/O N.J. Benson (D)   603 — 602
Sgt J. Bentley-Beard   249 — 1326
F/L H.R. Beresford (D)   257 — 858
P/O B. Bernas   302 — 1298
Sgt A. Berry (M)   264 — 497A
P/O Berry   603 — 1442
F/S F.G. Berry (D)   1 — 687
F/L M. Beytagh   73 — 958
Sgt A. Binham   64 — 162 220
P/O H. Bird-Wilson   17 — 1097
P/O Birkett (D)   219 — 1422
Sgt H.E. Black   46 — 1359
P/O K.H. Blair   151 — 247
F/L M. Blake   238 — 1010
Sublt A.G. Blake   19 — 902 1032 1129

107

P/O J.W. Bland (D)   501 — 224 430
Sgt J.C. Blessey   235 — 21
P/O C. Bodie   66 — 848 984 1187 1259
P/O Booth (D)   235 — 58
F/OJ. Boulter   603 — 1089
Adj H. Bouquillard   249 — 1327
P/O N.G. Bowen (D)   266 — 407
Sgt Bowen-Morris   92 — 1143 1360
LAC Bowers   48 — Imp 25/5
F/O Bowler   32 — 26
F/O B.H. Bowring   111 — 776 797 823
F/O J. Boyle (D)   41 — 1151
Sgt Braybrook   500 — 13
F/O E. Briese   1RCAF — 1027
Sgt Briggs   53 — 523
F/OV.M. Bright   229 — 1295 1490
Sgt J. Brimble (D)   73 — 951
P/O Brisbane (D)   65 — 121
Sgt Brooks   53 — 86 523
F/O R.E. Brooker   56 — 333
F/L Brothers   32/257 — 459 507 980
F/L Brown   53 — 86
P/O B. Brown   72 — 1086
P/O Brown   613 — 44
(Civil) K.K. Brown   Kent Fly. Club — 3
F/L G.A. Brown   253 — 632
LAC Brown (229) (D)   613 — 46
F/Sgt Brown   79 — 12
P/O R.C.Brown   229 — 1268
F/L D.C. Bruce (M)   111 — 754
P/O Bryant-Fenn   79 — 702
F/O Brzezina   74 — 321
Sgt M. Brezezowski (M)   303 — 1011
Sublt G.G. Bulmer (M)   32 — 180
Sgt J.H. Burgess   222 — 879 1365
P/O E. Burgogne (D)   19 — 1125
F/L N. Burnett   46 — 885
P/O P. Burton   249 — 708
Sgt B.M. Bush   504 — 855
P/O Bushell (M)   151 — 40
Sgt Butler   53 — 316
Sgt A. Butterick   3 — 7
F/L Byrne   92 — 27
Sgt Calderwood   85 — 1487
P/O F.W. Cale (D)   266 — 393
Sgt Callorrossi   500 — 534
S/L W.P. Cambridge (D)   253 — 807
Sgt Cameron   66 — 1135
P/O A. Campbell   54 — 116 459
P/O K.C. Campbell (D)   43 — 233
F/L Campbell-Colquhuon   264 — 485
Sgt Campion (M)   10 — 335
P/O C. Capon   257 — 1256
F/O B. Carbury   603 — 626 1209 1225
P/O D. Cardell (D)   603 — 1127 1128
   Add 1/9
F/O Carnaby   85 — 1484
Sgt R. Carnall   111 — 147 405
Sublt J.C. Carpenter (D)   46 — 883
P/O J.M. Carpenter   222 — 758

P/O K. Carswell   43 — 727
LAC Carter (D)   26 — 82
Sgt L.R. Carter   41 — 1239
Sgt H. Cartwright (D)   79 — 110
Sgt Cartwright (D)   82 — 1481
P/O K. Carver   229 — 923

Sgt Caryll   58 — 750A
P/O H.R. Case (D)   72 — 1244
P/O Casson   616 — Imp 1/9
Sgt Castle (D)   219 — 1422
F/O A. Cebrzynski (D)   303 — 928
P/O R.I. Chaffe   245 — Add 23/6
P/O Chaffey (D)   500 — 1415
P/O Chauffey (D)   500 — 156
P/O H.H. Chalder (D)   266/41 — 1149
F/O G.L. Chambers (D)   610 —   75
F/O Chambers (D)   500 — 73
Sgt Chamberlain   10 — 335
Sgt Chard   141 — 1036 1381 1496
P/O Chesters   74 — 1446
Sgt Chew   17 — 787
Sgt D. Chipping   222 — 788
F/L G.P. Christie   66 — 764 792 1452
P/O A. Clarke (M)   504 — 921
Sgt G.T. Clarke   151 — 495
Sgt Clayton   53 — 283
P/O J.K. Clifton (D)   253 — 693
P/O D.G. Cobden   74 — 145
F/O Coke   257 — 1317
P/O E. Coleman   54 — 118
F/O P. Collard (D)   615 — 166 347
Sgt G.R. Collett (D)   54 — 206 472
S/L Collins   72 — 745
Sgt Collorossi   500 — 534
P/O M. Constable-Maxwell   56 — 589
Sgt H. Cook   66 — 1303 1345
S/L D. Cooke (M)   65 — 124
P/O C.A. Cooke   66 — 759
A/C Combe   500 — 15
F/S C.J. Cooney (M)   56 — 223
Sgt S.F. Cooper   253 — 636
P/O T. Cooper-Slipper   605 — 992
P/O J.H. Copeman (D)   111 — 277
Sgt P. Copeland   616 — 557
P/O G. Corbett (D)   66 — 900 1137
   1213
F/L V.B. Corbett   1RCAF — 651
Sgt W.J. Corben   66 — 1380
Sgt D.F. Corfe   73/66/610 — 474 1048
F/L Cosby   72 — 1081
Sgt Coubrough   58 — 750A
F/O W.H. Coverley (D)   602 — 861
F/L P.A. Cox (M)   501 — 211
Sgt D.G. Cox   19 — 1120
P/O K.H. Cox (D)   610 — 591
Sgt Crawford (D)   82 — 1481
Sgt R. Crombie (M)   141 — 173
P/O Cronan   235 — 58
F/L R.P. Cross (D)   235 — 21 51
Sgt M. Crosskell   213 — 963
S/L M. Crossley   32 — 305 394 424 456
   460 521 524
P/O I. Cruikshanks   66 — 849 943
A/C Cullen   23 — 19
F/L J.L. Cunningham (M)   603 — 596
Sgt A.G. Curley (M)   141 — 170
P/O C. Currant   605 — 999 1179
Priv. C. Cuthbert   Homeguard — 191
F/O J.W. Cutts (M)   222 — 762
P/O M. Czernin   17 ' — 787 927 1376
F/O R. Dafforn   501 — 420 1278
Sgt E.V. Darling   41 — 1100 1118 1442
P/O J. Daszewski   303 — 852
Sgt H. Davidson   249 — 891 1464

Sgt Davidson (M)   139 — 1092
F/L C.R. Davies (D)   601 — 819
P/O C.G. Davies   222 — 668
Sgt M.P. Davies   1 — 1219
F/O J. Davies   79 — 12
F/O P.F. Davies   56 — 330
Sgt L. Davies   151 — 593
G/Capt E. Davis   ? — 317
Sgt W.L. Davis   249 — 916
F/O P.J. Davis-Cooke (D)   72 — 1112
P/O V. Daw   32 — 197
Sgt Day   75 — 1314
P/O K.B. Debenham   151 — 494
F/L A. Deere   54 — 133 282 310 311 359
    588
P/O R. De Grunne   32 — 461A
P/O A.V. D'Ertsenrijk (D)   501 — 988
Sgt A. Deller   43 — 847
F/O H. De Molson   1RCAF — 1181
S/L G. Denholm   603 — 603 615 966
F/O J.P. Desloges   1RCAF — 665
Sgt C. De Tilkin   58 — 750A
P/O P. Dexter   603 — 1128 1178
P/O R.B. Dewey (D)   603 — 1354
P/O Dews (M)   500 — Imp 29/5
Sgt D. D'Hamale (D)   46 — 914 1388
Sgt J.H. Dickenson (D)   253 — 635
LAC Dilnutt   48 — 62
P/O Dini   605 — 69
P/O R. Doe   234 — 781
P/O R. Don   501 — 239
F/O A. Donahue   64 — 245 262 304
F/L I.D. Donald (D)   141 — 174
S/L E. Donaldson   151 — 105
P/O B. Douthwaite   72 — 688
P/O G.L. Doutrepont (D)   229 — 970
P/O P.D.M. Down   56 — 431
F/O G.J. Drake (D)   607 — 895
P/O B. Draper   74 — 1291 1312
F/O G.G. Draper   41 — 1374
P/O Draw   500 — Imp 29/5
Sgt Dredge   253 — 945
Cpl J. Drew (D)   500 — 8
P/O J. Drummond   92 — 1079
P/O H.S. Dundas   616 — 476
F/O J. Dundas (D)   609 — 975
Sgt J.T. Dunmore   222 — 1279
P/O Dunn   48 — 57
Sgt S. Duszynski (M)   238 — 931
P/O D.A. Du Vivier   43 — 731
Sgt W.L. Dymond   111 — 379 395 432
F/O Dyn   77 — 1444
L/Cpl Ebbington   Army — 1081
P/O A.F. Eckford   32 — 460
F/L G. Edge   253 — 1104
Sgt D. Edgehill   229 — 71
P/O E.R. Edmunds   615 — 1364
P/O H.P. Edridge   222 — 638
P/O E.F. Edsell   54 — 291
P/O H.D. Edwards (D)   92 — 929 941
P/O A. Edy   602 — 1488
Sgt E.J. Egan (D)   501 — 1031
Sgt D.W. Elcome (D)   602 — Imp 26/10
Sgt F.W. Eley (D)   74 — 235
P/O J. Ellacombe   151 — 386
P/O R.D. Elliott   72 — 751 821

F/O Elliott   75 — 1314
Sgt Elliott (D)   235 — 58
F/L J. Ellis   610 — 93 190 205 210 449
Sgt J.H. Ellis (D)   85 — 697
Sgt W. Ellis   92 — 1096 1405
Sgt P. Else   610 — 538 553
F/O T. Elsdon   72 — 700A 869
W/C B. Embry   107 — 36
P/O P.T. Empson   4 — 1430
P/O C. English (D)   605 — 1204
P/O D.E. Evans   615 — 376
P/O Evans   49 — 1284
P/O Evershed (D)   54 — 136
Sgt P.R. Eyles (M)   92 — 1072
F/O A. Eyre   615 — 366
LAC Fairbrother   264 — 72
F/L Farley   46/605 — 1416
F/O E. Farnes   141 — 176
P/O K.A. Faulkner   53 — 1180
F/O Feric   303 — 742 825 1021
P/O H.M. Ferris (D)   111 — 325 378 400
    410
Sgt Fielder   53 — 1180
S/L D.O. Findlay   54 — 594
P/O A. Finnie (D)   54 — 203
P/O B. Finucane   65 — 194 309 338
P/O A. Fisher   111 — 165
F/L Fitzgerald   141 — 1466
F/O J. Fleming   605 — 884
P/O R.D. Fleming (D)   249 — 850
P/O Flinders   32 — 437
Sgt R. Fokes   92 — 1267 1341
F/L A. Forbes   303 — 818
Sgt Forest   421Flt — 1493
Sgt R. Forward   257 — 213
F/O Foxley-Norris   615 — 1491
P/O C.D. Francis (D)   253 — 614
F/S W. Franklin   65 — 131 206
Sgt J. Frantisek   303 — 746 770
Sgt R. Fraser (D)   257 — 1319
P/O J. Freeborn   74 — 141 268
Sgt E.T. Frith (D)   92 — 1222
Sgt G. Furst   310 — 867
P/O D. Gage   602 — 1377
F/O D.R. Gamblen (M)   41 — 225
Sgt B.G. Gardner   610 — 349
F/O F.T. Gardiner   610 — 201 286 530
P/O J.R. Gardner   141 — 172
P/O Garton (D)   54 — 132 135
Sgt L.A. Garvey (D)   41 — 1375
S/L D. Garvin   264 — 502 579
P/O R. Gaskell   264 — 498
F/L L. Gaunce   615 — 454 563
F/O J.R.H. Gaynor   615 — 166
Sgt Gethin (D)   4 — 1430
Sgt D. Gibbins   54 — 680
F/O J.A. Gibson   501 — 302 369 611
F/L H.S. Giddings   111 — 721 755
P/O E.G. Gilbert   64 — 380
P/O H.T. Gilbert   601 — 813
F/O J.C. Gilbert   609 — 68
F/L D.E. Gillam   616 — 634 737
F/S J. Gillies   421Flt — 1287 1486
F/L K.M. Gillies   66 — 984
P/O K.R. Gillman (M)   32 — 90 525
    Add. 4/7

109

P/O Gilroy   603 — 1357
S/L T. Gleave   253 — 612 627 656
Sgt N. Glew   72 — 1081 1214 1230
LAC Glover   49 — 1284
Sgt Glowacki   501 — 658
Sgt A. Gooderham   46 — 1282
P/O G.E. Goodman   1 — 436 445 812
F/O C.W. Goldsmith (D)   603 — 1353
S/L J. Gordon   151 — 339
P/O V. Goth (D)   501 — 1336
Sgt Gotham   53 — 1106
F/L N. Gracie   56 — 143 144
F/L E. Graham   72 — 732
P/O L.W. Graham   56 — 399
S/L J. Grandy   249 — 802
P/O G. Grant-Govern   2 — 32
P/O C. Gray   54 — 186 192 296 490 531
  643 675
Sgt Gray (M)   77 — 1444
P/O D.M. Gray   610 — 348 415 492
Sgt M. Gray (D)   72 — 775
F/L C.P. Green   92/421Flt — 38 1251
  1445
Sgt W.J. Green   501 — 482 609
Sgt Green   10 — 389
Sublt H.L. Greenshield (D)   266 — 366
F/O Gregory (D)   65 — 334
P/O D. Gribble   54 — 666 706
P/O D.N. Grice   32 — 89
F/O Grice (D)   600 — 259
Sgt J. Griffin   73 — 950
Sgt G. Griffiths   17 — 451 1379
LAC V. Griffiths   26 — 102
P/O Grisenthwaite   500 — Imp 25/5
F/O F. Gruszka (D)   65 — 428
P/O K. Gundry   257 — 1245
P/O H.R. Gunn (D)   74 — 236
F/O E.M. Gunter (D)   501 — 1123
P/O J.V. Gurteen (D)   504 — 989
Sgt Hadnam   53 — 1313
F/O L. Haines   19 — 773
Sgt S. Haines (D)   610 — 104
Sgt A. Hall (D)   53 — 1180
Sgt D.W. Halton (M)   615 — 377
F/L H.R. Hamilton   85 — 465
P/O A. Hamilton (D)   141 — 174
Sgt J. Hammerton (D)   615 — 1406
P/O O. Hanbury   602 — 843
Sgt Harding   10 — 1402
A/C Harding   48 — 62
Sgt O.A. Hardy   264 — 574
P/O F.N. Hargreaves (M)   92 — 929
P/O Harris   500 — 6
P/O F.C. Harrold (D)   501 — 1148
P/O Hart (K)   242 — 1403
P/O K. Hart   65 — 34 112
P/O P.McD. Hartas   603/421Flt — 1176
  1473 1493
Sgt Hawke   64 — 385
LAC Hawke (M)   500 — Imp 29/5
Sgt Hayes (D)   65 — 120
F/L G.D. Haysom   79 — 577 701 782
P/O J.C. Hayter   605 — 1342
Sgt D.A. Helcke (D)   504 — 1034
Sgt Hemsley (D)   53 — 1485
S/L M. Hendry (M)   139 — 1092
Sgt W. Henn   501 — 710

Sgt B. Henson   32 — 444
F/L L. Henstock   64 — 204 307
A/C Hopwood   500 — Imp 25/5
P/O H.M. Heron   266/66 — 1207
P/O N.B. Heywood (D)   257 — 1318
Sgt W.B. Higgins (D)   32/253 — 522 953
F/S F. Higginson   56 — 414
F/O T.P. Higgs (D)   111 — 142
Sgt C. Hilken   74 — 1311
P/O H.P. Hill (D)   92 — 1025 1071
Sgt Hill   65 — 509
LAC Hill   48 — 57
P/O R. Hillary   603 — 610 744
F/L H.B. Hillcoat   1 — 436
Sgt P. Hillwood   56 — 332
Sgt C. Hodson   229 — 1174
S/L H. Hogan   501 — 569 983 1049 1210
Sgt Hogg (D)   17 — 1421
P/O K.K. Holden   616 — 77
S/L A. Holland   501 — 295
P/O D.F. Holland (D)   72 — 1067
P/O R.H. Holland   92 — 985 1340
F/O M.G. Homer (D)   242 — 1124
P/O D.H. Hone   615 — 473 516
P/O B. Hooper   25 — 1023
F/O R. Hope   605 — 1153
A/C Hopwood   500 — Imp 25/5
Sgt O.V. Houghton (D)   501 — 804
Sgt E. Howarth   501 — 251
F/O F. Howell   609 — 67
Sgt Howes (D)   85/605 — 679 1476 1494
P/O P. Howes (D)   603 — 1040
P/O J. Howitt   242 — 55
P/O R. Howley (M)   141 — 170
Sgt J. Hubacek   310 — 993
A/C Hubbard (D)   500 — 156
F/L P.C. Hughes (D)   234 — 783 842
P/O P.H. Hugo   615 — 166 422
Sgt D. Hulbert   257 — 866
F/O J. Humpherson   32 — 168
S/L P.A. Hunter (M)   264 — 496
P/O Hunt   139 — 1094
Sgt C. Hurry   46 — 795 984 1052
Sgt I. Hutchinson   222 — 947 1056
Sgt Hutson   53 — 1313
P/O G.G. Hyde   1RCAF — 649
F/L Ingle   605 — 1474
Sgt R.A. Innes   253 — 1013 1070 1237
Sgt L.R. Isaac (M)   64 — 244
F/L Ives (M)   151 — 39
Lt M. Jacobs   Army — 1081
F/O Jameson   53 — 316
F/O W. Januszewicz (D)   303 — 827 1194
F/O M. Jebb (D)   504 — 998
F/O A.J. Jeffrey (D)   64 — 179 199
Sgt G.W. Jeffreys (D)   46 — 712 717 984
  1050
LAC Jeffreys   53 — 35
P/O C.G. Jeffries   3 — 11
P/O Jenkyns   613 — 46
Sgt A.C. Jepps   102 — Add 19/6
P/O C.E. Johnson   264 — 573
P/O J. Johnson   46 — 786
Sgt J.I. Johnson (D)   222 — 639
Sgt Johnson-Barrett   75 — 1314
S/L Johnston   602 — 871

110

P/O J.T. Johnston (D) 151 — 388
P/O J.T. Jones (M) 264 — 497
P/O Jones 10 — 1402
P/O R.E. Jones 605 — 969 1429
Sgt Jones 500 — 10
Sgt Jones 139 — 1093
LAC Jones (M) 264 — 60
LAC Jones (D) 2 — 32
S/L Joslin (D) 79 — 92 122
P/O C.C. Joubert 56 — 331
Sgt S. Karubin 303 — 806
P/O Kay 264 — 60
S/L K.R. Kayll 615 — 470
Sgt F.J. Keast (D) 600 — 259
Sgt E.H. Kee 253 — 1264
P/O G. Keighley 610 — 74 182
F/L P. Kelly 74 — 237 314
S/L R.G. Kellett 303 — 810 813 1020
P/O J.L. Kemp 54/141 — 173 289
P/O J. Kendal 66 — 1192
P/O P. Kennard-Davis (D) 64 — 260
P/O P.L. Kenner (D) 264 — 573
F/L J. Kent 92 — 1389
F/O Kerwin 1RCAF — 695
Sgt Kerr 58 — 750A
F/O Kerr-Wilson (M) 610 — 47 59
Sgt M. Keymer (D) 65 — 478
P/O R. Kidson (M) 141 — 171
Sgt F. Killingback 249 — 854
Sgt J.R. Kilner 65 — 113
P/O D.S. Kinder 92/73 — 1085 1383
S/L E.B. King (D) 151 — 617
P/O F.H. King (M) 264 — 496
Sgt D.E. Kingaby 92 — 1269 1361
F/L C.B. Kingcome 92 — 1082 1258 1265
Sgt T.B. Kirk (D) 74 — 1310
Sgt D.I. Kirton (D) 65 — 256
Sgt W. Klozinsky 54 — 362
P/O S. Kleczkowski 302 — 1294
P/O Knight 242 — 1400
A/C Knowles 53 — 86
Sgt Kominek 310 — 1392
Sgt Kosarz 302 — 1414
Sgt J. Koukal 310 — 876
P/O Kozlowski 501 — 450
S/L Z. Krasnowdebski 303 — 809
Sgt J. Lacey 501 — 299 607 629 774 944
  1030
Adj H. Lafont 615 — 1363 1457
F/O Lamb 610 — 552
F/O H.M. Lambert (D) 25 — 1023
Sgt Lancaster 235 — 58
F/O Lane 500 — 6
P/O N. Langham-Hobart 73 — 1083
P/O G.A. Langley (D) 41 — 934 981
Sgt J. Lansdell (D) 607 — 1029
P/O J.B. Latta 242 — 53
Sgt Laurence 141 — 1036 1381 1496
P/O K.A. Lawrence 421Flt — 1281 1434
  1449
Sgt N.A. Lawrence 54 — 361 371
P/O W. Lawson 19 — 1055
F/L R.A. Learoyd V.C. 49 — 1391
S/L J.A. Leathart 54 — 17 707
F/L W.S. Leather 611 — 984
Sgt Le Cheminant 92 — 1480

P/O J.G. Lecky (D) 41 — 1238
P/O K.N. Lee 501 — 425
Sgt M.A. Lee (D) 421Flt — 1224 1272
  1497
W/C R.B. Lees 72 — 734
P/O Leeson 500 — 730
P/O Lefevre 46 — 1051 1395
LAC Legassick 500 — 13
S/L R. Leigh 66/421Flt — 1260
Sgt M. Leng 73 — 949 1078
P/O J.D. Lenahan (D) 607 — 897
F/O Le Rougetel 600 — 264
P/O A.G. Lewis 249 — 1154
D.C. Lewis (D) Oxford Univ. Air Sqdn
  — 3
P/O T.S. Lewis 79 — 14
S/L R. Lister 41/92 — 956 1098
P/O P. Litchfield (D) 610 — 169
Sgt R.T. Llewellyn 213 — 1006
P/O Lloyd 615 — 97
P/O J. Lloyd 72 — 1047
P/O P.D. Lloyd (D) 41 — 1266
Sgt P. Lochnan 1RCAF — 932
Sgt E.S. Lock 41 — 790 1195
Sgt J. Lockhart 85 — 487
P/O K. Lofts 615/249 — 342 366 467 995
  1283
Sgt Lomax (D) 3 — 23
F/L M. Loudon 141 — 176
F/O A.D. Lovell 41 — 218 974 1175
Sgt J. Lowe 236 — 212
P/O D. Lowson 102 — Add 19/6
P/O K. Lukaszewicz (M) 501 — 292
P/O J. Lund 92 — 1275
P/O D. Lyne 19 — 42
F/O Mabey (D) 500 — 8
Sgt J. Macinski (M) 111 — 753
Sgt J. McAdam 41 — 1099 1322
P/O W.G. McArthur 102 — Add 19/6
P/O D.K. MacDonald (M) 603 — 595 P/O
P/O J.A. McClintock 615 — 560 281
F/L H.K. MacDonald (D) 603 — 662 1150
S/L A. McDonnell 64 — 200 257 446
P/O I. McDougall 141 — 175
P/O H.W. McGowan 92 — 959
P/O P. McGregor 46 — 886
LAC McIllvenney 48 — 57
Sgt P. McIntosh (D) 605 — 1250
P/O A.G. McIntyre 111 — 315
Sgt D.A. Mackay 501/421Flt — 429
  1450
S/L A. McKellar (D) 605 — 1302 1308
  1385
P/O J.D. McKenzie 54 — 17
P/O J.W. MacKenzie (M) 111 — 278
F/O J.N. MacKenzie 41 — 232 828 933
  1077 1371
P/O K.W. MacKenzie 501 — 1210 1212
  1337
Sgt McLaughlin 75 — 1314
P/O McLundie 500 — Imp 25/5
P/O D.A. McMullen 54/222 — 117 1289
  1330
P/O McNamara 603 — 1442
P/O T.F. McPhail 603 — 973
Sgt McQueen (D) 79 — 100
Sgt Macrae 23 — 19

Sgt MacRae 53 — 48
P/O S.J. Madle 615 — 578
S/L A. Malan 74 — 33 177 219 266
 319 1346 1478
P/O J.L. Malinski 302 — 1263
P/O Mallalieu (D) 500 — 1415
P/O Mallon 53 — 238
LAC Mansfield (M) 500 — Imp 29/5
Sgt J. Mann 64/92 — 257 409 961
P/O Mansell-Lewis 92 — 1111 1329
P/O R.A. Marchand 73 — 979
Sgt Marsden 500 — 730
P/O Marshall 85 — 606 616
Sgt A.E. Marshall 73 — 948
Sgt Marshall 10 — 335
P/O G. Marsland 245/253 — 66 1368
P/O Marsland 141 — 1396
P/O R. Marples 616 — 558
F/O Marston 56 — 547 548
P/O J.R. Mather (D) 66 — 793 1059 1344
F/O H.K. Matthews (D) 54/603 — 297 360
 1199
F/L G.C. Mattheson 222 — 640
Sgt W. Maxwell (M) 264 — 546
P/O D.A. Maxwell 603 — 1355
P/O P.F. Mayhew 79 — 700A
P/O Meakin 53 — 1313
Sgt W.H. Mechin (D) 264 — 498
P/O A.R. Medcalf 610 — Imp 27/5
Sgt Medway 610 — Imp 27/5
M. Mentz 222 — 655
Sgt Merchant 501 — 484
LAC F. Messent 500 — 8
Sgt J. Metham 253 — 705
P/O B. Mierzwa 303 — 1202
P/O D.E. Mileham 41 — 1191
F/O M.J. Miley (D) 25 — 1023
P/O Millard 615 — 1437 Imp 14/11
P/O Miller 107 — 37
P/O W.H. Millington (M) 79/249 — 667
 671 1372
P/O J.A. Milne 605 — 1179
P/O Mitchell 58 — 750A
P/O Mitchell (M) 79 — 127
F/O L. Mitchell 257 — 859
P/O G.E. Moberley (D) 616 — 544
Sgt Molyneux 49 — 1284
P/O C.R. Montgomery (D) 615 — 352
P/O H.W. Moody (M) 602 — 860
Sgt F.L. Moore (M) 77 — 1444
Sgt P.J. Moore 253 — 1373
P/O J. Morton 603 — 1193
P/O E.J. Morris 79 — 676
Sgt J. Morrison (D) 46 — 1316
P/O Mortimer 257 — 980
P/O R. Mottram 92 — 1041
Adj Mouchotte 615 — 1492
Sgt E. Mould 74 — 130 146 215
P/O Mounsdon 56 — 434
P/O K. Mrazek 46 — 1133 1435
P/O M.R. Mudie (D) 615 — 167
F/L I.J. Muirhead (D) 605 — 1206 1273
P/O L.C. Murch 253 — 743 766 1234
Sgt Musselwhite 75 — 1314
P/O T.F. Neil 249 — 1408
P/O Nelson (M) 74 — 1345 1348 1369
 1387
F/O A. Nesbit 1RCAF — 976 1197

Sgt H.S. Newton 111 — 423
Sgt Newton 500 — 534
P/O B.R. Noble 79 — 696
Sgt N.R. Norfolk 72 — 722 1044
P/O S.C. Norris 610 — 234
P/O G. North 257 — 1276
A/C North (D) 235 — 51
Sgt J. Norwell 54 — 666
P/O T. Nowak 253 — 1285
S/L J.S. O'Brien (D) 234 — 841
P/O A. O'Connell 264 — 484
Sgt O'Kelly (D) 500 — 10 155
Sgt T.G. Oldfield (D) 92 — 1142
P/O J. O'Malley 264 — 484 498
F/O J.J. O'Meara 421Flt — 1483 1495
F/O D.H. O'Neil 41 — 1240
Sgt H.C. Orchard 65 — 247 477
P/O Ortmans 229 — 1171 1295
Sgt Oughton 500 — 730
F/O R. Oxspring 66 — 1005 1061 1101
 1166 1258 1323
F/O A. Page 56 — 312
Sgt A. Page (D) 257 — 1412
P/O J.F. Pain 32 — 440
P/O Pain 500 — 10 15
F/O M. Park 74 — 274 1308 1426 1469
Sgt K.B. Parker (D) 92 — 1271
Sgt W. Parker (D) 610 — 160
P/O E.G. Parkin 501 — 239
P/O S. Parnell (D) 607 — 896
F/O D. Parrott 421Flt — 1300
P/O P.L. Parrott 145 — 43
Sgt Parrott 46 — 1436
Sgt Parson 66 — 1135
P/O Parsons (M) 10 — 335
Sgt Parton (M) 77 — 1444
F/O L.W. Paskiewicz (D) 303 — 1109
P/O Passey 605 — 1475
F/L J.A. Paterson (D) 92 — 939 1113
P/O Patterson 26 — 82
P/O Patterson (D) 500 — 8
F/O A.J.S. Pattinson (D) 92 — 1255
P/O J.G. Pattison 92 — 1080
P/O W.B. Pattullo (D) 151/46 — 677 1018
 1107
Sublt F.D. Paul (D) 64 — 112 163 208
Sgt L.H. Pearce 32/249/46 — 455 1261
Cpl D. Pearson G.M. Waaf — 73
Sgt G.W. Pearson (D) 501 — 805
P/O A.P. Pease (D) 603 — 749 1012
LAC Peebles 235 — 58
P/O C.C. Pegge 610 — 447
S/L Pemberton 1 — 466
A/C Penleve 23 — 19
P/O Penny 26 — 102
Sgt F.S. Perkins 73/421Flt — 1091 1343
Adj G. Perrin 249 — 1247
P/O P.W. Peters 500 — 534
F/O O.J. Peterson (D) 1RCAF — 1108
P/O J. Pfeiffer (D) 32 — 471 480
Sgt N.T. Phillips (D) 65 — 258
P/O J. Pickering 66 — 1232
Sgt T. Pickering 501 — 915
Sgt L.M. Pidd (D) 238 — 1009
F/O O.St.J. Pigg (D) 72 — 84 685

Sgt E. Pike   102 — Add 19/6
Pilkington   1 — 1219
S/L P.C. Pinkham (D)   19 — 772
P/O D. Pinkney   603 — 608 1442
Sgt Plant (D)   603 — 1439
S/L P. Plenderleith   73 — 1231
F/L G. Plinston   242 — 54
P/O K. Pniak   32 — 460 508 518
Sgt M.H. Pocock   72 —691
P/O Pollard   611 — 984
P/O W.A. Ponting (M)   264 — 497
P/O P. Poole   72 — 1228
Sgt R. Potter (D)   49 — 1284
W.A. Pragnell   Kent Fly. Club — 3
Sgt Prentice   500 — 156
Miss P.P. Price — 335
F/L C. Pritchard   600 — 355
F/L G. Proudman (D)   65 — 113 119
Sgt Purnell-Phillips   607 — 894
F/L A. Putt   501 — 368
P/O L.L. Pyman (D)   65 — 350 416
F/L A.C. Rabagliati   46 — 740 773 945
P/O J. Radomski   303 — 1169
P/O W.P. Rafter   603 — 767 1465
Sgt Ramsay   610 — Add 3/7
Sgt J.W. Ramshaw (D)   222 — 763
P/O A. Raven   610 — 128
P/O M. Ravenhill (D)   229 — 917 1163
Sgt Rayner   500 — 15
P/O J. Redman   257 — 124
? J.A. Reid   P.D.U. — 22
P/O H. Reilley (D)   66 — 1 01 1288
F/L R.C. Reynell   43 — 723 724
F/L W.H. Rhodes-Moorhouse (D)   601
   — 815
F/O A.L. Ricalton (D)   74 — 1290
P/O Richie   53 — 1106
Sgt M. Ridley (D)   616 — 543
A/C Ridley   500 — 15
P/O R.H. Robbins (M)   54/66 — 491 960
Sgt Roberts   53 — 283
F/L A.I. Robinson   222 — 669
F/L P.B. Robinson   601 — 655
S/L M. Robinson   616 — 50
P/O G. Robinson   264 — 485
Sgt J. Robinson   111 — 76
S/L M.W.S. Robinson   73 — 936 946
Sgt P.E. Robinson   56 — 433
Sgt Robson   53 — 1485
P/O F. Robshaw   229 — 1164
F/O Rochford   53 — 523
F/O E.B. Rogers   615/501 — 353 1147
Sgt Rogowski   303 — 817
Sgt Rolls   72 — 711
P/O J. Rose   32/17 — 479 527 1257
P/O A.T. Rose-Price (M)   501 — 736
P/O M. Rozwadowski (M)   151 —387
F/L F.W. Rushmer (M)   603 — 605 768
F/L H. Russell   609/32 — 68 442
F/L Ryder   41 — 1131
Sgt A. Sarre   603 — 633 752 863
Sgt A. St Aubin   616 — 541
P/O Salmond   64 — 1460
P/O W.M. Samolinski (M)   253 — 1103
S/L Sample   504 — 997
F/L C. Saunders   92 — 893 1073 1384
F/L G.A. Saunders   65 — 34

S/L H.C. Sawyer   65 — 193
Sgt C. Saward   501 — 1039
F/L L.H. Schwind (D)   213 — 1110
Sgt E. Scott (M)   222 — 1145
Sgt J.A. Scott (D)   74 — 1347
P/O L.D. Scott   145 — 83
F/O W.J. Scott   41 — 226 875 882
LAC Scott (D)   235 — 58
P/O E.G. Seghers   32 — 519
Sgt Shackleford   53 — 238
P/O M.M. Shand   54 — 529
Sgt Sharpe   10 — 335
F/O I.G. Shaw (M)   264 — 497A
P/O R.H. Shaw (M)   1 — 750
Sgt H.F. Shead   257 — 1332
F/O D.F. Sheen   72 — 686 785
Sgt Sheldrick   53 — 114
Sgt T. Sherrington   92 — 1076 1330
Sgt W. Shier (D)   500 — 155
Sgt F.H. Silk   111 — 771
Sgt Sillence   3 — 9
Sgt R.B. Sim   111 — 280
A/C Simmonds   500 — 10
F/O G.M. Simpson   229 — 1008
F/O G.L. Sinclair   310 — 1122
P/O S. Skalski   501 — 713 769
Sgt W.H. Skinner   74 — Imp 8/7
P/O D.M. Slatter (M)   141 — 172
Sgt A.V. Slocombe (D)   235 — 51
F/L S. Slocum (D)   P.D.U. — 22
S/L A.T. Smith (D)   610 — 148 188 202
F/L F.M. Smith   72 — 674
F/O D.S. Smith (D)   616 — 1121
F/O E.B. Smith   610 — 284
P/O R. Smith   229 — 972
P/O W. Smith   235 — 21
Sgt A.D. Smith (D)   66 — 757
Sgt E.C. Smith   600 — 264
Sgt W.B. Smith   602 — 1378
Sgt Smith   10 — 1402
LAC Smith   600 — 24
A/C S. Smith (D)   79 — 14
F/O R. Smither (D)   1RCAF — 977
Sgt R. Smithson   249 — 851
P/O Smyth   26 — 570
P/O R.F. Smythe   32 — 88 111 123 351
   354 517
F/O Smythe   249(?) — 1425
Sgt G. Smythe   56 — 598
P/O V.R. Snell   501 — 1335
Sgt H.J. Soars   74 — 1362
P/O S.F. Soden   266 — 411
P/O N.D. Solomon (D)   17 — 421
Sgt A.W. Spears   222/421Flt — 641 1286
   1301
Sgt D.C. Spencer   500 — 71A
Sgt G. Spencer   79 — Add 25/11/39
Lt Sperling (D)   Welsh Guards — 24
F/O Spiers   254 — 79
F/O Sprenger   1RCAF — 650
P/O R.L. Spurdle   74 — 1315 1394
Sgt P. Spyer   607 — 892
Sgt J. Squier   64 — 253
Sgt Stanley   500 — 534
P/O N. Stansfield   242/229 — 61 1162
Sgt F.R. Staples   72 — 1184
F/O B. Stapleton   603 — 865

S/L H.M. Starr (D)   253 — 646
P/O C. Stavert   1 — 436
P/O Steel (D)   53 — 1485
F/S J. Steere   72 — 1095 1186
P/O H.M. Stephen   74 — 1469
P/O I.R. Stephenson   264 — 546
P/O P.J. Stephenson   607 — 1014 1015
Sgt G. Steven s   213 — 1293
F/L Stevenson   53 — 283
P/O P.C. Stevenson   74 — 33 125   177
   216 273
Sgt G.A. Steward   17 — 670
P/O C. Stewart   54 — 511
P/O R.W. Stokes   264 — 72
Sgt A. Stokes   102 — Add 19/6
Sgt J. Stokoe   603 — 739
P/O D. Stones   79 — 868
F/L G.E. Stoney (D)   501 — 464
Sgt V. Sullivan (M)   77 — 1444
P/O F.B. Sutton   56 — 306 597
P/O N. Sutton (D)   72 — 1185
F/L N. Szczesny   74 — 320
P/O Tarlington (M)   79 — 18
Tarkowski   605 — 1416
Sgt N. Taylor   601 — 659
Sgt Terry (D)   26 — 570
F/S P.H. Tew   54 — 448
F/O E. Thomas   222 — 1223
S/L J.M. Thompson   111 — 315
F/O R.A. Thomson   72 — 689
Sgt E.R. Thorne   264 — 52 504 542
P/O Tiptree   53 — 35
P/O E. Tobin   609 — 975
P/O Tollemache   600 — 24
F/O J. Topolnicki   601 — 814
S/L P. Townsend   85 — 600 654
F/O O.V. Tracey   79 — 583
A/C (later Sgt) Trafford   53 — 48 1106
F/L R.S. Tuck   92 — 443 1243 1248
F/O Tucker   151 — 294
P/O Turley-George   54 — 198 290
F/O Turnbull   139 — 1093
F/S Turner   32 — 178
Sgt R.C. Turner (D)   264 — 505 572
Sgt L.J. Tweed   111 — 811
Sgt Tyrer   46 — 980 1107
F/S G.C. Unwin   19 — 940
Sgt F. Usmar   41 — 1119
P/O T. Vigors   222 — 898
F/O F. Villa   92 — 1306 1328
P/O Wade   92 — 935 942 1479
Sgt J. Wadham (D)   145 — 1249
P/O J.A. Walker   111 — 315
P/O W.L. Walker   616 — 539
Sgt Walker   65 — 246
Sgt Walker   10 — 1402
P/O J.R. Walker   41 — 1220
Sgt T.L. Wallace   111 — 756 877
LAC Walton   500 — 13
Sgt Ward   139 — 1093
Sgt R.A. Ward (D)   66 — 1217
F/L W.H. Warner (D)   610 — 413
A/C J.B. Warren (D)   600 — 259
Priv J. Waters (D) — 1014
P/O Watling   92 — 907
P/O E. Watson   605 — 1024
Sgt Watt   10 — 1402
F/L Watts   253 — 899 1477

F/L B.H. Way (D)   54 — 129 132 195
P/O L. Way   229 — 1173
F/O P.S. Weaver   56 — 328 439 590
P/O F.K. Webster (D)   610 — 550
F/L J.T. Webster   41 — 231
Sgt H. Webster   73 — 924
Sgt Wedzik   302 — 1274
P/O G.H. Welford   607 — 1028
P/O E.P. Wells   266/41 — 1447 1453
F/O P.H.V. Wells   249 — 856 1461
F/O K. Wendel   504 — 853
P/O R. West   245 — 64
Sgt T.E. Westmoreland (M)   616 — 528
F/O Wezelik   302 — 1413
P/O Wharry   48 — 62
P/O H. Whitbread (D)   222 — 905 1068
Sgt White   74 — 109
Sgt J. White   72 — 844 1114
Sgt Whitehouse   501 — 1334
P/O D. Whitley   264 — 483 505 572
P/O Wicks   56 — 499 549
Mid. Wightman   151 — 137
P/O E.J. Wilcox (D)   72 — 678
Sgt Wilcox   53 — 238
Sgt W.A. Wilkinson   501 — 252
S/L R.L. Wilkinson (D)   266 — 406
Sgt P.H. Willcocks (D)   610/66 — 962 1155
   1229 1458
P/O Williams   603 — 1442
F/S E.E. Williams (M)   46 — 1280
P/O Williams(?)   264 — 63 70
Sgt Williamson   53 — 35
P/O R.R. Wilson (M)   111 — 85 279
Sgt Wilson   610 — 205
Sgt J. Wilson   500 — 155
P/O Winskill   603 — 1442
F/O D.C. Winter   72 — 784
Sgt J. Wise (M)   141 — 175
F/O S. Witorzenc   501 — 367 463
P/O Wlasnowolski   32 — 357 441 459
Sgt Wojciechowski   303 — 1004 1035
Sgt S. Wojtowicz (D)   303 — 748 922
S/L Wolfe   141 — 1455
P/O J.E. Wood   79 — 126
F/O P.P. Woods-Scawen (D)   85 — 601
   673 726
F/O Woodward   64 — 303
S/L Worrall   32 — 181 394
Sgt Worton   500 — 155
P/O A.R. Wright   92 — 906
Sgt B. Wright   66 — 1188
LAC Wyatt (D)   25 — 1023
F/L R.E. Wynn   249 — 704
Sgt York   500 — 730
P/O C.R. Young   615/46 — 470 1482
P/O J.H.R. Young (D)   74 — 214
P/O C.R. Young   615 — 470
F/O A. Yuile   1RCAF — 698
P/O P. Zenker (M)   501 — 462 489
P/O A. Zukowski (D)   302 — 1297

INDEX OF LUFTWAFFE PERSONNEL

Uffz F. Burger (D)   II/LG2 — 111
Gfr F. Burger (M)   8/KG1 — 113
Gfr A. Burghardt (M)   6/KG3 — 571
Uffz Burkart (M)   9/KG77 — 1060
Lt Busch (P)   I/JG3 — 1352
Fw Busch (M)   8/JG51 — 481
Obfw Buttlik (M)   Stab/StG1 — 1468
Oblt Butterweck (D)   I/JG26 — 310
Uffz Buttler (P)   II/KG53 — 1002
Fw Carnot (M)   II/KG77 — Imp 25/10
Oblt H. Christinnecke (P)   7/JG26 — 834
Uffz Clauser (D)   9/JG27 — 1073
Obfw Dabusga (M)   6/JG3 — 336
Oblt K. Dähn (D)   I/JG26 — 945
Uffz Dahnke (P)   I/ZG2 — 857
Uffz Damerius (D)   3/KG77 — 1135
Fw Damschen (D)   8/KG77 — 1058
Fw Dannisch (D)   7/KG2 — 327
Obfw A. Dau (P)   7/JG51 — 599
Oblt Deicke (P)   8/JG27 — 1277
Uffz Depenheuer (D)   6/KG3 — 383
Uffz Deuker (M)   II/ZG2 — 733
Lt J. Deutsch (M)   7/JG53 — 765
Gfr R. Deutsch (D)   4/KG53 — 1438
Uffz F. Dilthey (P)   II/JG2 — 1081
Uffz Disch (D)   8/KG76 — 436
Gfr K. Donner (M)   III/LG1 — 1295
Obgfr K. Döpfer (P)   14/LG1 — 648
Lt Z.S. Drews (M)   1/KGr126 — 1101
Oblt Drehs (M)   III/JG54 — 305
Uffz Dreyer (P)   2/KG26 — 918
Uffz Dubs (M)   4/KG76 — 504
Obgfr Duda (P)   6/KG3 — 383
Fw Duensnig (D)   1/EproGr210 — 1189
Uffz Ebben (D)   3/ZG26 — 328
Hptm Ebbinghausen (M)   II/JG26 — 353
   412
Oblt H. Ebeling (D)   9/JG26 — 1397
Uffz Ebeling (D)   7/LG2 — 1304
Fw Eberhard (P)   9/KG76 — 426
Lt Eberle (D)   9/JG54 — 1220
Fw Ebertz (D)   9/JG26 — 206
Fw F. Eckert (D)   6/KG53 — 623
Gfr Eckert (M)   9/ZG26 — 936
Lt Eggert (D)   7/KG3 — 554
Uffz Eggert (D)   8/KG77 — 1058
Oblt H. Ehrig (P)   1/JG77 — 655
Fw Eichinger (D)   6/KG77 — 1138
Lt K. Eichorn (D)   14/LG1 — 647
Obfw Eichorn (D)   II/KG76 — 427
Uffz H. Elbers (P)   8/JG54 — 738
Uffz K. Elbing (P)   7/JG3 — 1089
Uffz Elfner (P)   2/EproGr210 — 395
Hptm W. Ennslen (M)   II/JG52 — Imp 2/11
Fw W. Erdniss (P)   3/JG51 — 1451
Oblt Erlich (M)   8/JG52 — 192
Lt H. Escherhaus (P)   I/JG77 — 1221
Fw W. Essmert (P)   7/KG3 — 567
Fw H. Ettler (P)   I/JG77 — 952
Fw W. Evers (D)   I/JG77 — 662
Obfw Faschinger (D)   I/KG54 — 1036
Uffz Fahrian (P)   6/JG3 — 1376
Fw Falke (P)   II/KG3 — 967
Uffz Fasz (M)   I/KG26 — 830

Gfr N. Feierabend (P)   II/KG1 — 620
Uffz K. Feldmann (P)   3/JG53 — 986
Oblt Fermer (D)   7/JG52 — 188
Oblt Fiel (P)   8/JG53 — 1176
Obgfr Fietmeyer (P)   9/StG1 — 1426
Oberst J. Fink (?)   Stab/KG2 — 323
Lt G. Finke (P)   7/KG1 — 1418
Uffz W. Finke (D)   4/JG3 — 547
Lt S. Fischer (or Flischer) (M)   1/JG53 —
   1478
Oblt Flebbe (D)   8/JG3 — 337
Uffz Fleming (M)   III/KG2 — Imp 15/9
Fw Flessner (M)   II/KG76 — 502
Uffz Flisk (D)   5/KG2 — 888
Oblt Floerke (D)   3/JG3 — 607
Hptm Föcö (?)   II/JG51 — 236 276 543 858
   488 1266
Gfr Foelinger (M)   8/KG77 — 1062
Lt Forster (M)   4(F)122 — 185
Gfr Frank (D)   7/JG52 — 190
Fw Franke (D)   5/KG3 — 967
Obfw W. Freidmann (M)   6/JG52 — 1307
Uffz Freimann (M)   4/KG76 — 504
Oblt Freyer (M)   Stab/StG1 — 1468
Fw H. Friebe   Seenotflkdo — 1445A
Fw Friedrich (P)   I/KG26 — 918
Obfw H. Frischmuth (P)   8/KG1 — 112
Uffz Froba (M)   4/KG76 — 504
Oblt W. Fronhofer (P)   9/JG26 — 256 675
Oblt Fuchs (D)   3/ZG26 — 328
Oblt Fuchs (D)   8/KG77 — 1062
Uffz Fuchs (M)   IV/KG30 — 1159
Lt Furnwagner (M)   II/LG1 — 221
Fw J. Gaertner (P)   8/JG26 — 1328
Gfr W. Gailer (P)   6/KG3 — 571
Uffz Galla (D)   II/ZG2 — 874
Maj A. Galland   Stab/JG26 — 191 579
   736 993
Lt Ganzlmayr (D)   I/KG54 — 1036
Uffz Garnith (P)   I/JG51 — 1175
Uffz Gebauer (M)   I/ZG26 — 437
Uffz Gebhardt (D)   6/KG77 — 1138
Gefr Gebhardt (M)   2/JG51 — 219
Oblt Geghardt (D)   I/JG53 — 800
Lt Gehalsis (or Gehlhaar) (M)   II/JG52 —
   313
Uffz Gehsla (P)   1/JG53 — 1191
Fw Geier (D)   9/KG76 — 426
Gfr Geisinger (P)   I/KG1 — 1417
Lt Geist (P)   4/JG52 — 1134
Uffz Geiswinkler (D)   6/JG53 — 1341
Lt Geller (M)   2/JG52 — 613
Gfr E. Genter (D)   3/KG2 — 402
Fw George (P)   I/KG26 — 918
Obfw Gerber (D)   I/JG52 — 683
Uffz Gericke (D)   2/KG1 — 424
Uffz Gericke (M)   13/LG1 — 1020
Lt Gerlach (M)   2/JG54 — 366
Fw Gey (P)   I/KG1 — 1417
Uffz F. Geyer (M)   6/KG76 — 816
Lt H. Gichi (M)   2/KG53 — Imp 26/10

116

Fw Gierga (P)   4/ZG26 — 458
Fw Giess (M)   II/KG26 — Imp 11/9
Uffz Glaeschker (P)   9/KG77 — 1060
Fw Glaser (D)   9/KG2 — 1022
Uffz E. Glaeska (P)   Eprogr210 — 657
Gfr Glöckner (P)   9/JG27 — 1053
Uffz A. Glomb (P)   4/JG2 — 717
Gfr F. Glück (P)   6/KG53 — 623
Uffz Goebels (M)   4/AufKlGr — 679
Lt Goedsche (D)   4(F)14 — 838
Fw Goern (P)   8/KG77 — 1063
Fw V. Goertz (P)   4/KG3 — 996
Uffz W. Goetting (P)   I/LG1 — 867
Oblt Goettmann (D)   III/JG3 — 846
Gfr Golob (D)   3/KG2 — 401
Oblt Goltzsche (P)   I/JG77 — 871
Uffz Gonschorrek (P)   5/JG27 — 1357
Lt Gorisch (M)   V/LG1 — 1020
Fw F. Gottlob (D)   IV/LG1 — 648
Fw Gottschalk (P)   7/KG1 — 1418
Fw W. Gottschalk (P)   II/LG2 — 824
Oblt S. Gottshalt (P)   I/ZG2 — 747
Oblt A. Gotz (P)   1/JG2 — 878
Uffz H. Grabow (P)   I/JG3 — 781
Gfr W. Grafer (M)   4/KG3 — Imp 2/11
Uffz Gramling (D)   10/LG1 — 342
Fw Grassl (D)   II/KG53 — 982
Uffz Grasser (P)   7/KG53 — 465
Obgfr H. Greil (M)   II/KG3 — Imp 2/11
Lt Grell (M)   4/KG76 — 505
Sgte Mag G. Grillo (M)   18°Gruppo CT —
  1442
Lt E. Grote (M)   4/JG54 — 1390
Uffz R. Growe (D)   IV/LG1 — 647
Maj Grube (P)   II/KG53 — 982
Lt Gruel (D)   I/JG26 — 78
Obfw O. Grunke   II/KG76 — Imp 2/11
Obfw G. Gryzmalla (P)   8/JG26 — 1082
Fw E. Gudat (P)   5/KG3 — 664
Lt E. Gudenatz (M)   KGr100 — 17
Uffz H. Gueltgen (P)   II/LG2 — 826
Uffz Guetting   I/LG2 — 867
Obgfr Gurnkrantz (M)   III/KG77 —
  Imp 25/10
Fw Gutacker (M)   II/KG26 — Imp 11/9
Maj M. Gutzmann (P)   2/KG2 — 568
Gfr K. Haak (M)   7/KG53 — 789
Oblt J. Haase (D)   3/JG53 — 973
Oblt Habische (P)   2/EproGr210 — 395
Gfr Haeck (M)   III/KG3 — 791
Uffz H. Haenel (D)   6/KG76 — 816
Gefr Hagabiel (D)   4/KG3 — 1438
Maj Handrich (?)   JG26 — 317
Uffz Handsburg (D)   II/KG3 — 997
Fw Hansgen (P)   III/KG2 — 325
Lt Hanau (M)   2/KG53 — Imp 26/10
Obfw K. Harbauer (D)   4/JG2 — 634
Uffz Harheim (M)   8/JG51 — 481
Uffz Hartleib (D)   2/JG52 — 564
Uffz Haslache (M)   I/KG26 —830
Uffz Hastriche (D)   3/KG77 — 1135
Uffz Haupt (P)   7/KG53 — 554

Uffz Hausdorf (D)   I/KG3 — 1356
Uffz Hauswald (P)   3/KG26 — 919
Uffz Hautkappe (P)   5/JG54 — 364
Uffz Hechmaier (D)   I/LG2 — 930
Obfw Heidrich   (P)   3/KG1 — 902
Lt H. Heinemann (D)   1/JG26 — 1483
Fw Heise (D)   3/JG3 — 265
Uffz Heitmann (M)   8/KG76 — 971
Fw Heitsch (P)   8/KG76 — 975
Uffz Hekers (M)   II/KG77 — Imp 25/10
Oblt H. Held (P)   I/JG54 — 531
Oblt H. Hellmuth (D)   6/ZG26 — 434
Lt Hellermann (M)   5/F/122 — 503
Uffz Hemmersbach (D)   6/ZG26 — 433
Fw E. Hemmerling (M)   6/JG51 — 227
Uffz Hempel (D)   8/JG53 — 822
Uffz Henneberg (D)   4/KG76 — 505
Oblt Henken (D)   6/ZG26 — 927
Uffz Henker (D)   I/KG51 — 1065
Fw Henson (D)   5/KG3 — 1014
Fw Hermes (M)   2/JG2 — 1157
Uffz Herms (D)   3/KG26 — 919
Oblt S. Hertel (D)   2/KG2 — 568
Uffz Hertlein (D)   2/KG77 — 1115
Fw Herwath-Bittenfeld (P)   1/JG3 — 1195
Uffz Hess (M)   3/KG2 — 401
Uffz Hesse (M)   3/ZG26 — 439
Obfw P. Hessel (P)   1/JG3 — 938 1003
Gfr H. Heucht (M)   2/KG53 — Imp 26/10
Uffz W. Heyer (D)   6/JG26 — 643
Obfw Heyse (D)   10/LG1 — 392
Gfr H. Hildebrandt (P)   IV/KG1 — 620
Oblt Hilderbrandt (M)   KuflGr3/906 — 179
Lt Himmelheber (P)   Stab/JG2 — 832
Fw Himsel (P)   III/KG77 — 1064
Oblt Hintze (P)   2/EproGr210 — 1366
Gfr K. Hirsch (D)   3/KG2 — 402
Uffz Hirsch (P)   3/KG1 — 933
Obfw Hoebel (P)   5/KG3 — 994
Uffz Hoehn (P)   4/JG51 — 1267
Fw Hofelich (D)   3/JG3 — 266
Lt Hofer (M)   AufKlGr d.L — 514
Uffz U. Hoffenden (D)   I/StG3 — 1410
Oblt F. Hoffmann (M)   7/JG53 —
  Imp 2/11
Fw H. Hoffmann (P)   5/JG52 — 1130
Fw Hoffmann (D)   13/LG1 — 1021
Uffz M. Hoffmann (P)   I/ZG2 — 747
Uffz Hoffmann (P)   I/KG26 — 918
Obgfr Hoffmann (P)   5/KG2 — 889
Obgfr Hoffmann (M)   III/KG77 —
  Imp 25/10
Obgfr Hoffmann (D)   6/ZG26 — 926
Gfr Hoffmann (P)   9/KG2 — 1018
Gfr Hoffman (D)   II/KG53 — 1002
Lt Hohagen (?)   JG51 — 237
Obfw A. Hohn (M)   II/KG77 — Imp 25/10
Fw Holz (P)   Stab/KG2 — 323
Gfr P. Holzapfel (M)   7/JG26 — 801
Fw H. Honisch (P)   I/JG53 — 904
Oblt Hopp (D)   Stab/JG3 — 1087

Uffz Hoppe (D)   9/KG2 — 1018
Fw Horn (D)   2/KG26 — 920
Gfr H. Hornatschek (D)   9/JG26 — 1160
Uffz Hotzelmann (P)   I/JG54 — 773
Obfw Howind (P)   5/KG3 — 994
Flgr K. Hubel (D)   7/JG51 — 1165
Uffz Huber (D)   5/KG2 — 1005
Uffz Hubner (M)   1/EproGr210 — 1182
Gfr Huhn (D)   7/KG3 — 567
Lt Hurck (M)   5(F)122 — 503
Fw A. Iburg (P)   9/JG54 — 1302
Obfw W. Illg (P)   9/KG76 — 699
Uffz F. Imspringt (D)   I/StG3 — 1411
Fw M. Jäckel (D)   15/LG1 — 700A
Uffz Jäckel (D)   4/ZG26 — 457
Lt F. Jäger (D)   5/JG51 — 1395A
Uffz Jahme (M)   2/KG26 — 830
Uffz Jahn (D)   II/LG1 — 1179
Fw Jahnke (M)   2(F)122 — Imp 2/9
Fw Jessen (M)   2/KG26 — 830
Fw D. Junger (M)   II/JG52 — Imp 2/11
Oblt Junghans (M)   9/ZG26 — 936
Uffz W. Kaffenberger (P)   6/ZG26 — 431
Fw Kalucza (D)   II/KG54 — Imp 7/9
Fw W. Kaminski (D)   1/JG26 — 1454
Uffz Kamolz or Uffz Kanotz (M)
    4/AufklGr d.L — 679
Oblt Kapsch (M)   9/KG77 — 108
Uffz W. Karl (P)   1/JG53 — 712
Gfr W. Karrach (M)   5/StG1 — 1382
Lt Kastner (P)   6/ZG26 — 431
Obfw Katzmarski (P)   2/KG1 — 424
Fw Kaufmann (M)   7/ZG26 — 799
Fw Keck (D)   8/KG76 — 971
Uffz F. Keck (P)   I/JG77 — 661
Oblt Keidel (M)   7/JG52 — 205
Obfw Keifel (D)   6/ZG26 — 433
Oblt Keller (?)   1/JG3 — 938
Uffz G. Kemen (P)   I/JG26 — 351
Fw Keppitsch (D)   1/EproGr210 — 1189
Uffz Kern (D)   II/JG52 — 285
Lt J. Kernbach (P)   6/KG76 — 835
Uffz G. Keuerleben (P)   6/KG53 — 624
Uffz E. Kind (D)   I/JG52 — 774
Uffz Kirchbauer (M)   II/LG1 — 1179
Oblt Kirchoff (D)   3/ZG26 — 461
Uffz Kirchubel (P)   6/KG3 — 384
Oblt E. Kircheis (P)   Stab/JG51 — 576
Lt Kislinger (D)   I/ZG2 — 857
Oblt Kittmann (P)   8/KG2 — 1013
Oblt Kiunka (P)   3/KG1 — 902
Gfr A. Klapp (P)   6/KG53 — 623
Gfr W. Klappholz (P)   II/KG1 — 620
Fw M. Klar (P)   7/JG26 — 673
Uffz Klaus (M)   I/KG77 — Imp 9/11
Fw J. Kleditzsch (D)   8/KG3 — 1395
Uffz Kleemann (M)   II/JG54 — 584
Uffz Kleiber (M)   4/ZG26 — 925
Lt J. Kleppmeier (P)   2/KG76 — 677
Uffz W. Klemm (P)   7/KG1 — 1418
Maj Kless (D)   III/KG77 — 1064
Lt Klüge (D)   III/JG2 — 725
Uffz A. Klick (P)   I/LG2 — 1001
Gfr Kling (M)   2/ZG2 — 913

Fw F. Klotz (D)   9/JG51 — 991
Fw Klumb (D)   7/KG76 — 400
Fw Knedler (M)   3/JG54 — 403A
Obfw Knippscheer (D)   3/JG54 — 1088
Lt Knittel (D)   II/JG51 — 1358
Obgfr W. Knockenmuss (M)7/KG3 — 554
Obfw Kobert (D)   IV/LG1 — 694
Fw Koch   II/JG26 — 635
Gfr Koch (M)   9/StG1 — 1426
Flgr H. Koch (D)   3/KG2 — 402
Hptm Kogler (P)   I/ZG26 — 274
Kreigsberichter Köhler (P)   8/KG2 — 1013
Uffz Koehn (D)   9/KG77 — 1060
Obgfr Kohn (D)   6/KG76 — 816
Flgr Kohl (P)   5/KG2 — 889
Gfr H. Köler (D)   6/KG53 — 623
Uffz Kollmansmager (P)   1/KG77 — 1116
Oblt Kothe (M)   II/LG1 — 222
Oblt V. Kraft (P)   II/LG2 — 1489
Oblt Kraftschick (M)   I/JG27 — 1037
Fw Kramer (P)   1/JG77 — 659
Uffz Kramer (P)   3/KG1 — 933
Uffz Krapp (M)   II/ZG2 — 733
Uffz F. Kraus (D)   10/LG1 — 391
Fw Krebs (D)   2/KG77 — 1115
Fw Krebs (D)   6/KG76 — 432
Hptm Kreiger (P)   3/KG2 — 150
Oblt Kretschmann (M)   I/KG77 — 106
Lt H. Kringler (D)   6/KG3 — 383
Fw Kripmann (D)   8/KG77 — 1063
Uffz F. Krohn (D)   I/StG3 — 1411
Gfr W. Krohn (D)   8/KG3 — 1395
Uffz Kroll (D)   9/JG51 — 522
Gfr Kronberg (D)   2(F)122 — Imp 2/9
Gfr Krostopotsch (P)   4/KG3 — 663
Uffz Kross (M)   II/LG1 — 1179
Uffz Kruell (D)   II/KG76 — 504
Fw Krueshpow (P)   2/ZG26 — 937
Oblt Krug (M)   II/JG26 — 353 836
Lt P. Krug (P)   6/KG3 — 571
Uffz Kruger (?)   I/KG1 — 1417
Fw Krummheuer (D)   9/KG2 — 1022
Obfw E. Kuehlmann (M)   I/JG53 — 719
Obfw A. Kuepper (P)   8/JG26 — 1079
Uffz T. Kuhn (P)   6/KG4 — 95
Oblt Kuhnert (D)   8/JG53 — 880
Lt Kuhrke (M)   8/ZG26 — 143
Lt W. Kummer (D)   I/StG3 — 1410
Uffz Kunz (M)   1/KG77 — Imp 19/9
Oblt H. Kunze (D)   I/JG77 — 1016
Uffz Kurella (D)   III/ZG76 — 901
Uffz Kurtz (D)   9/KG77 — 1060
Uffz Lackner (M)   5/JG27 — 272
Fw Laege (M)   IV/KG30 — 1159
Oblt Lamberty (P)   9/KG76 — 426
Oblt Lammers (P)   I/JG3 — 777
Lt Landenberger (D)   5/KG2 — 890
Lt Landry (D)   I/JG3 — 592
Obfw H. Lang (P)   2/KG76 — 677
Lt Lange (D)   9/JG51 — 163
Obfw W. Lange (P)   4/KG3 — 663
Uffz Lange (D)   II/KG53 — 1008
Uffz J. Lange   Seenotflkdo — 1445A
Oblt Langenheim (M)   II/KG53 — 967
Obfw Langer (D)   III/KG2 — 325

Uffz Langer (P)   8/KG2 — 1013
Uffz M. Langer (D)   9/JG53 — 1035
Oblt Lauth (D)   III/KG77 — 1064
Lt H. Leder (D)   8/KG76 — 436
Uffz Lederer (P)   5/JG27 — 1205
Uffz Lehner (D)   3/KG53 — 1019
Fw Lehrmann (D)   III/JG27 — 612
Gfr Leichsenring (M)   I/KG77 — Imp 9/11
Oblt Lemmerich (P)   7/LG2 — 1304
Uffz Leng (D)   9/KG2 — 1022
Uffz H. Lenger (P)   III/KG53 — 794
Lt L. Lenz (D)   I/LG2 — 1269
Oblt Leppla (?)   I/JG51 — 216
Lt Lessing (D)   5/JG51 — 463
Fw Lichtenhagen (P)   II/KG53 — 1008
Uffz H. Liebeck (P)   7/JG26 — 666
Fw Liebernecht (M)   II/KG54 — Imp 7/9
Uffz R. Lindemann (P)   7/JG26 — 1490
Fw Linsner (P)   4/AugklGr d.L — 1043
Uffz Loeffler (P)   6/KG76 — 432
Gfr H. Loeffler (D)   4/KG3 — 1438
Obgfr Lohmann (D)   EproGr210 — 394
Obgfr G. Loppach   2/JG77 — 1440
Obgfr Lotter (D)   5/KG2 — 890
Obfw Luckhard (D)   I/KG51 — 1065
Uffz Ludwig (P)   I/KG77 — 1135
Oblt Lutze (D)   II/KG77 — 1139
Uffz M. Maasen (P)   9/KG76 — 699
Lt Mader (M)   I/LN Regt 32 — 461
Uffz Mahringer (P)   7/KG2 — 326
Uffz Mai (M)   1/ZG26 — 437
Gfr Mailander (P)   7/KG53 — 465
Uffz Mairl (D)   3/LG2 — 1308
Obgfr W. Malecki (P)   2/JG52 — 562
Lt Malischewski (P)   II/JG54 — 1248
Uffz Malter (D)   9/KG76 — 980
Uffz Marck (P)   3/KG1 — 902
Uffz R. Marckovitz (M)   8/KG1 — 113
Fw H. Marte (M)   II/KG51 — 1296
Gfr F. Martinek (M)   8/KG1 — 113
Lt H. Marx (P)   2/EproGr210 — 397
Uffz Massmann (P)   3/JG3 — 903
Fw Maul (M)   I/JG51 — 467
Fw Mavrer (D)   4/AufklGr d L — 679
Hptm Mayer (D)   I/JG53 — 1289
Fw Mayer (D)   II/KG53 — 1002
Uffz R. Mayer (D)   2/EproGr210 — 343
Uffz Mayer (?)   III/JG51 — 178
Hptm W. Mayerweissflog (P)   Stab/JG53
    791
Uffz Maywald (P)   Seenotflkdo — 138
Lt G. Mazza (M)   18°Stormo CT — 1442
Uffz Meier (M)   II/KG76 — 502
Fw Meining (P)   IV/LG1 — 694
Uffz Meixner (M)   3/JG77 — 968
Uffz W. Melchert (P)   5/JG2 — 875
Uffz Mellin (M)   1/KGr126 — 1101
Uffz Menz (M)   8/JG27 — 275
Uffz Merschen (D)   I/KG77 — 1135
Oblt Metz (P)   III/JG2 — 786
Fw Meudner (M)   3/JG51 — 1102
Oblt Meuncheberg (D)   III/JG26 —
    214 258
Uffz Meussel (D)   II/KG26 — Imp 11/9
Lt E. Meyer (P)   2/JG51 — 1210
Obfw Meyer (P) 8/ZG26 — 152

Fw Meyer (D)   II/KG76 — 502
Uffz W. Miesala (D)   9/JG51 — 1473
Uffz Mileska (D)   1/KG1 — 1432
Lt Michaelis (P)   II/KG3 — 997
Uffz Mobius (M)   5/KG2 — 1005
Uffz Mobius (P)   I/ZG26 — 446
Gfr Mökel (D)   1/KG77 — Imp 19/9
Lt Moellenbrok (M)   3/KG2 — 401
Uffz H. Moeller (D)   2/LG2 — 512
Uffz G. Moerschel (P)   4/LG2 — 1209
Maj Mölders (?)   Stab/JG51 — 216 218
    1024 1071 1072 1232 1233 1288
Oblt Morch (D)   8/KG2 — 325
Maj Moricke (D)   II/KG76 — 501
Fw L. Mugge (D)   1/KG1 — 1432
Oblt Muller (P)   III/KG2 — 325
Oblt Muller (M)   II/JG2 — Imp 4/9
Obfw Muller (P)   I/JG53 — 966
Fw R. Muller (M)   II/KG77 — Imp 25/10
Uffz Muller (M)   4/JG3 — 535
Uffz Muller (M)   9/STG1 — 1426
Oblt Muller (D)   13/LG1 — 1021
Obfw H. Muller (P)   1/KG77 — 1116
Obfw Muller (M)   3/JG26 — 1409
Obfw R. Muller (P)   1/KG77 — 1116
Lt Muller-Duhe (D)   7/JG26 — 459
Gfr E. Mummert (P)   II/JG52 — 1167
Hptm Munchenhagen (P)   10/LG1 — 392
Fw Nagel (P)   II/KG53 — 982
Fw Natzke (D)   2/KG1 — 424
Uffz Neidermaier (D)   9/JG54 — 396
Hptm Neumann (?)   I/JG27 — 1028 1029
Obgfr Neumann (D)   II/KG53 — 864
Gfr Neiweg (M)   8/KG77 — 1063
Fw B. Nickel (D)   5/KG3 — 664
Obfw Niebler (D)   I/KG76 — 984
Fw Nitsche (D)   I/KG3 — 1356
Obgfr Nitsche (D)   7/KG2 — 327
Uffz E. Nittmann (P)   7/JG27 — 828
Fw Nolte (D)   III/KG77 — Imp 18/9
Gfr A. Nowotny (P)   III/KG53 — 794
Gfr Odene (D)   II/ZG76 — 761
Obgfr T. Oehl (D)   II/ZG2 — 715
Oblt Oehm (M)   8/JG26 — 257
Fw Oglodek (D)   1/JG51 — 500
Hptm Oligschlager   I/ZG2 — 872
Lt Ortner (P)   EproGr210 — 394
Oblt Oswald (P)   Stab/KG2 — 323
Uffz Osenow (D)   8/KG76 — 971
Fw Osinsky (M)   3/KG2 — 150
Fw J. Ottersbach (D)   I/ZG2 — 872
Lt Pannhas (D)   3(F)22 — 319
Hptm Peters (P)   9/KG76 — 426
Fw H. Pfachler (P)   2/KG76 — 677
Fw Pfeiffer (P)   8/KG76 — 975
Uffz Pfeiffer (M)   III/JG3 — 604
Gfr Pfeiffer (P)   3/KG1 — 933
Obgfr H. Pfieffer (M)   III/LG1 — 1295
Fw Phillips (?)   II/JG26 — 477
Oblt G. Piduhn (D)   II/ZG76 — 761
Uffz Pieronczyk (P)   6/KG3 — 384
Uffz Pirschan (M)   III/KG77 — Imp 25/10
Obfw Pitzkar (D)   II/KG53 — 864
Uffz Pohling (M)   8/KG30 — Imp 2/11
Oblt Pointer (P)   8/JG27 — 1348

Uffz Poschenrieder (P)   7/JG52 — 1168
Obfw Potthast (M)   5/JG52 — 346
Lt Prampesberger (D)   i/KG1 — 1432
Oblt E. Priebe (P)   2/JG77 — 652
Oblt J. Priller (?)   II/JG51 — 180
Lt M. Probst (P?)   1/KG1 — 1417
Hptm H. Prochnow (D)   4/KG4 — 96
Uffz Proebst (P)   III/KG77 — 1064
Oblt R. Proske (P)   I/ZG26 — 446
Uffz Puempel (P)   3/KG1 — 933
Hptm Puettemann (D)   II/KG3 — 967
Fw Puschnerus (M)   I/ZG26 — 268
Fw Raab (P)   9/KG76 — 980
Fw Radelmeier (D)   6/ZG26 — 927
Uffz K. Ramm (M)   II/KG3 — 554
Uffz Rascher (P)   II/KG53 — 624
Oblt Rath (P)   II/JG54 — 619
Uffz A. Rauwolf (P)   6/JG27 — 905
Fw X. Ray (P)   8/JG53 — 1394
Lt Regenauer (P)   I/JG26 — 303
Uffz Reichenbach (D)   4/JG52 — 1242
Gefr Reiner (P)   3/KG77 — 1140
Uffz H. Reinhardt (M)   7/KG3 — 567
Gfr Reinhardt (P)   7/KG53 — 465
Gfr Reinecke (D)   I/KG2 — 401
Gfr Reinecke (P)   3/KG1 — 902
Uffz Reith (P)   8/JG2 — 625
Gfr R. Reisel (P)   II/KG76 — 835
Uffz Reiss (P)   8/JG52 — 207
Fw A. Reitzig (D)   6/KG4 — 95
Oblt H. Rheumschuessel (P)   3/JG53 —
   990
Oblt Richter (M)   IV/KG30 — 1159
Uffz Richter (P)   3/KG77 — 1140
Gfr Richter (P)   3/KG53 — 1019
Uffz Richter (P)   3/KG77 — 1140
Lt R. Riedel (D)   I/JG3 — 1433
Obfw Riedel (M)   7/KG76 — 400
Oblt Riegel (M)   3/JG53 — 798
Lt H. Riegel (M)   I/JG53 — 724
Gfr Riesel (P)   6/KG76 — 835
Obfw Rilling (D)   5/KG3 — 994
Lt Ripke (D)   8/JG26 — 1330
Uffz Ritzel (M)   7/KG3 — 567
Oblt E. Roch (M)   II/JG26 — 749
Obfw K. Rochel (P)   5/ZG26 — 714
Obgfr Rockstrol (M)   2(F)122 — Imp 2/9
Lt Roden (M)   II/StG2 — 196
Gfr Roeder (M)   I/KG51 — 1065
Uffz W. Roempert (P)   6/KG53 — 624
Gfr H. Roggemann (P)   II/KG1 — 620
Gfr Rohde (M)   8/ZG26 — 152
Gfr Rohleder (D)   6/KG3 — 383
Gfr F. Rohmer (M)   III/LG1 — 1295
Fw Rosche (P)   Stab/KG76 — 873
Uffz F. Rosenberger (M)   7/KG53 — 789
Flgr H. Rösler (D)   15/LG1 — 700A
Hptm Roth (P)   9/KG76 — 426
Uffz R. Roth (D)   Stab/ZG26 — 808
Uffz Rudermond (M)   8/KG30 — Imp 2/11
Fw Rudinger (D)   9/KG3 — 470
Uffz Rudolf (M)   9/KG76 — 436
Uffz Ruetig (D)   3/KG53 — 1019
Uffz Ruhlandt (P)   3/KG77 — 1140
Uffz H. Ruhn (M)   4/KG3 — Imp 2/11
Fw Rungen (P)   7/JG3 — 1258

Oblt W. Rupp (P)   3/JG53 — 1291
Uffz Rupprecht (D)   Stab/KG76 — 873
Oblt Russel (D)   4(F)14 — 838
Oblt Rutters (P)   4/ZG26 — 457
Obfw Ruttinger (M)   4/JG52 — 339
Lt G. Rüttkowski (D)   1/JG51 — 706
Fw Saal (M)   I/KGr126 — 1101
Lt Sachse (D)   7/KG3 — 561
Gfr Sailer (D)   II/KG53 — 1008
Uffz Salomo (M)   8/KG3 — 1158
Gfr Sandmann (M)   III/KG2 — Imp 15/9
Oblt Sauer (P)   2/JG52 — 1253
Fw Sauter (P)   8/KG76 — 975
Lt Schactebeck (D)   2/KG26 — 830
Uffz Schall (P)   6/KG53 — 624
Gfr A. Schank (P)   2/EproGr210 — 355
Uffz Schatz (D)   3/KG76 — 984
Fw Schauer (P)   6/KG3 — 384
Lt J. Schauf (D)   III/JG26 — 186
Uffz Scheidt (D)   6/JG27 — 1129
Oblt E. Schelcher (D)   III/JG54 — 716
Uffz Schersand (D)   I/JG53 — 965
Uffz Schiele (P)   Seenotflkdo — 138
Fw Schierling (M)   8/KG3 — 1158
Fw L. Schieverhofer (P)   3/JG52 — 1349
Lt R. Schiffbauer (P)   3/JG26 — 1428
Gfr Schild (P)   4/KG3 — 996
Uffz Schilling (P)   II/KG53 — 982
Obgefr Schindlhauer   I/KG77 — Imp 9/11
Lt G. Schipper (P)   I/ZG2 — 718
Oblt Schirming (P)   II/KG53 — 982
Oblt H. Schlegel (P)   Stab/KG2 — 323
Uffz Schlitt (M)   4/JG53 — 1345
Uffz Schloessler (D)   I/KG54 — 1036
Obfw Schmid (D)   I/JG51 — 182 242
Fw Schmid (D)   8/KG76 — 975
Oblt R. Schmidt (D)   2/JG53 — 987
Lt Schmidt (M)   7/JG52 — 210
Obfw H. Schmidt (?)   6/JG53 — 1471
Uffz Schmidt (P)   2/KG77 — 1115
Fw Schmidt   I/JG26 — 1399
Obgfr Schmitt (D)   9/StG1 — 1426
Obfw Schmittborn (P)   II/KG53 — 982
Uffz A. Schmolzer (P)   2/KG2 — 568
Lt H. Schnabel (P)   I/JG3 — 770
Oblt Schneider (P)   5/KG2 — 889
Obfw Schneider (D)   Stab/KG76 — 873
Uffz Schneider (P)   2/KG1 — 424
Obgfr Schneider (D)   Stab/KG76 — 873
Uffz K. Schneiderberger (M)   II/JG51 —
   131
Oblt Schnell   9/JG51 — 1423
Gfr T. Schockenhoff (P)   I/ZG2 — 718
Uffz W. Schoefler (P)   5/ZG26 — 714
Gfr Schoeffmann (D)   II/LG1 — 1179
Oblt G. Schöpfel (?)   I/JG54 — 429 450
   425 430
Fw Schoettle (P)   I/JG54 — 603
Oblt Schon (D)   8/JG54 — 1117
Uffz Schonn (M)   8/KG3 — 1158
Fw Schreiber (D)   I/KG3 — 1356
Uffz Schroff (M)   8/KG3 — 1158
Obfw Schutegh-Mader (M)   8/KG30 —
   Imp 2/11
Oblt W. Schueller (P)   3/JG27 — 825
Fw Schuetz (D)   2/ZG26 — 711
Fw Schuetz (D)   4/AufklGr — 1043
Flgr Schuetz (D)   5/KG2 — 890

120

Uffz A. Schuebauer (M)   2/KG53 —
   Imp 26/10
Gfr E. Schuller (P)   6/JG3 — 1379
Oblt Schulte (D)   II/KG76 — 501
Uffz G. Schulte (P)   7/JG53 — 829
Oblt Schulte-Blank   4/JG53 — 910
Uffz Schulz (M)   6/JG53 — 1321
Fw E. Schulz (D)   9/JG27 — 1054
Obfw W. Schumacher (P)   6/KG76 — 835
Uffz Schumacher (P)   5/KG2 — 889
Gfr Schumacher (M)   II/JG2 — 1156
Gfr Schumann (M)   7/ZG26 — 799
Obgfr K. Schweda (D)   EproGr210 — 657
Fw Schwertfeger (D)   III/KG2 — 327
Fw Schwesers (P)   7/JG54 — 1223
Oblt J. Schypek (P)   5/JG54 — 1324
Uffz Sehert (P)   9/KG2 — 1022
Oblt Seif (D)   6/KG77 — 1138
Oblt Seiler (P)   I/JG54 — 246 247
Oblt H. Seliger (M)   III/JG53 — 1033
Uffz Selter (D)   5/KG2 — 888
Obfw Semerau (D)   8/KG77 —1058
Uffz Sergocki (P)   2/KG77 — 1115
Oblt Siegmund (P)   8/ZG26 — 151
Fw Simon (D)   III/KG2 — Imp 15/9
Gfr Skuthan (D)   II/KG76 — 427
Oblt Sonnberg (D)   11/LG1 — 166
Uffz W. Sonntag (D)   5/KG3 — 664
Lt J. Sonntag (M)   II/KG51 — 1296
Lt W. Sonnenberg (D)   8/KG3 — 1395
Gfr Sossner (M)   2/ZG2 — 913
Fw A. Spehr (P)   7/KG1 — 1418
Gfr G. Speiss (D)   9/KG76 — 699
Oblt G. Sprick (?)   III/JG26 — 259
Gfr Stabner (M?)   III/JG54 — 300
Obtw Staib (D)   9/KG2 — 1018
Uffz Stamfer (P)   8/KG2 — 1013
Gfr Stamminger (P)   3/KG53 — 1019
Obfw H. Stange (M)   3/ZG26 — 439
Fw Stange (P)   6/ZG26 —445
Oblt A. Stangl (P)   II/JG54 — 684
Uffz H. Steding (P)   2/EproGr210 — 355
Obfw A. Stegmuller (M)   II/KG51 — 1296
1296Fw Steigenberger (P)   5/JG51 — 382
Uffz Steinecke (P)   3/KG1 — 933
Lt Dr Steinert (M)   KuFlGr906 — 179
Oblt U. Steinhilper (P)   3/JG52 — 1350
Uffz Stenzel (M)   II/KG26 — 787
Obgfr Stief (M)   14/LG1 — 964
Fw Stier (P)   8/KG77 — 1062
Gfr Still (D)   I/JG77 — 1038
Uffz Stirnemann (P)   I/KG26 — 918
Uffz Stocker (D)   5/JG51 — 145A
Fw K. Stockl (P)   6/KG53 — 623
Oblt Stoll (M)   9/JG53 — 1032
Oberst Lt J. Stollbrock (D)   Stab/KGr100
   — 17
Obfw — Strack (D)   1/JG52 — 1340
Obfw Strahl (M)   1/KG77 — Imp 19/9
Fw K. Straub (P)   7/JG26 — 580 587
Uffz H. Streibing (P)   1/LG2 — 1004
Obfw Streit (P)   9/KG76 — 980
Lt Striberny (M)   3/LG2 — 129
Lt H. Ströbel (D)   5/JG27 — 795
Obfw Ströbel (P)   5/KG2 — 890
Obfw Stroehlein (M)   2/JG51 — 845

Oblt Stronk (D)   8/JG53 — 1177
Uffz Struwe (P)   9/JG3 — 1146
Gfr Stuewe (P)   2/ZG26 — 711
Uffz Stumbaum (P)   3/KG1 — 902
Uffz Stumpf (M)   II/KG76 — Imp 2/11
Uffz Szyminski (D)   8/KG76 — 436
Fw Teuffert (P)   9/KG76 — 980
Lt W. Teumar (P)   II/JG51 — 1452
Obfw Thalmann (P)   3/KG2 — 150
Lt H. Thoerl (P)   1/JG51 — 707
Fw Thomas (M)   4/KG76 — 505
Oblt H. Tiedmann (P)   I/JG3 — 448
Hptm J. Tietzen (D)   II/JG51 — 169 235
   462
Gfr W. Tilger (D)   4/KG53 — 1438
Uffz Toepfer (D)   7/JG26 — 1371
Lt Tornow (D)   4/JG51 — 1369
Hptmn H. Trautloft(?)   III/JG51 — 253
Obfw K. Trebing (D)   III/JG3 — 586
Lt Treibel (M)   II/JG51 — 134
Oblt C. Treiber (P)   II/JG52 — 1132
Uffz Treutmann (D)   8/KG77 — 1058
Uffz E. Trost (D)   5/KG2 — 888
Oblt Troha (P)   9/JG3 — 1368
Gfr Tscentke (M)   II/KG77 — Imp 25/10
Fw H. Tschoppe (P)   1/JG53 — 974
Gfr Ulbrich (M)   8/KG76 — 436
Gfr Ulrich (P)   II/KG53 — 864
Gfr B. Valkmann (D)   4/KG3 — 1438
Lt Vaupel (M)   I/KG77 — Imp 9/11
Fw H. Verlings (P)   1/JG52 — 741
Obfw Vetter (M)   II/KG26 — 787
Obfw Vetter (D)   5/KG76 — 427
Fw Vetter (M)   II/KG76 — 502
Oblt F. Viertel (P)   Stab/ZG26 — 808
Oblt Vogel (M)   4/JG53 — 1225
Obfw Vogel (M)   II/KG76 — Imp 2/11
Uffz Vogel (P?)   7/KG2 — 326
Uffz Vogel (D)   4/AugKlGr — 679
Oblt Voigt (P)   4/JG3 — 1218
Lt Volk (M)   6/ZG26 — 926
Hptm von Brauschitsch (?)   LG1 — 317
Hptm H. von Claer (M)   II/KG51 — 1296
Lt von Fonderen (D)   III/JG3 — 435
Oblt von Groben (D)   7/KG2 — 324
Fw von Hewarth-Bittenfeld (P)   I/JG3 —
   1195
Hptm von Houwald (D)   III/JG52 — 189
Lt R. von Larisch (D)   4/JG3 — 672
Lt von Rosen (M)   II/StG2 — 370
Uffz von Stein (P)   4/JG2 — 723
Obfw Graf von Treuberg (D)   I/JG26 —
   604
OberstLt von Wedel (P)   Stab/JG3 — 978
Oblt H. von Werra (P)   II/JG3 — 783
Fw Voss (P)   3/JG52 — 1254
Fw Vosshagen (P)   I/KG3 — 1356
Magg F. Vosilla (M)   83ªSqdla Regia
   Aeronautica — 1442
Obfw Wachter (D)   7/KG76 — 400
Uffz Wagelein (D)   5/JG53 — 1469
Oblt R. Wagner (M)   6/KG76 — 816
Lt E. Wagner (P)   5/JG54 — 1331
Uffz G. Wagner (P)   8/KG1 — 113
Uffz H. Wagner (P)   6/KG53 — 624

Sonderfuhrer Wagner (D)   II/KG76 — 501
Fw Waier (D)   III/KG53 — 794
Uffz W. Waldeim   Seenotflkdo — 1445A
Oblt Waller (P)   3/JG52 — 820
Lt Walter (P)   II/KG3 — 384
Fw Walter (M)   I/KG51 — 1065
Lt Waltermann (M)   I/KG77 — Imp 9/11
Fw Walz (M)   5/JG51 — 282
Fw Wart (M)   II/KG26 — 787
Fw Watermann (P)   6/KG76 — 432
Oblt Weber (D)   8/KG77 — 1063
Fw Weber (D)   10/LG1 — 391
Lt A. Weckner (M)   Stab/KGr100 — 17
Oblt Weimann (M)   1/EproGr210 — 1182
Obfw Weiss (D)   4/JG52 — 339
Uffz Wemhoner (P)   5/JG26 — 329
Uffz Wendtland (D)   I/KG1 — 1432
Oblt Werdin (D)   7/LG2 — 419
Gfr H. Werner (P)   3/JG51 — 870
Oblt K. Westerhof (P)   6/JG3 — 671
Fw Westfalen (D)   3/KG26 — 919
Uffz Wetzker (M)   4/KG76 — 505
Gfr Weymar (P)   4/KG3 — 996
Uffz Wiemann (?)   5/JG27 — 1236
Uffz Wien (P)   4/KG3 — 996
Uffz Wiesen (P)   4/AufKlGr — 1043
Fw Wilde (M)   II/KG26 — 787
Oblt Wilke (P)   3/KG76 — 984
Fw Winkelmann (D)   I/KG77 — Imp 19/9
Fw W. Winkelmann (M)   3/KG2 — 150
Fw F. Winter (D)   6/ZG26 — 434
Lt Wesemann (P)   II/KG26 — Imp 11/9

Fw Wissmann (D)   3/KG76 — 984
Oblt Witmeier (M)   I/JG53 — 880 881
Oblt Witt (M)   I/JG54 — 755
Fw H. Wöhner (P)   9/KG76 — 699
Gfr Woite (M)   I/KG77 — Imp 9/11
Uffz H. Wolf (P)   2/JG26 — 1463
Uffz G. Wollin (D)   6/ZG26 — 445
Gfr Worsch (P)   III/KG53 — 465
Fw E. Wortbach (D)   1/JG51 — 1425
Fw W. Wowereit (M)   8/KG30 — Imp 2/11
Fw H. Wuensch (P)   4/KG3 — 663
Gfr Zabel (D)   1/KG77 — 1116
Gfr H. Zag (P)   8/JG53 — 1178
Gfr Zaehle (D)   3/KG76 — 919
Fw Zahn (M)   8/KG76 — 971
Lt O. Zauner (P)   5/KG53 — 1441
Lt Zeiss (P)   I/JG53 — 1190
Fw Zeller (D)   II/KG77 — 1139
Lt Ziegler (P)   II/JG54 — 619
Fw A. Ziegler (P)   3/JG52 — 537
Oblt Ziems (D)   5/KG2 — 888
Gfr Zierer (P)   9/KG2 — 1018
Uffz Zilling (P)   II/KG53 — 1008
Fw Zimmermann (P)   5/KG3 — 994
Uffz A. Zimmermann (P)   7/JG54 — 1351
Fw Zinsmeister (P)   6/KG77 — 1138
Oblt Zipse (P)   7/KG53 — 465
Uffz Zremer (P)   3/KG76 — 984
Gfr F. Zumbrock (D)   8/KG3 — 1395
Uffz R. Zurlage (P)   3/JG51 — 840

123

141	170 171 172 173 174 175 176 1036 1320 1381 1396 1455 1456 1466 1496
142	532
145	43 83 1249
151	39 40 105 137 247 270 293 294 339 386 387 388 390 494 495 514 582 593 617 677
213	963 1006 1110 1292 1293
219	1422
222	621 622 638 639 640 641 642 655 668 669 758 762 763 788 879 898 905 947 1056 1068 1145 1223 1279 1289 1330 1365
229	71 917 923 970 972 1008 1090 1162 1163 1164 1171 1173 1174 1268 1270 1295 1366 1490
234	781 783 841 842
235	20 21 49 51 58
236	212
238	931 1009 1010
242	53 54 55 61 1124 1126 1400 1403
245	64 65 66
249	704 708 709 715 718 733 802 850 851 854 856 891 916 995 1144 1154 1226 1247 1283 1326 1327 1372 1407 1408 1461 1464
253	16 612 614 627 632 635 636 646 656 693 705 720 743 766 807 899 945 953 954 955 1013 1017 1069 1070 1103 1104 1227 1234 1237 1264 1285 1373 1477
254	79 80
257	213 858 859 866 980 1084 1203 1245 1246 1256 1276 1317 1318 1319 1332 1412
264	31A 52 60 63 70 72 483 484 485 496 497 501 502 504 505 542 545 546 554 572 573 574 579
266	322 366 375 393 406 407 408 411 412 452 453
302	1263 1274 1294 1297 1298 1413 1414
303	716 742 746 748 770 806 809 810 817 818 825 827 852 922 928 1004 1007 1011 1020 1021 1035 1062 1087 1105 1109 1169 1182 1183 1189 1194 1202
310	664 867 876 993 1122 1392 1401
500	6 8 10 13 15 71A 73 155 156 317 533 534 700 729 730 1415
501	211 224 239 239A 251 252 292 295 299 302 367 368 369 420 425 429 430 450 462 463 464 482 489 503 506 520 569 607 609 611 629 658 710 713 735 736 769 774 803 804 805 915 944 983 988 996 1030 1031 1039 1049 1123 1147 1148 1161 1190 1198 1210 1212 1278 1325 1334 1335 1336 1337
504	220 853 855 921 989 997 998 1034
600	24 103 259 264 298 340 341 418 468
601	655 659 813 814 815 819
602	800 843 860 861 862 871 1377 1378 1488
603	595 596 602 603 605 608 610 615 626 633 662 739 744 749 752 767 768 863 865 966 973 1012 1040 1089 1127 1128 1150 1176 1178 1193 1199 1209 1225 1353 1354 1355 1357 1439 1442 1465
605	69 884 969 992 994 999 1024 1153 1179 1204 1205 1206 1250 1273 1302 1342 1385 1386 1416 1428 1429 1474 1475 1476
607	892 894 895 896 897 1014 1015 1028 1029
609	68 975
610	47 59 74 75 93 94 104 128 148 158 160 169 182 188 189 190 201 202 205 207 209 210 234 254 255 284 285 286 287 288 313 344 345 348 349 413 415 447 449 474 488 492 493 530 537 538 550 552 591 620
611	984
613	44 46
615	1 97 167 281 342 347 352 353 366 376 377 422 454 467 469 470 473 516 535 560 563 578 1363 1364 1406 1437 1457 1491 1492
616	41 50 77 476 528 539 540 541 543 544 557 558 618 634 737 1121
421Flt	1224 1235 1251 1272 1281 1286 1287 1300 1301 1343 1434 1445 1445A 1449 1450 1467 1473 1483 1486 1493 1495 1497
1RCAF	649 650 651 665 695 698 932 976 977 1027 1046 1108 1181 1197

P.D.U. (Photographic Development Unit)
  22
1 C.A.C.U. (1 Coastal Artillery Co-operation Unit)   1077
16 Group Communications Flight
  241
826(FAA)
  912
Stn Flt Hawkinge
  238A
O.U. Air Sqdn
  3

INDEX OF LUFTWAFFE UNITS

In each Geschwader the incidents referring to Gruppen are given first followed by those concerning the Staffeln.

KG1	I/	1417
	1/	1432
	2/	424
	3/	902 933
	7/	1418
	8/	113
	10/	620
KG2	Stab/	234 323
	2/	551 568
	3/	149 150 142 401 402
	5/	888 889 890 1005
	7/	324 325 326 327
	8/	1013
	9/	469 1018 1022
KG3	1/	1356
	3/	142
	4/	663 996 997 1438
	5/	664 967 994 1014
	6/	383 384 571
	7/	554 561 567
	8/	1158 1395
	9/	470
KG4	4/	96
	6/	95
	9/	269
KG26	I/	918
	II/	787
	2/	830 920
	3/	919
KG30	IV/	1159
	3/	33
	6/	1219
KG51	I/	1065 1066
	II/	1296
	III/	506
KG53	II/	373 864 982 1002 1008 1438
	III/	794 1470
	3/	1019
	6/	623 624
	7/	465 789
KG54	I/	1036
KG76	Stab/	873
	II/	501 502
	III/	1393
	2/	677
	3/	984
	4/	504 505
	5/	427
	6/	432 816 835
	7/	400 410 835
	8/	436 971 975
	9/	426 699 980
KG77	II/	1139
	III/	1064
	1/	1116

	2/	106 1115
	3/	1135 1140
	6/	1138
	8/	107 1057 1058 1062 1063
	9/	108 1060
KGr100	Stab/	17
KGr126	1/	1101
KuFlGr906		
	3/	179
AufKlGr Ob d L		
	3/	514
	4/	679 1043
4(F)14		838
3(F)22		319
2(F)122		45
3(F)122		12
4(F)122		185
5(F)122		363 503

STUKA

StG1	Stab/	1468
	I/	365 1429
	II/	196 271 1382
	III/	1426
StG2	II/	184 271 370 371 374
StG3	I/	1411

Air/Sea Rescue

SeeNotFlKdo		138 208 272 486 601 604 630 631 642 644 728 729A 756 760 777 778 839 920 938 1075 1339 1445A
	3/	467

FIGHTERS

JG2	Stab/	832
	II/	644 1156
	1/	878
	2/	1157
	4/	634 717 723 1081
	5/	875
	8/	625 786
	9/	725
JG3	Stab/	978 1087
	I/	592 770 777 781 1352
	II/	783
	III/	435 507 586 604 846 1089
	1/	770 938 1003 1195 1433
	2/	448
	3/	265 266 296 297 607 990
	4/	535 547 672 1218
	5/	776
	6/	336 548 671 1376 1379
	7/	601 903 911 1089 1258
	8/	337 466 839 1268
	9/	515 1146 1368
JG26	Stab/	581
	I/	78 303 310 338 351 604 631 945 1399

	II/	353 412 456 477 630 635 744 749 836 837 1199		5/	1441 1469
	III/	186 193 214 258 259		6/	1321 1341 1471
	1/	242 1454 1483		7/	765 829
	2/	1317 1463		8/	822 880 1176 1177 1178 1394
	3/	1409 1428		9/	1032 1033 1035 1470
	5/	329	JG54	Stab/	1248
	6/	643		I/	247 531 603 773
	7/	459 460 486 580 666 673 801 831 834 1371 1490		II/	584 619 684 778
				III/	300 305 396 716
	8/	257 1079 1082 1328 1330 1370		1/	909
				2/	366
	9/	206 214 256 675 746 1160 1397 1398		3/	309 358 403A 755 756 908 1088
JG27	I/	280A 642 1028		4/	1390
	II/	682		5/	364 1324 1331
	III/	612 1354		7/	1223 1351
	1/	1037		8/	738 1117
	3/	626 627 825		9/	396 1166 1220 1302
	5/	272 795 833 1205 1236 1357	JG77	I/	661 662 760 1016
				1/	655 659 871 952 1038 1221
	6/	905 1129		2/	652 1440
	7/	828		3/	645 968 1135
	8/	275 1277 1348	ZG2	I/	718 747 857 872
	9/	1053 1054 1073 1208		II/	715 733 874
JG51	Stab/	576 1024 1232 1288 1333		2/	913
	I/	182 216 585	ZG26	Stab/	808
	II/	131 134 181 235 1358		I/	268 274 446
	III/	132 142 170 178 189 253		II/	708 711
				III/	140
	1/	242 467 500 706 707 1175 1425		1/	437
				2/	937
	2/	219 845 1210 1440 1452		3/	328 439 461
	3/	840 870 1102 1367 1447 1448 1451		4/	457 458 925
				5/	709 714
	4/	130 235 404 1266 1267 1369		6/	431 433 434 445 926 927
	5/	145A 169 282 382 462 463 1395A	7/99		
				8/	143 151 152 681
	6/	227 403 499		9/	936
	7/	131 599 999 1165 1325	ZG76	II/	761
	8/	481 729A		III/	901
	9/	157 163 522 746 991 1322 1423	LG1	I/	
				II/	154 221 222 1179
JG52	I/	510 683 774 1000		III/	1295
	II/	313 285 1132		IV/	270
	III/	189 211		V/	249
	1/	741 1252 1340		10/	342 344 345 391 392
	2/	559 562 564 565 613 1253		11/	166
				13/	1020 1021
	3/	537 820 1254 1349 1350		14/	647 648 694 964
	4/	339 1134 1136 1141 1167 1242		15/	700A
			LG2	Stab/	1269 1489
	5/	346 1130 1309		I/	490 491 867 930 1004 1107
	6/	1307		II/	824 826
	7/	188 190 205 209 210 1168		2/	512 1243
				3/	129 1001 1308
	8/	192 207		4/	111 1205 1209 1211
JG53	Stab/	791		5/	1075
	I/	719 724 728 800 881 887 904 965 966 1289 1478		6/	957
				7/	419 1304
	II/	1061	EproGr210		298 311 330 340 394 657 1183 1365
	III/	703		1/	1182 1189
	1/	712 974 1190 1191		2/	343 355 395 397 1366
	2/	987			
	3/	798 986 973 1291			
	4/	910 1225 1339 1345			

Corpo Aereo Italiano
18ºGruppo C.T.   1442

Books by members of the Kent Aviation Historical Research Society

PRELUDE TO WAR: KENT AVIATION 1938-39
A selection of articles by members of the Society about the impact of the threat of war on Kent's airfields.   Paperback £2.50

FLIGHT IN KENT
Nine articles by members of the Society on a variety of subjects from a three day aviation meeting in Folkestone to the daring exploits of pilots intercepting Doodlebugs in 1944.   Paperback £1.95

TARGET FOLKESTONE by Roy Humphreys
During the Second World War Folkestone was very much in the front line, being in range of shelling from across the Channel as well as an obvious target for enemy bombers. This thoroughly researched book is in diary form, detailing all recorded incidents with details of casualties and personal memories of those involved. Well illustrated.
                 Paperback £7.95

FROM MOTHS TO MERLINS by Robin J. Brooks
The story of West Malling Airfield.   Paperback £4.95

KENT'S OWN by Robin J. Brooks
The history of 500 (County of Kent) Squadron of the Royal Auxiliary Air Force 1931-1957. Well illustrated.   Hardback £5.95

AVIATION IN KENT by Robin J. Brooks
A large format pictorial history from 19th century ballooning to 1939.
                 Paperback £2.95

KENT AIRFIELDS IN THE BATTLE OF BRITAIN
The story of nine airfields in the Battle of Britain told by members of the Society. Reprint planned for 1991.

HAWKINGE 1912-1961 by Roy Humphreys
A well-illustrated history of the former RAF station. Reprint planned for 1991.

These books are available from most bookshops in Kent, including the Rainham Bookshop, 17 Station Road, Rainham, Kent.

They are also available by post from Meresborough Books, 17 Station Road, Rainham, Kent. ME8 7RS. Medway (0634) 388812. Please add 10% towards p&p (minimum 30p, orders over £25 post free).

Meresborough Books

17 Station Road, Rainham, Gillingham, Kent. ME8 7RS
Telephone: Medway (0634) 388812

We are a specialist publisher of books about Kent. Our books are available in most bookshops in the county, including our own at this address. Alternatively you may order direct, adding 10% for post (minimum 30p, orders over £25 post free). ISBN prefix 0 905270 for 3 figure numbers, 094819 for 4 figure numbers. Titles in print December 1990.

HARDBACKS

AIRCRAFT CASUALTIES IN KENT Part One 1939-40 compiled by G.G. Baxter, K.A. Owen and P. Baldock. ISBN 3506. £12.95.

BARGEBUILDING ON THE SWALE by Don Sattin. ISBN 3530. £9.95.

EDWARDIAN CHISLEHURST by Arthur Battle. ISBN 3433. £9.95.

FISHERMEN FROM THE KENTISH SHORE by Derek Coombe. ISBN 3409. £10.95.

THE GILLS by Tony Conway. ISBN 266. £5.95. **BARGAIN OFFER £1.95.**

JUST OFF THE SWALE by Don Sattin. ISBN 045. £5.95.

KENT CASTLES by John Guy. ISBN 150. £7.50.

KENT'S OWN by Robin J. Brooks. The history of 500 (County of Kent) Squadron of the R.A.A.F. ISBN 541. £5.95.

LIFE AND TIMES OF THE EAST KENT CRITIC by Derrick Molock. ISBN 3077. **BARGAIN OFFER £1.95.**

THE LONDON, CHATHAM & DOVER RAILWAY by Adrian Gray. ISBN 886. £7.95.

THE NATURAL HISTORY OF ROMNEY MARSH by Dr F.M. Firth, M.A., Ph.D. ISBN 789. £6.95.

A NEW DICTIONARY OF KENT DIALECT by Alan Major. ISBN 274. £7.50.

THE PAST GLORY OF MILTON CREEK by Alan Cordell and Leslie Williams. ISBN 3042. £9.95.

ROCHESTER FROM OLD PHOTOGRAPHS compiled by the City of Rochester Society. Large format. ISBN 975. £7.95.(Also available in paperback ISBN 983. £4.95.)

SHERLOCK HOLMES AND THE KENT RAILWAYS by Kelvin Jones. ISBN 3255. £8.95.

SOUTH EAST BRITAIN: ETERNAL BATTLEGROUND by Gregory Blaxland. A military history. ISBN 444. £5.95. **BARGAIN £2.95.**

STRATFORD HOUSE SCHOOL 1912-1987 by Susan Pittman. ISBN 3212. £10.00.

TALES OF VICTORIAN HEADCORN or The Oddities of Heddington by Penelope Rivers (Ellen M. Poole). ISBN 3050. £8.95. (Also available in paperback ISBN 3069. £3.95).

TEYNHAM MANOR AND HUNDRED (798-1935) by Elizabeth Selby, MBE. ISBN 630. £5.95.

TROOPSHIP TO CALAIS by Derek Spiers. ISBN 3395. £11.95.

TWO HALVES OF A LIFE by Doctor Kary Pole. ISBN 509. £5.95.

US BARGEMEN by A.S. Bennett. ISBN 207. £6.95.

A VIEW OF CHRIST'S COLLEGE, BLACKHEATH by A.E.O. Crombie, B.A. ISBN 223. £6.95.

LARGE FORMAT PICTORIAL PAPERBACKS

ARE YOU BEING SERVED, MADAM? by Molly Proctor. ISBN 3174. £3.50.

AVIATION IN KENT by Robin J. Brooks. ISBN 681. £2.95.

BEFORE AND AFTER THE HURRICANE IN AND AROUND CANTERBURY by Paul Crampton. ISBN 3387. £3.50. BARGAIN £1.95.

THE BLITZ OF CANTERBURY by Paul Crampton. ISBN 3441. £3.50.

EAST KENT FROM THE AIR by John Guy. ISBN 3158. £3.50.

EAST SUSSEX RAILWAYS IN OLD POSTCARDS by Kevin Robertson. ISBN 3220. £3.50.

GEORGE BARGEBRICK Esq. by Richard-Hugh Perks. ISBN 479. £4.50.

HEADCORN: A Pictorial History by the Headcorn Local History Society. ISBN 3271. £3.50.

KENT TOWN CRAFTS by Richard Filmer. ISBN 584. £2.95.

THE LIFE AND ART OF ONE MAN by Dudley Pout. ISBN 525. £2.95.

THE MEDWAY TOWNS FROM THE AIR by Piers Morgan and Diane Nicholls. ISBN 3557. £4.95.

MORE PICTURES OF RAINHAM by Barbara Mackay Miller. ISBN 3298. £3.50.

THE MOTOR BUS SERVICES OF KENT AND EAST SUSSEX — A brief history by Eric Baldock. ISBN 959. £4.95.

OLD BROADSTAIRS by Michael David Mirams. ISBN 3115. £3.50.

OLD CHATHAM: A THIRD PICTURE BOOK by Philip MacDougall. ISBN 3190. £3.50. BARGAIN £1.95.

OLD FAVERSHAM by Arthur Percival. ISBN 3425. £3.50.

OLD GILLINGHAM by Philip MacDougall. ISBN 3328. £3.50.

OLD MAIDSTONE'S PUBLIC HOUSES by Irene Hales. ISBN 533. £2.95. BARGAIN £1.95.

OLD MAIDSTONE Vol.3 by Irene Hales. ISBN 3336. £3.50. BARGAIN £1.95.

OLD MARGATE by Michael David Mirams. ISBN 851. £3.50.

OLD PUBS OF TUNBRIDGE WELLS & DISTRICT by Keith Hetherington and Alun Griffiths. ISBN 300X. £3.50.

PEMBURY IN THE PAST by Mary Standen. ISBN 916. £2.95.

A PICTORIAL STUDY OF ALKHAM PARISH by Susan Lees and Roy Humphreys. ISBN 3034. £2.95.

A PICTORIAL STUDY OF HAWKINGE PARISH by Roy Humphreys. ISBN 328X. £3.50.

A PICTUREBOOK OF OLD NORTHIAM by Lis Rigby. ISBN 3492. £3.95.

A PICTUREBOOK OF OLD RAINHAM by Barbara Mackay Miller. ISBN 606. £3.50.

REMINISCENCES OF OLD CRANBROOK by Joe Woodcock. ISBN 331X. £3.50.

ROCHESTER FROM OLD PHOTOGRAPHS — see under hardbacks.

SMARDEN: A Pictorial History by Jenni Rodger. ISBN 592. £3.50.

THOMAS SIDNEY COOPER OF CANTERBURY by Brian Stewart. ISBN 762. £2.95.

WEST KENT FROM THE AIR by John Guy. ISBN 3166. £3.50.

STANDARD SIZE PAPERBACKS

BIRDS OF KENT: A Review of their Status and Distribution by the Kent Ornithological Society. ISBN 800. £6.95.

BIRDWATCHING IN KENT by Don Taylor. ISBN 932. £4.50.

THE CANTERBURY MONSTERS by John H. Vaux. ISBN 3468. £2.50.

THE CHATHAM DOCKYARD STORY by Philip MacDougall. ISBN 3301. £6.95.

CHIDDINGSTONE — AN HISTORICAL EXPLORATION by Jill Newton. ISBN 940. £1.95.

A CHRONOLOGY OF ROCHESTER by Brenda Purle. ISBN 851. £1.50.

COBHAM. Published for Cobham Parish Council. ISBN 3123. £1.00.

CRIME AND CRIMINALS IN VICTORIAN KENT by Adrian Gray. ISBN 967. £3.95.

CURIOUS KENT by John Vigar. ISBN 878. £1.95.

CYCLE TOURS OF KENT by John Guy. No. 1: Medway, Gravesend, Sittingbourne and Sheppey. ISBN 517. £1.50.

EXPLORING KENT CHURCHES by John E. Vigar. ISBN 3018. £3.95.

EXPLORING SUSSEX CHURCHES by John E. Vigar. ISBN 3093. £3.95.

FLIGHT IN KENT. ISBN 3085. £1.95.

FROM MOTHS TO MERLINS: The History of West Malling Airfield by Robin J. Brooks. ISBN 3239. £4.95.

THE GHOSTS OF KENT by Peter Underwood. ISBN 86X. (Reprinting)

A HISTORY OF CHATHAM GRAMMAR SCHOOL FOR GIRLS, 1907-1982 by Audrey Perkyns. ISBN 576. £1.95.

KENT AIRFIELDS IN THE BATTLE OF BRITAIN by the Kent Aviation Historical Research Society. ISBN 3247. (Reprinting)

KENT COUNTRY CHURCHES by James Antony Syms. ISBN 3131. £4.50.

KENT COUNTRY CHURCHES CONTINUED by James Antony Syms. ISBN 314X. £5.95.

KENT COUNTRY CHURCHES CONCLUDED by James Antony Syms. ISBN 345X. £5.95.

KENT INNS AND SIGNS by Michael David Mirams. ISBN 3182. £3.95.

LET'S EXPLORE THE RIVER DARENT by Frederick Wood. ISBN 770. £1.95.

LULLINGSTONE PARK: THE EVOLUTION OF A MEDIAEVAL DEER PARK by Susan Pittman. ISBN 703. £3.95.

PENINSULA ROUND (The Hoo Peninsula) by Des Worsdale. ISBN 568. £1.50.

PRELUDE TO WAR: Aviation in Kent 1938-39 by KAHRS. ISBN 3476. £2.50.

RADIO KENT GARDENERS' GUIDE by Harry Smith and Bob Collard. ISBN 3549. £3.95.

REAL ALE PUBS IN KENT by CAMRA in Kent. ISBN 3263. Was £1.95. Now 95p.

SAINT ANDREW'S CHURCH, DEAL by Gregory Holyoake. ISBN 835. 95p.

SHORNE: The History of a Kentish Village by A.F. Allen. ISBN 3204. £4.95.

SIR GARRARD TYRWHITT-DRAKE AND THE COBTREE ESTATE, MAIDSTONE by Elizabeth Melling B.A. ISBN 3344. £1.50.

SITTINGBOURNE & KEMSLEY LIGHT RAILWAY STOCKBOOK AND GUIDE. ISBN 843. 95p.

STEAM IN MY FAMILY by John Newton. ISBN 3417. £4.95.

STOUR VALLEY WALKS from Canterbury to Sandwich by Christopher Donaldson. ISBN 991. £1.95.

TALES OF VICTORIAN HEADCORN — see under hardbacks.

TARGET FOLKESTONE by Roy Humphreys. ISBN 3514. £7.95.

WADHURST: Town of the High Weald by Alan Savidge and Oliver Mason. ISBN 3352. £5.95.

WARTIME KENT 1939-40 compiled by **Oonagh Hyndman** from the BBC Radio Kent broadcasts. ISBN 3611. £6.95.

WHERE NO FLOWERS GROW by George Glazebrook. ISBN 3379. £2.50.

WHO'S BURIED WHERE IN KENT by Alan Major. ISBN 3484. £5.95.